Kate L- ... *1968*

KU-427-270

PENGUIN BOOKS

2365

ABINGER HARVEST

Edward Morgan Forster was born in London in 1879,
attended Tonbridge School as a day boy, and went on to
King's College, Cambridge, in 1897. With King's he has had
a lifelong connexion and was elected to an honorary fellow-
ship in 1946. He has had honarary degrees conferred on him
by many universities. He declares that his life as a whole has
not been dramatic and he is unfailingly modest about his
achievements. Interviewed by the B.B.C. on his eightieth
birthday he said: 'I have not written as much as I'd like to . . .
I write for two reasons: partly to make money and partly to
win the respect of people whom I respect . . . I had better
add that I am quite sure I am not a great novelist.' Eminent
critics and the general public have judged otherwise; in
Penguins alone *A Passage to India* has sold well over half a
million copies.

In addition to five famous novels and a collection of short
stories available as Penguins, E. M. Forster has published
about fourteen other works; they include two biographies;
two books about Alexandria, the result of his sojourn there
in the First World War, when he was with the Red Cross;
a film script; and, with Eric Crozier, the libretto for Britten's
opera, *Billy Budd*.

ABINGER HARVEST

E. M. Forster

Penguin Books

Penguin Books Ltd, Harmondsworth, Middlesex, England
Penguin Books Australia Ltd, Ringwood, Victoria, Australia

—

First published by Edward Arnold 1936
Published in Penguin Books 1967

—

Copyright © E. M. Forster, 1936

—

Made and printed in Great Britain
by Hazell Watson & Viney Ltd,
Aylesbury, Bucks
Set in Monotype Bembo

PREFATORY NOTE

THIS book reprints about eighty articles, essays, reviews, poems, etc., chosen out of a number of contributions to various periodicals. They are arranged not in their order of composition but according to subjects. They fall into five sections.

(i) A commentary on passing events. This section is prefaced by some remarks on the English character, criticizes a few of our aims and diversions, and concludes with a speech which was delivered last summer to an international congress of writers at Paris.

(ii) Literary criticism. This deals with some creative writers, mainly my contemporaries, whom I have admired or loved. The short prefatory essay answers the question, 'What use is literature today?' as well as I can answer it. I know that there are other answers.

(iii) The past. Beginning with a few reflections upon the consolations of history, I proceed to angle in the stream, and draw out of it objects ranging in date from a Greek toilet-case to a house which once belonged to my great-grandfather.

(iv) The East. The fourth section, after saluting the Orient, strays from the nearer east on the tracks of the Emperor Babur into India, and comes to rest there in the Bhagavad-Gita.

(v) Text of our local pageant. This section, furthermore, provides a general title for the book. Relatives of mine have been connected with Abinger, a village in Surrey, for nearly sixty years, and I have known the place all my life myself, so the name *Abinger Harvest* suggested itself as possible for the whole collection. Something is not quite right with this title, but no one could hit on a better, and it is at all events supported by the respectable precedents of *Winterslow* and *Walden*.

Acknowledgements. Thanks are due to the editors of the following periodicals for allowing republication: the *Atlantic Monthly*, the *Calendar*, the *Egyptian Mail*, the *Independent Review*, *Life and Letters*, the *Listener*, the *London Mercury*, the *New Criterion*, the *New Leader*, the *New Statesman* (incorporating the *Athenaeum* and the *Nation*), the *New Weekly*, the *Oxford and Cambridge Review*, the *Spectator*, *Time and Tide*, the *Times Literary Supplement*. My relationship with editors has almost invariably been friendly, and it is a great pleasure to record this.

As for dedication. A miscellany can have no value as an offering. All the same, I should like to offer this one to some of the friends in a younger generation who have encouraged me to compile it; most particularly to William Plomer, and also to J. R. Ackerley, R. J. Buckingham, and Christopher Isherwood.

ABINGER HAMMER
   January, 1936

CONTENTS

CONTENTS

PART III — THE PAST

PART IV — THE EAST

CONTENTS

PART V – THE ABINGER PAGEANT

PART I
THE PRESENT

NOTES ON THE ENGLISH CHARACTER

First Note. I had better let the cat out of the bag at once and record my opinion that the character of the English is essentially middle-class. There is a sound historical reason for this, for, since the end of the eighteenth century, the middle classes have been the dominant force in our community. They gained wealth by the Industrial Revolution, political power by the Reform Bill of 1832; they are connected with the rise and organization of the British Empire; they are responsible for the literature of the nineteenth century. Solidity, caution, integrity, efficiency. Lack of imagination, hypocrisy. These qualities characterize the middle classes in every country, but in England they are national characteristics also, because only in England have the middle classes been in power for one hundred and fifty years. Napoleon, in his rude way, called us 'a nation of shopkeepers'. We prefer to call ourselves 'a great commercial nation' – it sounds more dignified – but the two phrases amount to the same. Of course there are other classes: there is an aristocracy, there are the poor. But it is on the middle classes that the eye of the critic rests – just as it rests on the poor in Russia and on the aristocracy in Japan. Russia is symbolized by the peasant or by the factory worker; Japan by the samurai; the national figure of England is Mr Bull with his top hat, his comfortable clothes, his substantial stomach, and his substantial balance at the bank. Saint George may caper on banners and in the speeches of politicians, but it is John Bull who delivers the goods. And even Saint George – if Gibbon is correct – wore a top hat once; he was an army contractor and supplied indifferent bacon. It all amounts to the same in the end.

13

*Second Note.*Just as the heart of England is the middle classes, so the heart of the middle classes is the public-school system. This extraordinary institution is local. It does not even exist all over the British Isles. It is unknown in Ireland, almost unknown in Scotland (countries excluded from my survey), and though it may inspire other great institutions – Aligarh, for example, and some of the schools in the United States – it remains unique, because it was created by the Anglo-Saxon middle classes, and can flourish only where they flourish. How perfectly it expresses their character – far better, for instance, than does the university, into which social and spiritual complexities have already entered. With its boarding-houses, its compulsory games, its system of prefects and fagging, its insistence on good form and on *esprit de corps*, it produces a type whose weight is out of all proportion to its numbers.

On leaving his school, the boy either sets to work at once – goes into the army or into business, or emigrates – or else proceeds to the university, and after three or four years there enters some other profession – becomes a barrister, doctor, civil servant, schoolmaster, or journalist. (If through some mishap he does not become a manual worker or an artist.) In all these careers his education, or the absence of it, influences him. Its memories influence him also. Many men look back on their school days as the happiest of their lives. They remember with regret that golden time when life, though hard, was not yet complex; when they all worked together and played together and thought together, so far as they thought at all: when they were taught that school is the world in miniature and believed that no one can love his country who does not love his school. And they prolong that time as best they can by joining their Old Boys' society; indeed, some of them remain Old Boys and nothing else for the rest of their lives. They attribute all good to the school. They worship it. They quote the remark that 'the battle of Waterloo was won on the playing-fields of

Eton'. It is nothing to them that the remark is inapplicable historically and was never made by the Duke of Wellington, and that the Duke of Wellington was an Irishman. They go on quoting it because it expresses their sentiments; they feel that if the Duke of Wellington didn't make it he ought to have, and if he wasn't an Englishman he ought to have been. And they go forth into a world that is not entirely composed of public-school men or even of Anglo-Saxons, but of men who are as various as the sands of the sea; into a world of whose richness and subtlety they have no conception. They go forth into it with well-developed bodies, fairly developed minds, and undeveloped hearts. And it is this undeveloped heart that is largely responsible for the difficulties of Englishmen abroad. An undeveloped heart – not a cold one. The difference is important, and on it my next note will be based.

For it is not that the Englishman can't feel – it is that he is afraid to feel. He has been taught at his public school that feeling is bad form. He must not express great joy or sorrow, or even open his mouth too wide when he talks – his pipe might fall out if he did. He must bottle up his emotions, or let them out only on a very special occasion.

Once upon a time (this is an anecdote) I went for a week's holiday on the Continent with an Indian friend. We both enjoyed ourselves and were sorry when the week was over, but on parting our behaviour was absolutely different. He was plunged in despair. He felt that because the holiday was over all happiness was over until the world ended. He could not express his sorrow too much. But in me the Englishman came out strong. I reflected that we should meet again in a month or two, and could write in the interval if we had anything to say; and under these circumstances I could not see what there was to make a fuss about. It wasn't as if we were parting for ever or dying. 'Buck up,' I said, 'do buck up.' He refused to buck up, and I left him plunged in gloom.

The conclusion of the anecdote is even more instructive. For when we met the next month our conversation threw a good deal of light on the English character. I began by scolding my friend. I told him that he had been wrong to feel and display so much emotion upon so slight an occasion; that it was inappropriate. The word 'inappropriate' roused him to fury. 'What?' he cried. 'Do you measure out your emotions as if they were potatoes?' I did not like the simile of the potatoes, but after a moment's reflection I said, 'Yes, I do; and what's more, I think I ought to. A small occasion demands a little emotion, just as a large occasion demands a great one. I would like my emotions to be appropriate. This may be measuring them like potatoes, but it is better than slopping them about like water from a pail, which is what you did.' He did not like the simile of the pail. 'If those are your opinions, they part us forever,' he cried, and left the room. Returning immediately, he added: 'No – but your whole attitude toward emotion is wrong. Emotion has nothing to do with appropriateness. It matters only that it shall be sincere. I happened to feel deeply. I showed it. It doesn't matter whether I ought to have felt deeply or not.'

This remark impressed me very much. Yet I could not agree with it, and said that I valued emotion as much as he did, but used it differently; if I poured it out on small occasions I was afraid of having none left for the great ones, and of being bankrupt at the crises of life. Note the word 'bankrupt'. I spoke as a member of a prudent middle-class nation, always anxious to meet my liabilities. But my friend spoke as an Oriental, and the Oriental has behind him a tradition, not of middle-class prudence, but of kingly munificence and splendour. He feels his resources are endless, just as John Bull feels his are finite. As regards material resources, the Oriental is clearly unwise. Money isn't endless. If we spend or give away all the money we have, we haven't any more, and must take the consequences, which are frequently unpleasant. But, as regards the resources of the spirit, he may be right. The emotions may be endless. The more we express them, the more we may have to express.

> True love in this differs from gold and clay,
> That to divide is not to take away,

says Shelley. Shelley, at all events, believes that the wealth of the spirit is endless; that we may express it copiously, passionately, and always; and that we can never feel sorrow or joy too acutely.

In the above anecdote, I have figured as a typical Englishman. I will now descend from that dizzy and somewhat unfamiliar height, and return to my business of note-taking. A note on the *slowness* of the English character. The Englishman appears to be cold and unemotional because he is really slow. When an event happens, he may understand it quickly enough with his mind, but he takes quite a while to feel it. Once upon a time a coach, containing some Englishmen and some Frenchmen, was driving over the Alps. The horses ran away, and as they were dashing across a bridge the coach caught on the stonework, tottered, and nearly fell into the ravine below. The Frenchmen were frantic with terror: they screamed and gesticulated and flung themselves about, as Frenchmen would. The Englishmen sat quite calm. An hour later the coach drew up at an inn to change horses, and by that time the situations were exactly reversed. The Frenchmen had forgotten all about the danger, and were chattering gaily; the Englishmen had just begun to feel it, and one had a nervous breakdown and was obliged to go to bed. We have here a clear physical difference between the two races – a difference that goes deep into character. The Frenchmen responded at once; the Englishmen responded in time. They were slow and they were also practical. Their instinct forbade them to throw themselves about in the coach, because it was more likely to tip over if they did. They had this extraordinary appreciation of *fact* that we shall notice again and again. When a disaster comes, the English instinct is to do what can be done first, and to postpone the feeling as long as possible. Hence they are splendid at emergencies. No doubt they are brave – no one will deny that – but bravery is partly an affair of the nerves, and the English nervous system is well equipped for meeting a physical emergency. It acts promptly and feels slowly. Such a combination is fruitful, and anyone who possesses it has gone a long way toward being brave. And when the action is over, then the Englishman can feel.

There is one more consideration – a most important one. If the English nature is cold, how is it that it has produced a great literature and a literature that is particularly great in poetry? Judged by its prose, English literature would not stand in the first rank. It is its poetry that raises it to the level of Greek, Persian, or French. And yet the English are supposed to be so unpoetical. How is this? The nation that produced the Elizabethan drama and the Lake Poets cannot be a cold, unpoetical nation. We can't get fire out of ice. Since literature always rests upon national character, there must be in the English nature hidden springs of fire to produce the fire we see. The warm sympathy, the romance, the imagination, that we look for in Englishmen whom we meet, and too often vainly look for, must exist in the nation as a whole, or we could not have this outburst of national song. An undeveloped heart – not a cold one.

The trouble is that the English nature is not at all easy to understand. It has a great air of simplicity, it advertises itself as simple, but the more we consider it, the greater the problems we shall encounter. People talk of the mysterious East, but the West also is mysterious. It has depths that do not reveal themselves at the first gaze. We know what the sea looks like from a distance: it is of one colour, and level, and obviously cannot contain such creatures as fish. But if we look into the sea over the edge of a boat, we see a dozen colours, and depth below depth, and fish swimming in them. That sea is the English character – apparently imperturbable and even. The depths and the colours are the English romanticism and the English sensitiveness – we do not expect to find such things, but they exist. And – to continue my metaphor – the fish are the English emotions, which are always trying to get up to the surface, but don't quite know how. For the most part we see them moving far below, distorted and obscure. Now and then they succeed and we exclaim, 'Why, the Englishman has emotions! He actually can feel!' And occasionally we see that beautiful creature the flying fish, which rises out of the water altogether into the air and the sunlight. English literature is a flying fish. It is a sample of the life that goes on day after day beneath the surface; it is a proof that beauty and emotion exist in the salt, inhospitable sea.

And now let's get back to terra firma. The Englishman's attitude toward criticism will give us another starting-point. He is not annoyed by criticism. He listens or not as the case may be, smiles and passes on, saying, 'Oh, the fellow's jealous'; 'Oh, I'm used to Bernard Shaw; monkey tricks don't hurt me.' It never occurs to him that the fellow may be accurate as well as jealous, and that he might do well to take the criticism to heart and profit by it. It never strikes him – except as a form of words – that he is capable of improvement; his self-complacency is abysmal. Other nations, both Oriental and European, have an uneasy feeling that they are not quite perfect. In consequence they resent criticism. It hurts them; and their snappy answers often mask a determination to improve themselves. Not so the Englishman. He has no uneasy feeling. Let the critics bark. And the 'tolerant humorous attitude' with which he confronts them is not really tolerant, because it is insensitive, and not really humorous, because it is bounded by the titter and the guffaw.

Turn over the pages of *Punch*. There is neither wit, laughter, nor satire, in our national jester – only the snigger of a sub-urban householder who can understand nothing that does not resemble himself. Week after week, under Mr Punch's super-vision, a man falls off his horse, or a colonel misses a golf ball, or a little girl makes a mistake in her prayers. Week after week ladies show not too much of their legs, foreigners are depre-cated, originality condemned. Week after week a bricklayer does not do as much work as he ought and a futurist does more than he need. It is all supposed to be so good-tempered and clean; it is also supposed to be funny. It is actually an out-standing example of our attitude toward criticism: the middle-class Englishman, with a smile on his clean-shaven lips, is engaged in admiring himself and ignoring the rest of mankind. If, in those colourless pages, he came across anything that really was funny – a drawing by Max Beerbohm, for instance – his smile would disappear, and he would say to himself, 'The fellow's a bit of a crank,' and pass on.

This particular attitude reveals such insensitiveness as to suggest a more serious charge: is the Englishman altogether indifferent to the things of the spirit? Let us glance for a moment at his religion – not, indeed, at his theology, which would not merit inspection, but at the action on his daily life of his belief in the unseen. Here again his attitude is practical. But an innate decency comes out: he is thinking of others rather than of himself. Right conduct is his aim. He asks of his religion that it shall make him a better man in daily life; that he shall be more kind, more just, more merciful, more desir-ous to fight what is evil and to protect what is good. No one could call this a low conception. It is, as far as it goes, a spiritual one. Yet – and this seems to me typical of the race – it is only half the religious idea. Religion is more than an ethical code with a divine sanction. It is also a means through which man may get into direct connexion with the divine, and, judging by history, few Englishmen have succeeded in doing this. We have produced no series of prophets, as has Judaism or Islam. We have not even produced a Joan of Arc, or a Savon-arola. We have produced few saints. In Germany the Reformation was due to the passionate conviction of Luther. In England it was due to a palace intrigue. We can show a steady level of piety, a fixed determination to live decently according to our lights – little more.

Well, it is something. It clears us of the charge of being an unspiritual nation. That facile contrast between the spiritual East and the materialistic West can be pushed too far. The West also is spiritual. Only it expresses its belief, not in fasting and visions, not in prophetic rapture, but in the daily round, the common task. An incomplete expression, if you like. I agree. But the argument underlying these scattered notes is that the Englishman is an incomplete person. Not a cold or an unspiritual one. But undeveloped, incomplete.

The attitude of the average orthodox Englishman is often misunderstood. It is thought that he must know that a doctrine – say, like that of the Trinity – is untrue. Moslems in particular feel that his faith is a dishonest compromise between polytheism and monotheism. The answer to this criticism is that the average orthodox Englishman is no theologian. He regards the Trinity as a mystery that it is not his place to solve. 'I find difficulties enough in daily life,' he will say. 'I concern myself with those. As for the Trinity, it is a doctrine handed down to me from my fathers, whom I respect, and I hope to hand it down to my sons, and that they will respect me. No doubt it is true, or it would not have been handed down. And no doubt the clergy could explain it to me if I asked them; but, like myself, they are busy men, and I will not take up their time.'

In such an answer there is confusion of thought, if you like, but no conscious deceit, which is alien to the English nature. The Englishman's deceit is generally unconscious.

For I have suggested earlier that the English are sometimes hypocrites, and it is now my duty to develop this rather painful subject. Hypocrisy is the prime charge that is always brought against us. The Germans are called brutal, the Spanish cruel, the Americans superficial, and so on; but we are perfide Albion, the island of hypocrites, the people who have built up an Empire with a Bible in one hand, a pistol in the other, and financial concessions in both pockets. Is the charge true? I think it is; but while making it we must be quite clear as to what we mean by hypocrisy. Do we mean *conscious* deceit? Well, the English are comparatively guiltless of this; they have little of the Renaissance villain about them. Do we mean *unconscious* deceit? Muddle-headedness? Of this I believe them to be guilty. When an Englishman has been led into a course of wrong action, he has nearly always begun by muddling himself. A public-school education does not make for mental clearness, and he possesses to a very high degree the power of confusing his own mind. We have seen this tendency at work in the domain of theology; how does it work in the domain of conduct?

Jane Austen may seem an odd authority to cite, but Jane Austen has, within her limits, a marvellous insight into the English mind. Her range is limited, her characters never attempt any of the more scarlet sins. But she has a merciless eye for questions of conduct, and the classical example of two English people muddling themselves before they embark upon a wrong course of action is to be found in the opening chapters of *Sense and Sensibility*. Old Mr Dashwood has just died. He has been twice married. By his first marriage he has a son, John; by his second marriage three daughters. The son is well off; the young ladies and their mother – for Mr Dashwood's second wife survives him – are badly off. He has called his son to his death-bed and has solemnly adjured him to provide for the second family. Much moved, the young man promises, and mentally decides to give each of his sisters a thousand pounds; and then the comedy begins. For he announces his generous intention to his wife, and Mrs John Dashwood by no means approves of depriving their own little boy of so large a sum. The thousand pounds are accordingly reduced to five hundred. But even this seems rather much. Might not an annuity to the stepmother be less of a wrench? Yes – but though less of a wrench it might be more of a drain, for 'she is very stout and healthy, and scarcely forty'. An occasional present of fifty pounds will be better, 'and will, I think, be amply discharging my promise to my father'. Or, better still, an occasional present of fish. And in the end nothing is done, nothing; the four impecunious ladies are not even helped in the moving of their furniture.

Well, are the John Dashwoods hypocrites? It depends upon our definition of hypocrisy. The young man could not see his evil impulses as they gathered force and gained on him. And even his wife, though a worse character, is also self-deceived. She reflects that old Mr Dashwood may have been out of his mind at his death. She thinks of her own little boy – and surely a mother ought to think of her own child. She has muddled herself so completely that in one sentence she can refuse the ladies the income that would enable them to keep a carriage and in the next can say that they will not be keeping a carriage and so will have no expenses. No doubt men and women in other lands can muddle themselves, too, yet the state of mind of Mr and Mrs John Dashwood seems to me typical of England. They are slow – they take time even to do wrong; whereas people in other lands do wrong quickly.

There are national faults as there are national diseases, and perhaps one can draw a parallel between them. It has always impressed me that the national diseases of England should be cancer and consumption – slow, insidious, pretending to be something else; while the diseases proper to the South should be cholera and plague, which strike at a man when he is perfectly well and may leave him a corpse by evening. Mr and Mrs John Dashwood are moral consumptives. They collapse gradually without realizing what the disease is. There is nothing dramatic or violent about their sin. You cannot call them villains.

Here is the place to glance at some of the other charges that have been brought against the English as a nation. They have, for instance, been accused of treachery, cruelty, and fanaticism. In these charges I have never been able to see the least point, because treachery and cruelty are conscious sins. The man knows he is doing wrong, and does it deliberately, like Tartuffe or Iago. He betrays his friend because he wishes to. He tortures his prisoners because he enjoys seeing the blood flow. He worships the Devil because he prefers evil to good. From villainies such as these the average Englishman is free. His character, which prevents his rising to certain heights, also prevents him from sinking to these depths. Because he doesn't produce mystics he doesn't produce villains either; he gives the world no prophets, but no anarchists, no fanatics – religious or political.

Of course there are cruel and treacherous people in England – one has only to look at the police courts – and examples of public infamy can be found, such as the Amritsar massacre. But one does not look at the police courts or the military mind to find the soul of any nation; and the more English people one meets the more convinced one becomes that the charges as a whole are untrue. Yet foreign critics often make them. Why? Partly because they fix their eyes on the criminal classes, partly because they are annoyed with certain genuine defects in the English character, and in their irritation throw in cruelty in order to make the problem simpler. Moral indignation is always agreeable, but nearly always misplaced. It is indulged in both by the English and by the critics of the English. They all find it great fun. The drawback is that while they are amusing themselves the world becomes neither wiser nor better.

The main point of these notes is that the English character is incomplete. No national character is complete. We have to look for some qualities in one part of the world and others in another. But the English character is incomplete in a way that is particularly annoying to the foreign observer. It has a bad surface – self-complacent, unsympathetic, and reserved. There is plenty of emotion further down, but it never gets used. There is plenty of brain power, but it is more often used to confirm prejudices than to dispel them. With such an equipment the Englishman cannot be popular. Only I would repeat: there is little vice in him and no real coldness. It is the machinery that is wrong.

I hope and believe myself that in the next twenty years we shall see a great change, and that the national character will alter into something that is less unique but more lovable. The supremacy of the middle classes is probably ending. What new element the working classes will introduce one cannot say, but at all events they will not have been educated at public schools. And whether these notes praise or blame the English character – that is only incidental. They are the notes of a student who is trying to get at the truth and would value the assistance of others. I believe myself that the truth is great and that it shall prevail. I have no faith in official caution and reticence. The cats are all out of their bags, and diplomacy cannot recall them. The nations *must* understand one another, and quickly; and without the interposition of their governments, for the shrinkage of the globe is throwing them into one another's arms. To that understanding these notes are a feeble contribution – notes on the English character as it has struck a novelist.

[1920]

MRS GRUNDY AT THE PARKERS'

WHEN Mrs Grundy called recently at the Nosey Parkers', she was informed by the maid that they were 'Not at home'.

'Do you mean that your mistress is out or is not out?' she asked. Doris collapsed, and said that Mrs Parker was in, but had rather a headache, and so was resting.

'Then have the goodness to tell her I am here, without further prevarication,' said Mrs Grundy, and seated herself in the austere drawing-room – such a contrast to her own cosy parlour. The Parkers enjoyed making themselves as well as other people uncomfortable, which she had never been able to understand.

'Ah, Amelia,' said her friend, coming in. 'Quite a voice from the past!'

'Edith, I called about something or other, but Doris's untruthfulness has put it clean out of my head. Why did she say you were not at home when you are?'

'Well, it is only a form of words; a modern convention. One has to keep pace with the times if one is to guide them and they sorely need our guidance.'

'And have you the headache or have you not?' Mrs Grundy persisted.

'I have. Still I am glad you forced your way in, for I want to talk about our methods of work. You don't interfere with people in quite the right way, you know. You are too desultory and impetuous. That was all right in the nineteenth century, when life was slow, and one could point to one impropriety after another with one's umbrella as they crossed the street – but today! Why, you'll get knocked down. You'll be run over by a motor bicycle, and before you can see whether it was a girl on the pillion she will have disappeared. Today one must select and one must plan; civilization is so complicated. Think of our triumph the other month – that man who was arrested for bathing at Worthing.'

'Ah, don't talk to me about bathing. I often wish there was no such place in these islands as the sea-shore.'

'That is shallow of you. If there was no sea-shore, how could we catch people on it? Besides, I approve of bathing, provided it is so regulated that no one can enjoy it. We are working toward that. You were a great pioneer, but you made the mistake of trying to suppress people's pleasure. I try to spoil their pleasure. It's much more effective. I don't say, "You shan't bathe." I say, "You shall bathe in an atmosphere of self-consciousness and fear," and I think I am succeeding. I certainly have at Worthing.'

'I expect I read about Worthing, but where everything is so shameless one gets bewildered.'

'Why, the case of the visitor who bathed, properly clad, and then returned to his bathing machine to dry. Thinking no one could see him, since the machine faced the ocean, he left its door open. He had reckoned without my foresight. I had arranged that a policewoman should be swimming out at sea. As soon as she observed him, she signalled to a policeman on shore, who went to the machine and arrested him. Now, Amelia, would you have ever thought of that?'

'I certainly shouldn't have. I don't like the idea of women policemen at all. A woman's proper place is in her home.'

'But surely there can't be too many women anywhere.'

'I don't know. Anyhow, I am glad the visitor was arrested. It will stop him and others going to English seaside resorts, which is a step in the right direction, and I hope the magistrate convicted.'

'Oh, yes. Magistrates nearly always convict. They are afraid of being thought to condone immorality. As my husband points out, that is one of our strong cards. In his private capacity the magistrate was probably not shocked. The average man simply doesn't mind, you see. He doesn't mind about bathing costumes or their absence, or bad language, or indecent literature, or even about sex.' At this point she rang the bell. 'Doris, bring the smelling salts,' she said, for Mrs Grundy had fainted. When consciousness had been restored, she continued: 'No, nor even about sex, and we social workers of the twentieth century cannot ignore sex; what we can do is to make it a burden. And we are faced with the difficulty that the average man, if left to himself, does not brood, and forgets to persecute. He has habits instead of ideals. Isn't that too dreadful! He says in effect, "I go my way about sex or whatever it is, and I let others go theirs, even if I think it queer. It isn't my funeral." But it is going to be his funeral – at least I hope so.'

'And what of the average woman?'

'She is a little more satisfactory, a little more apt to be scared. Though I have known sad cases of women saying, "Pore thing, we don't take no notice although she did 'ave a little Unwanted, we treats her like one of ourselves." You see what we are up against – tolerance, good temper, and unsuspiciousness. It has been no easy matter to cover England with regulations from end to end.'

Mrs Grundy sighed. 'I admit you manage to interfere more than I did,' she said. 'I expect it is as you say, and I was too impulsive. I hurried too much from vice to vice when I was young. I stood outside the music halls, to stop people going in, and then I heard profanity in the cab-shelter, and went to silence that, and while I was doing so the music hall filled up. I went to Africa to make the cannibals monogamous, and during my absence the Deceased Wife's Sister's Bill became law in England. When it's daylight I can see people, which is scandalous, and at night-time I can't see them, which is worse. I simply don't know where to turn, and while I am insisting on ulsters for sunbathing the Deceased Husband's Brother's Bill will probably become law, too. You have a sounder method, Edith. You have brought in education, of which I never dreamt, and I am not surprised that your wonderful work gives you the headache.'

'My headache, to which you now refer, has nothing to do with my work,' replied her hostess. 'It has been caused by a piece of bad news which has just arrived from the Continent. Even my husband is upset by it.'

'If I had my way there never would have been any Continent,' cried Mrs Grundy, and proceeded to ask a series of agitated questions, such as had the bad news to do with chocolates being allowed in theatres, were sweepstakes to be legalized, was Sunday cricket spreading, had the King been seen patting a race-horse, and so on.

'No, you are quite off the lines. It has to do with something inside us.'

'And pray, what can the Continent have to do with my inside?'

'Amelia, you must make an effort to understand. It concerns you as much as myself. It is a sort of discovery that has been made by a kind of doctor. Just as our work was prospering and we were making people stodgy and self-conscious under the pretence of building better citizens, just as we had bullied the lay authorities and coaxed the clerical into supporting us, just as interference was about to be launched on a colossal scale —. But I despair of explaining what it is. Perhaps my husband will be able to.' And she called out, 'Nosey!'

Mr Nosey Parker, who now joined the ladies, was scarcely their equal as a field worker. Where he excelled was on committees. Without being obtrusive, he managed to generate that official uneasiness upon which all their work depended. Let me explain. Each member of any committee has, of course, broken the law at some time or other, and desires to prove to his colleagues that he hasn't; he can do this best by being timid in discussion, and by voting for any measure that deprives the public of enjoyment. Furthermore, each member either has a daughter or feels that he ought to have one, and dares not oppose any censorship of art or literature in consequence. Mr Parker realized all this. He had only to say 'We must think of our daughters' and everyone thought of their skins. He had only to say 'I am not narrow-minded, but ...' and broadness became impossible. He raised the banner of respectability and called it idealism. *Sauve qui peut* was embroidered in brown on its folds. And under it the municipal councillors or the board of magistrates or the jurymen gathered, all afraid of being found out, and when their duties concluded they had not done at all what they intended (which was, generally speaking, to let their fellow creatures alone), but had stopped one man from doing this and another from doing that, and had sent a third man to prison.

'Nosey, do explain what has happened,' his wife said.

'Nothing has happened. It is only an idea.'

'Ideas have never troubled me, especially from abroad,' said Mrs Grundy.

'You are fortunate. I own myself worried by this one. The idea is that we, who have helped others, ought now to be helped, and it is proposed to help us by pulling us to pieces.' He shuddered. 'To you that means little. But I have always had doubts of my own solidity. How can I bring it home to you? They desire to examine your intimate fabric, Mrs Grundy: they suspect it of being diseased. My wife's and my own they assert to be even fouler than yours. They believe that we all three try to improve people because we envy their happiness and had bad luck ourselves when we were young.

What so alarms me is that there is no bitterness in the new attack. We are actually objects of pity.'

'And, pray, is that all?' said Mrs Grundy, with her dry little laugh. 'You may have given Edith a headache over this, but you have no such effect on me. I am quite accustomed to pity. I got a lot as a girl. It is merely a term of abuse, and I shall castigate it in due season. Good-bye, my dear sir, and take an old woman's advice: keep away from foreign newspapers in the future.' And, gathering up her skirts, she left their house – perhaps for her doom.

'Poor thing, she doesn't know the danger,' said Mrs Parker, looking after their friend anxiously, and observing how she first scowled at Doris and then lectured some navvies for using a word which had been devitalized twenty years previously by Mr Bernard Shaw. 'She is brave because she is out of date. But we – oh Nosey, Nosey! Fancy, if it gets known that interference is a disease which ought to be interfered with. Men and women will live as they like, they will be natural and decent about one another, and we shall boss and nag at them no more.'

'Too true, too true,' said her husband, 'and yet I see a ray of hope. Our enemies cannot interfere with us unless they organize. As individuals they are helpless. They will have to form Freedom Leagues, or Anti-Fuss Societies or sign Beach Pyjama Covenants, and they cannot do so without constituting themselves into committees. And as soon as they meet on committees . . . yes, I think we shall survive after all.'

Will they survive? Only Doris, who is the future, can tell.

[1932]

'IT IS DIFFERENT FOR ME'

Bishop Welldon, Dean of Durham, in a letter to The Times, *censures the 'vulgar profanity' of the language used by the Labour Party in the House of Commons, and inquires whether there is 'no adequate means of preventing or punishing it'.*

My brethren, nothing on earth is finer
Than a truly refined inarticulate miner
(Or may we say 'under the earth,' for there
Is a miner's place, not up in the air?);
But he must be refined, he must be meek,
Expert at his job, yet unable to speak,
He must not complain or use swear words or spit;
Much is expected of men in the pit.

It is different for me. I have earned the right,
Through position and birth to be impolite.
I have always been used to the best of things,
I was nourished at Eton and crowned at King's,
I pushed to the front in religion and play,
I shoved all competitors out of the way;
I ruled at Harrow, I went to Calcutta,
I buttered my bread and jammed my butter,
And returned as a bishop, enormous of port,
Who stood in a pulpit and said what he thought.
Yes, I said what I thought, and thought what I said,
They hadn't got butter, they hadn't got bread,
They hadn't got jam or tobacco or tea,
They hadn't a friend, but they always had me.
And I'm different to them. I needn't be meek,
Because I have learned the proper technique;
Because I'm a scholar, a don, and a dean,

32

It's all in good taste when I'm vulgar or mean.
I can bully or patronize, just which I please;
I am different to them. . . . But those Labour M.P.s,
How *dare* they be rude? They ought to have waited
Until they were properly educated.
They must be punished, they've got to be stopped,
Parliamentary privilege ought to be dropped.
They shall be scourged and buried alive
If they trespass on My prerogative.

May I most clearly state, ere I lay down my pen,
That rudeness is only for gentlemen?—
As it was in the beginning, it shall be . . . Amen!

[1923]

MY WOOD

A FEW years ago I wrote a book which dealt in part with the difficulties of the English in India. Feeling that they would have had no difficulties in India themselves, the Americans read the book freely. The more they read it the better it made them feel, and a cheque to the author was the result. I bought a wood with the cheque. It is not a large wood – it contains scarcely any trees, and it is intersected, blast it, by a public footpath. Still, it is the first property that I have owned, so it is right that other people should participate in my shame, and should ask themselves, in accents that will vary in horror, this very important question: What is the effect of property upon the character? Don't let's touch economics; the effect of private ownership upon the community as a whole is another question – a more important question, perhaps, but another one. Let's keep to psychology. If you own things, what's their effect on you? What's the effect on me of my wood?

In the first place, it makes me feel heavy. Property does have this effect. Property produces men of weight, and it was a man of weight who failed to get into the Kingdom of Heaven. He was not wicked, that unfortunate millionaire in the parable, he was only stout; he stuck out in front, not to mention behind, and as he wedged himself this way and that in the crystalline entrance and bruised his well-fed flanks, he saw beneath him a comparatively slim camel passing through the eye of a needle and being woven into the robe of God. The Gospels all through couple stoutness and slowness. They point out what is perfectly obvious, yet seldom realized: that if you have a lot of things you cannot move about a lot, that furniture requires dusting, dusters require servants, servants require insurance stamps, and the whole tangle of them makes you think twice before you accept an invitation to dinner or go for a bathe in the Jordan. Sometimes the Gospels proceed further and say with Tolstoy that property is sinful; they approach the difficult ground of asceticism here, where I cannot follow them. But as to the immediate effects of property on people, they just show straightforward logic. It produces men of weight. Men of weight cannot, by definition, move like the lightning from the East unto the West, and the ascent of a fourteen-stone bishop into a pulpit is thus the exact antithesis of the coming of the Son of Man. My wood makes me feel heavy.

In the second place, it makes me feel it ought to be larger. The other day I heard a twig snap in it. I was annoyed at first, for I thought that someone was blackberrying, and depreciating the value of the undergrowth. On coming nearer, I saw it was not a man who had trodden on the twig and snapped it, but a bird, and I felt pleased. My bird. The bird was not equally pleased. Ignoring the relation between us, it took fright as soon as it saw the shape of my face, and flew straight over the boundary hedge into a field, the property of

Mrs Henessy, where it sat down with a loud squawk. It had become Mrs Henessy's bird. Something seemed grossly amiss here, something that would not have occurred had the wood been larger. I could not afford to buy Mrs Henessy out, I dared not murder her, and limitations of this sort beset me on every side. Ahab did not want that vineyard – he only needed it to round off his property, preparatory to plotting a new curve – and all the land around my wood has become necessary to me in order to round off the wood. A boundary protects. But – poor little thing – the boundary ought in its turn to be protected. Noises on the edge of it. Children throw stones. A little more, and then a little more, until we reach the sea. Happy Canute! Happier Alexander! And after all, why should even the world be the limit of possession? A rocket containing a Union Jack, will, it is hoped, be shortly fired at the moon. Mars. Sirius. Beyond which . . . But these immensities ended by saddening me. I could not suppose that my wood was the destined nucleus of universal dominion – it is so very small and contains no mineral wealth beyond the blackberries. Nor was I comforted when Mrs Henessy's bird took alarm for the second time and flew clean away from us all, under the belief that it belonged to itself.

In the third place, property makes its owner feel that he ought to do something to it. Yet he isn't sure what. A restlessness comes over him, a vague sense that he has a personality to express – the same sense which, without any vagueness, leads the artist to an act of creation. Sometimes I think I will cut down such trees as remain in the wood, at other times I want to fill up the gaps between them with new trees. Both impulses are pretentious and empty. They are not honest movements towards money-making or beauty. They spring from a foolish desire to express myself and from an inability to enjoy what I have got. Creation, property, enjoyment form a sinister trinity in the human mind. Creation and enjoyment are both very very good, yet they are often unattainable without a material basis, and at such moments property pushes itself in as a substitute, saying, 'Accept me instead – I'm good enough for all three.' It is not enough. It is, as Shakespeare said of lust, 'The expense of spirit in a waste of shame': it is 'Before a joy proposed; behind, a dream.' Yet we don't know how to shun it. It is forced on us by our economic system as the alternative to starvation. It is also forced on us by an internal defect in the soul, by the feeling that in property may lie the germs of self-development and of exquisite or heroic deeds. Our life on earth is, and ought to be, material and carnal. But we have not yet learned to manage our materialism and carnality properly; they are still entangled with the desire for ownership, where (in the words of Dante) 'Possession is one with loss'.

And this brings us to our fourth and final point: the blackberries.

Blackberries are not plentiful in this meagre grove, but they are easily seen from the public footpath which traverses it, and all too easily gathered. Foxgloves, too – people will pull up the foxgloves, and ladies of an educational tendency even grub for toadstools to show them on the Monday in class. Other ladies, less educated, roll down the bracken in the arms of their gentlemen friends. There is paper, there are tins. Pray, does my wood belong to me or doesn't it? And, if it does, should I not own it best by allowing no one else to walk there? There is a wood near Lyme Regis, also cursed by a public footpath, where the owner has not hesitated on this point. He has built high stone walls each side of the path, and has spanned it by bridges, so that the public circulate like termites while he gorges on the blackberries unseen. He really does own his wood, this able chap. Dives in Hell did pretty well, but the gulf dividing him from Lazarus could be traversed by vision, and nothing traverses it here. And perhaps I shall come to this in time. I shall wall in and fence out until I really taste the sweets of property. Enormously stout, endlessly avaricious, pseudo-creative, intensely selfish, I shall weave upon my forehead the quadruple crown of possession until those nasty Bolshies come and take it off again and thrust me aside into the outer darkness.

[1926]

ME, THEM, AND YOU

I HAVE a suit of clothes. It does not fit, but is of stylish cut. I can go anywhere in it and I have been to see the Sargent pictures at the Royal Academy. Underneath the suit was a shirt, beneath the shirt was a vest, and beneath the vest was Me. Me was not exposed much to the public gaze; two hands and a face showed that here was a human being; the rest was swathed in cotton or wool.

Yet Me was what mattered, for it was Me that was going to see Them. Them what? Them persons what governs us, them dukes and duchesses and archbishops and generals and captains of industry. They have had their likenesses done by this famous painter (artists are useful sometimes), and, for the sum of one and six, they were willing to be inspected. I had one and six, otherwise I should have remained in the snow outside. The coins changed hands. I entered the exhibition, and found myself almost immediately in the presence of a respectable family servant.

'Wretched weather,' I remarked civilly. There was no reply, the forehead swelled, the lips contracted haughtily. I had begun my tour with a very serious mistake, and had addressed a portrait of Lord Curzon. His face had misled me into thinking him a family servant. I ought to have looked only at the

clothes, which were blue and blazing, and which he clutched
with a blue-veined hand. They cost a hundred pounds perhaps.
How cheap did my own costume seem now, and how impossible it was to imagine that Lord Curzon continues beneath
his clothes, that he, too (if I may venture on the parallel), was
a Me. Murmuring in confusion, I left the radiant effigy and
went into the next room. Here my attention was drawn by a
young Oriental, subtle and charming and not quite sure of his
ground. I complimented him in flowery words. He winced,
he disclaimed all knowledge of the East. I had been speaking to
Sir Phillip Sassoon. Here again I ought to have looked first at
the clothes. They were slightly horsey and wholly English,
and they put mine to shame. Why had he come from Tabriz,
or wherever it was and put them on? Why take the long
journey from Samarkand for the purpose of denouncing our
Socialists? Why not remain where he felt himself Me? But
he resented analysis and I left him.

The third figure – to do her justice – felt that she was Me
and no one else could be, and looked exactly what she was:
namely, the wife of our Ambassador at Berlin. Erect she stood
with a small balustrade and a diplomatic landscape behind her.
She was superbly beautiful and incredibly arrogant, and her
pearls would have clothed no mere hundreds of human beings
but many of her fellow-portraits on the walls. What beat in
the heart – if there was a heart – I could not know, but I heard
pretty distinctly the voice that proceeded from the bright red
lips. It is not a voice that would promote calm in high places,
not a voice to promote amity between two nations at a difficult
moment in their intercourse. Her theme was precedence, and
perhaps it is wiser to allow her to develop it in solitude.

And I drifted from Them to Them, fascinated by the hands
and faces which peeped out of the costumes. Lord Roberts upheld with difficulty the rows of trinkets pinned on his uniform;
Sir Thomas Sutherland was fat above a fat black tie; a riding

costume supported the chinless cranium of a Duke; a Mr John Fife 'who showed conspicuous ability in the development of the granite industry' came from Aberdeen in black; and a Marquess actually did something: he was carrying the Sword of State on the occasion of King Edward's Coronation; while a page carried his train. Sometimes the painter saw through his sitters and was pleasantly mischievous at their expense; sometimes he seemed taken in by them – which happens naturally enough to a man who spends much time dangling after the rich. In spite of the charm of his work, and the lovely colours, and the gracious pictures of Venice, a pall of upholstery hung over the exhibition. The portraits dominated. Gazing at each other over our heads, they said, 'What would the country do without us? We have got the decorations and the pearls, we make fashions and wars, we have the largest houses and eat the best food, and control the most important industries, and breed the most valuable children, and ours is the Kingdom and the Power and the Glory.' And, listening to their chorus, I felt this was so, and my clothes fitted worse and worse, and there seemed in all the universe no gulf wider than the gulf between Them and Me – no wider gulf, until I encountered You.

You had been plentiful enough in the snow outside (your proper place), but I had not expected to find You here in the place of honour, too. Yours was by far the largest picture in the show. You were hung between Lady Cowdray and the Hon. Mrs Langman, and You were entitled 'Gassed'. You were of godlike beauty – for the upper classes only allow the lower classes to appear in art on condition that they wash themselves and have classical features. These conditions you fulfilled. A line of golden-haired Apollos moved along a duckboard from left to right with bandages over their eyes. They had been blinded by mustard gas. Others sat peacefully in the foreground, others approached through the middle distance.

The battlefield was sad but tidy. No one complained, no one looked lousy or over-tired, and the aeroplanes overhead struck the necessary note of the majesty of England. It was all that a great war picture should be, and it was modern because it managed to tell a new sort of lie. Many ladies and gentlemen fear that Romance is passing out of war with the sabres and the chargers. Sargent's masterpiece reassures them. He shows that it is possible to suffer with a quiet grace under the new conditions, and Lady Cowdray and the Hon. Mrs Langman as they looked over the twenty feet of canvas that divided them, were still able to say, 'How touching', instead of 'How obscene'.

Still, there You were, though in modified form, and in mockery of your real misery, and though the gulf between Them and Me was wide, still wider yawned the gulf between us and You. For what could we do without you? What would become of our incomes and activities if you declined to exist? You are the slush and dirt on which our civilization rests, which it treads under foot daily, which it sentimentalizes over now and then, in hours of danger. But you are not only a few selected youths in khaki, you are old men and women and dirty babies also, and dimly and obscurely you used to move through the mind of Carlyle. 'Thou wert our conscript, on Thee the lot fell. . . .' That is as true for the twentieth century as for the nineteenth, though the twentieth century – more cynical – feels that it is merely a true remark, not a useful one, and that economic conditions cannot be bettered by booming on about the brotherhood of man. 'For in Thee also a godlike frame lay hidden, but it was not to be unfolded,' not while the hard self-satisfied faces stare at each other from the walls and say, 'But at all events we founded the Charity Organization Society – and look what we pay in wages, and look what our clothes cost, and clothes mean work'.

The misery goes on, the feeble impulses of good return to

the sender, and far away, in some other category, far away from the snobbery and glitter in which our souls and bodies have been entangled, is forged the instrument of the new dawn.

[1925]

A VOTER'S DILEMMA

Nice Mr Grey and Mr Brown
Have recently arrived from town,
Their country's interests to promote.
I wonder how I ought to vote?
Each is so pleasant and so rich
I scarce remember which is which.
Each has a wife and a cigar,
Two daughters and a motor-car.
Each wears a watch-chain, and of course
Each has a Military Cross,
Won, during the Allies' advance,
Somewhere behind the lines in France.
And shares in steel and poison-gas,
And oil, and coal, so that – alas! —
I scarce distinguish what they say,
Nice Mr Brown and Mr Grey.

'Our difference' (they say to me)
'Lies in our fiscal policy'.
Mr Brown's a Conservative,
And certain products that arrive
From certain countries, he would tax —
I think he mentioned sealing-wax —
While Mr Grey's a Liberal,
And wouldn't tax such things at all.
Each of them wears a fur great-coat:
I wonder how I ought to vote?

For if to either I impart
The word that's graven on my heart,
Nineteen-fourteen, they smile and say
'We do not want a war today,
We don't want war as yet; our aim
Is (save for sealing-wax) the same.
We're merely wanting to get in,
And then – why then we can begin.'
And behind Mr Brown there stands,
With glittering prizes in his hands,
And jolly words about the dead,
The Lord High Galloper Birkenhead.
And behind Mr Grey I see
Great Churchill of Gallipoli,
Who did immortal glory win
Through Kolchak and through Denikin,
Saved Antwerp, pacified the Turk,
And now is needing further work.

And thus, whichever way I vote,
I get into the same old boat,
And Mr Brown and Mr Grey
Are rowing it the same old way —
The way of blood and fire and tears
And pestilence and profiteers —
The way that all mankind has been
Since nineteen hundred and fourteen.
Nice Mr Grey! Nice Mr Brown,
Why trouble to come down from town?

[1923]

OUR GRAVES IN GALLIPOLI

Scene: the summit of Achi Baba, an exposed spot, looking out across the Dardanelles towards Asia and the East. In a crevice between the rocks lie two graves covered by a single heap of stones. No monument marks them, for they escaped notice during the official survey, and the heap of stones has blended into the desolate and austere outline of the hill. The peninsula is turning towards the sun, and as the rays strike Achi Baba the graves begin to speak.

FIRST GRAVE: We are important again upon earth. Each morning men mention us.

SECOND GRAVE: Yes, after seven years' silence.

FIRST GRAVE: Every day some eminent public man now refers to the 'sanctity of our graves in Gallipoli'.

SECOND GRAVE: Why do the eminent men speak of 'our' graves, as if they were themselves dead? It is we, not they, who lie on Achi Baba.

FIRST GRAVE: They say 'our' out of geniality and in order to touch the great heart of the nation more quickly. *Punch*, the great-hearted jester, showed a picture lately in which the Prime Minister of England, Lloyd George, fertile in counsels, is urged to go to war to protect 'the sanctity of our graves in Gallipoli'. The elderly artist who designed that picture is not dead and does not mean to die. He hopes to illustrate this war as he did the last, for a sufficient salary. Nevertheless he writes 'our' graves, as if he was inside one, and all persons of position now say the same.

SECOND GRAVE: If they go to war, there will be more graves.

FIRST GRAVE: That is what they desire. That is what Lloyd George, prudent in counsels, and lion-hearted Churchill intend.

SECOND GRAVE: But where will they dig them?

FIRST GRAVE: There is still room over in Chanak. Also, it is well for a nation that would be great to scatter its graves all over the world. Graves in Ireland, graves in Irak, Russia, Persia, India, each with its inscription from the Bible or Rupert Brooke. When England thinks fit, she can launch an expedition to protect the sanctity of her graves, and can follow that by another expedition to protect the sanctity of the additional graves. That is what Lloyd George, prudent in counsels, and lion-hearted Churchill, have planned. Churchill planned this expedition to Gallipoli, where I was killed. He planned the expedition to Antwerp, where my brother was killed. Then he said that Labour is not fit to govern. Rolling his eyes for fresh worlds, he saw Egypt, and fearing that peace might be established there, he intervened and prevented it. Whatever he undertakes is a success. He is Churchill the Fortunate, ever in office, and clouds of dead heroes attend him. Nothing for schools, nothing for houses, nothing for the life of the body, nothing for the spirit. England cannot spare a penny for anything except for her heroes' graves.

SECOND GRAVE: Is she really putting herself to so much expense on our account?

FIRST GRAVE: For us, and for the Freedom of the Straits. That water flowing below us now – it must be thoroughly free. What freedom is, great men are uncertain, but all agree that the water must be free for all nations; if in peace, then for all nations in peace; if in war, then for all nations in war.

SECOND GRAVE: So all nations now support England.

FIRST GRAVE: It is almost inexplicable. England stands alone. Of the dozens of nations into which the globe is divided, not a single one follows her banner, and even her own colonies hang back.

SECOND GRAVE: Yes . . . inexplicable. Perhaps she fights for some other reason.

FIRST GRAVE: Ah, the true reason of a war is never known

until all who have fought in it are dead. In a hundred years' time we shall be told. Meanwhile seek not to inquire. There are rumours that rich men desire to be richer, but we cannot know.

SECOND GRAVE: If rich men desire more riches, let them fight. It is reasonable to fight for our desires.

FIRST GRAVE: But they cannot fight. They must not fight. There are too few of them. They would be killed. If a rich man went into the interior of Asia and tried to take more gold or more oil, he might be seriously injured at once. He must persuade poor men, who are numerous, to go there for him. And perhaps this is what Lloyd George, fertile in counsels, has decreed. He has tried to enter Asia by means of the Greeks. It was the Greeks who, seven years ago, failed to join England after they had promised to do so, and our graves in Gallipoli are the result of this. But Churchill the Fortunate, ever in office, ever magnanimous, bore the Greeks no grudge, and he and Lloyd George persuaded their young men to enter Asia. They have mostly been killed there, so English young men must be persuaded instead. A phrase must be thought of, and 'the Gallipoli graves' is the handiest. The clergy must wave their Bibles, the old men their newspapers, the old women their knitting, the unmarried girls must wave white feathers, and all must shout 'Gallipoli graves, Gallipoli graves, Gallipoli, Gally Polly, Gally Polly', until the young men are ashamed and think, What sound can that be but my country's call? and Chanak receives them.

SECOND GRAVE: Chanak is to sanctify Gallipoli.

FIRST GRAVE: It will make our heap of stones for ever England, apparently.

SECOND GRAVE: It can scarcely do that to my portion of it. I was a Turk.

FIRST GRAVE: What! a Turk! You a Turk? And I have lain beside you for seven years and never known!

SECOND GRAVE: How should you have known? What is there to know except that I am your brother?

FIRST GRAVE: I am yours . . .

SECOND GRAVE: All is dead except that. All graves are one. It is their unity that sanctifies them, and some day even the living will learn this.

FIRST GRAVE: Ah, but why can they not learn it while they are still alive?

His comrade cannot answer this question. Achi Baba passes beneath the sun, and so long as there is light warlike preparations can be seen on the opposite coast. Presently all objects enter into their own shadows, and through the eneral veil thus formed the stars become apparent.

[1922]

HAPPINESS!

O BEAUTIFUL book!* What would the art critics, whose rightful property you are, say about you? They would not say 'O beautiful book!' for they have the gift of words and can state with precision which of your pages are Illustrations and which Significant Forms. O fifty pages, each lovelier than its brother, so gorgeous in your colours, so moving in your theme that the beholder falls a-doting, and phrases of music come into his ear, and quotations from poetry to his lips! Your scene is an island – a kingless continent sinless as Eden, and no one lives upon it but Adam and Eve.

Qui pourrait dire comment Macao et Cosmage vinrent dans cette île, comment la destinée put les unir? Personne! Ni toi, ni moi, nous ne le saurons jamais.

* The book was *Macao et Cosmage*, by Edy. Legrand. I think it is still obtainable. Published by the N.R.F.

They have lived there as long as they can remember amongst birds and flowers; they have ridden giraffes and turtles, and danced in the shades and lights of the forest; they have played by the cataract at sunset; and at night, when all the island except its stars became azure, they have slept beneath plumèd trees, while their innocence enclosed them in a shell of white light, in a magical fruit that gleamed in the highways of the darkness. New joys in the morning. By listening to the song of the birds Cosmage learned how to sing, and by watching their nests Macao learned how to build a house. They made a path through the wood, and found at the end of it the sea, and the sea opened her treasures to them – great fish that slithered, and scuttling crabs. Macao and Cosmage were not dignified, they had not the faked simplicity of Genesis or Greece, but he was chinless, like all truly good men, and she goggle-eyed and black. They neither toiled nor posed, nor did they give thanks.

And during a morning of that eternal spring they saw 'une apparition inexpliquable' upon the blue and white of the sea. It was the Commandant Létambot and his jolly tars, who had been chasing the Boche. He landed on the island, exclaimed, 'Quelle trouvaille!' and hoisted the tricolour upon a lofty palm. After many days he returned. The whole horizon was black with smoke this time. An immense fleet arrived, full of soldiers, colonists, officials, photographers, commercial travellers, botanists, electricians, policemen; and the Commandant made a speech in which he told the two inhabitants that their island's name was 'L'île du Coin du Monde', and that he was bringing to it 'le bonheur', happiness. Before long the giraffes were exterminated and the waterfalls diverted for industrial purposes; the trees were cut down, and a public garden installed where they had grown; the birds were chased by gallant airmen out of the sky; and the mountains were scored with funiculars, and crowned with hotels for ladies and their dogs. Macao and Cosmage grew old. They could not find the happiness that they had been promised, they had lost the solitude that they loved, and they went upon the matter before the Governor, weeping. The Governor was a young and energetic man. He removed his cigar for a moment, and spoke over his shoulder to Macao and Cosmage as follows:

Vous vivez à l'époque des grandes inventions; l'activité humaine, sous toutes ses formes, est sans limites! Le bonheur est dans le travail.

'I don't understand what you mean by work', replied Macao 'and I am too old to learn.' However, he obtained permission to depart, together with Cosmage, and to seek out some corner which civilization had not yet blessed. They set out, followed by their faithful animals, and, having walked for many, many days, came to a place where the sky was not covered with smoke. It was a poor place compared to the home of their youth, but the trees, though scanty, were beautiful; the birds, though rare, still sang; and there was a little stream. Here they built a small house, and sitting on its doorstep, in extreme old age, they had the experience of happiness. . .

O beautiful book! O wisest of books! What help do you bring after all? You only underline the nevitable. As the author remarks, '*Enfant, Macao était un sag , mais le gouverneur avait raison.*' But your scarlet birds, your purple precipices and white ponds, are part of a dream from which humanity will never awake. In the heart of each man there is contrived, by desperate devices, a magical island such as yours. We place it in the past or the future for safety, for we dare not locate it in the present, because of the Commandant Létambot, who sails upon every sea. We call it a memory or a vision to lend it solidity, but it is neither really; it is the outcome of our sadness, and of our disgust with the world that we have made.

[1920]

ROGER FRY: AN OBITUARY NOTE

ROGER FRY'S death is a definite loss to civilization. He was a great critic and a fine lecturer, and according to some a good painter; he was in touch with the best continental opinion, particularly French opinion; he was charming, polite, courageous, and gay in his private life; he was generous and energetic; he was always helping people, especially the young and the obscure. On all these counts he will be missed, but the definite loss lies elsewhere. What characterized him and made him so precious in twentieth-century England was that, although he was a modern, he believed in reason.

Belief in reason was common enough among the educated a couple of hundred years back, but it is rare today, because our knowledge has become greater and our problems more complicated. We can no longer divide mankind into philosophers, priests, and dupes, as Gibbon or Voltaire could. Even when we style ourselves philosophers, we know that we are sometimes duped, and not always by the priests. We know that each of us carries about a mass of inherited instincts which enters into our judgements and complicates our actions. How is it possible for so mixed a being as man to be reasonable? One might as well expect brass to behave as if it were unalloyed copper. Is not belief in reason based upon a misconception of human nature which we should correct? Since the war, an increasing number of people have come to feel this, and are taking refuge instead in authority or in intuition. Authority attracts our dictators and our serfs, because it seems to promise a stable society. Intuition attracts those who wish to be spiritual without any bother, because it promises a heaven where the intuitions of others can be ignored.

Now Roger Fry rejected authority, mistrusted intuition. That is why his loss is so irreparable. There is no one now living – no one, that is to say, of his calibre – who stands exactly where he stood. He rejected authority absolutely. It is fairly easy for a recluse to reject it or at all events to elude it, but he was not a recluse, he was always in the world and keenly interested in its details, and it is difficult for such a man to avoid being overawed by the imposing figures who surround him and try to set the pace. He is tempted to listen not to what they say but to their names. But a name meant nothing whatever to Fry. He had, in this respect, the unworldliness of his Quaker forebears, and he could always shake an opinion out of its husk, and hold it up to the light of reason, where it often shrivelled to nothing at all. If you said to him, 'This must be right, all the experts say so, all the Trustees of the National Gallery say so, all the art-dealers say so, Hitler says so, Marx says so, Christ says so, *The Times* says so,' he would reply in effect, 'Well. I wonder. Let's see.' He would see and he would make you see. You would come away realizing that an opinion may be influentially backed and yet be tripe. Needless to add, his rise in the official world was slow. It was not until recently that he was elected to a Slade professorship – an extraordinary delay in view of his outstanding claims. And after his death the obituary announcer of the B.B.C. spoke not of him but of a ninety-two-year-old admiral who once captured a Chinese fort. Roger would have found the admiral entertaining and appropriate, almost a sedative. 'Yes, well . . .' comes his veiled, beautiful voice, 'well, yes, of course, he would capture it.' And his eye travels back to the canvas or his hand to the chessboard. He was not an aggressive man, but he was not conciliatory. His integrity and his independence were more to him than official seemliness, and if he wanted to make a devastating remark about Sir Lawrence Alma Tadema, O.M., he made it, and scandalized authority.

Intuition he did not reject. He knew that it is part of our equipment, and that the sensitiveness which he valued in himself and in others is connected with it. But he also knew that it can make dancing dervishes of us all, and that the man who believes a thing is true because he feels it in his bones, is not really very far removed from the man who believes it on the authority of a policeman's truncheon. So he was suspicious of intuition, subjecting it, as it were, to a fumigating process, and not allowing it into his life until it was well aired. Here, it can be argued, he showed himself more of a critic than of a creative artist. Certainly he never tired in applying logic to the illogical – an endless task, though in his case no labour of Ixion. New vistas kept opening as he rose. In his latter years he became more and more fascinated by the implications of modern psychology, and he would not if he could have exchanged his complicated inheritance for the simpler domain of the eighteenth century, where reason reigned unchallenged, or was challenged only by ignorance.

As a young man, he took a science degree at Cambridge; then he devoted himself to art. It was he who introduced the post-impressionists to England and it was his ideas for furniture and decoration which were taken up by commercial firms after the Omega workshops failed. But his aesthetic achievement will be recorded by others; I have no qualifications for referring to it, and though I knew him for many years I only entered into a corner of his rich and varied life. It just seemed worth while, in this brief notice to emphasize the belief which underlies his aesthetics and all his activity; the belief that man is, or rather can be, rational, and that the mind can and should guide the passions towards civilization. He is a terrible loss. Yet somehow he cannot be mourned. There is something anti-funereal about him, just as there was something anti-pi. Enthusiastic, yet comprehending, he moves down the sinister corridor of our age, and those of us who knew him or listened to him or listen to him are heartened to go ahead without him.

[1934]

OUR DIVERSIONS

1. *The Scallies*

EIGHT stools in a row. On each of them a lady or a gentleman sat who, as the curtain rose, broke into unpremeditated song. They were the Scallies, they told us, the Scallies, the Scallies, they were the Scallies. Yes. They were the Scallies, the black and white Scallies, and black and white was their dress. So it was, and when they got up their stools proved to be black and white too, and on the first stool was an S, and on the second stool was a C, and on the third stool was an A, and on the fourth – I hesitate to press the lesson home, but they did not. Each pointed with one hand at his or her stool, and with the other hand at us, and said pleasantly but firmly 'Scallies'. We consulted our programmes. It was so, and they sat down.

The vast auditorium was crammed.* Khaki of the simplest cut predominated. But stars were not absent, nor Crowns, nor even Swords, while Sisters – a little clump of grey touched up with scarlet and white – sat huddled together in a box like seedlings. There were a few civilians – not civilians of the cosmopolitan type – who so laxly throng our cinemas and cafés, but God-fearing patriotic men, who had been told that the Scallies ought to be supported, and had left their homes in consequence. Clouds of smoke arose from the pit. Woodbines, Black Cats, Flags, Scissors, Half-a-Moes, mingled their odours with pipes. An officer lit a cigar. All felt happy.

* Alexandria: during the First World War.

The second item, unlike the first, was not original. It was that song about Ireland. To anyone who has either seen or been an Irishman it is an unconvincing sort of song, and the lady Scally to whom it had been entrusted intoned it without enthusiasm. However, there it was recognizable, and we recognized it, and Tennessee, and the song about the daughters, and many of the jokes, and when the whole troupe ran round their stools and sat down again it was in no unfamiliar fashion. Well satisfied we clapped, and relit our cigarettes, they go out as soon as you stick them behind your ear, while the Scallies spoke humorously to one another about Sergeant Majors, and stopped, with concerted shrieks, one of their number who kept trying to play the piano. It was as soothing as a plate of soup, and as it slipped down the tired limbs relaxed drowsily and the big mouths parted, asking for more.

During the interval we discussed, not whether the Scallies were good, but whether they were better or worse than the Wags. They were less hot stuff, that was admitted on all sides, but on the other hand there were twice as many of them. The Wags were in deep disgrace. There is so little art in the army that it is narrowly watched, and while the Wags ran round their stools the theologico-military authorities had observed that they displayed too much of their legs. Censure was pronounced, and one of the company – he who had sat upon the letter G – seceded to found an entertainment that should be draped beyond reproach. He called unto himself for this purpose a lady then singing in the Boboes, and on the wrecks of these previous institutions the Scallies had been erected. Would it last? Would it split in its turn? It stood firm at present. It represented all that was healthy and official in the way of entertainment for the troops. But the interval was a little long. The audience a little tired and suddenly, from no one in particular, the whole house began singing the Banks of Loch Lomond to pass the time. This was disturbing, because it was beautiful, spontaneous, creative, all that the Scallies were not, and never could be.

The second part opened with an item that did not quite go down. Loch Lomond was to blame perhaps. What happened was that the man who had not played the piano in the first part took the extreme right-hand stool and the extreme left-hand, and put them together, placed on their left the stool marked A, and pointed out the result to one of the other men. Generals and that sort of person in the audience tumbled to the joke at once, but the rank and file were rather puzzled. Neither the Wags nor the Boboes nor the Quips had ever arranged three of their stools in such an order as to spell Ass. However, the cloud passed, and we were back on familiar ground again in an imitation of a Sergeant Major, drilling a squad of seven recruits, and in China Town, and in the 'Long, Long Trail'. 'Chorus, Boys,' the leading lady would say politely, and the boys would chorus with unexpected beauty, and the leading lady, taking care to avert her eyes from anyone in particular, would nod. They all nodded a great deal but never at us. It was one of the familiarities that the theologico-military authorities were discouraging, and when they smiled it was at one another or the ceiling. Their real names? The rank – when they were wives – of their husbands? It is possible to answer such questions but idle to ask them. Art is impersonal.

The programme ended at an early hour. Some took cars, others trams, the clump of Sisters were swiftly transplanted from their box into a motor ambulance. 'Quite what is wanted,' said the most scarlet of them, 'yet I'm still not certain that I, for my own part, do not personally regret the Wags.' I rather regret them, too, but not acutely. For among these changings and choppings of companies' permutations of the alphabet I find this abiding consolation: all are British.

[1917]

2. *The Birth of an Empire*

Feeling a bit lost, and lifting my feet like a cat, I entered the grounds of the British Empire Exhibition at Wembley a few days before their official opening. It was the wrong entrance, or at all events not the right one, which I could not find, and I feared to be turned back by the authorities, but they seemed a bit lost too, though they no longer lifted their feet. Useless for pussy to pick and choose in such a place; slap over one's ankles at the first step flowed the mud. A lady in the Victoria League had told me there was to be no mud; 'There was some, but we have dealt with it,' said she, and perhaps there is none at the proper entrance; the hundreds of shrouded turnstiles that I presently viewed from the inside were certainly clean enough. But the authorities seemed covered with mud; it disputed with grey paint the possession of their faces; they made no bones about mud at all, and were without exception courteous and cheerful. They were even leisurely; the idea that they were completing an entertainment which should be opened in less than a week had evidently been dismissed from their minds, and they went on living their lives. In this they showed their high imperial vision. Pray, did Clive settle the date when he would win Plassey, or Stanley and Livingstone decide exactly when and where they would shake hands? Certainly not. They were making history, not keeping to it, and Wembley does the same. Clocks may strike, suns rise and set, the moon herself accomplish an entire revolution, but the loftier enterprises of man have always ignored such promptings. What is time? And, after all (I thought), why should the Exhibition not be opened in a day or two. It is even open now.

I was bound for the Indian section, and received a good deal of sympathy and advice from the navvies I consulted. They agreed India was no ordinary journey, and far-away looks came into their eyes. 'It's a bit mucky that way. . . . Best try through that large building, but don't bear too much to the left or you'll get mixed up in the stuff.' I was already glad to be inside a building, for the mud seethed with railway trains, and if I attempted open country, gardeners complained it was their new grass lawn. But the building was so large that it failed in the normal immunities of an interior; more railway trains ran down its stupendous galleries, and there was the extra terror of motions overhead that shaved one's scalp. Some of the machines were exhibits and stood still, but, just as at Madame Tussaud's, one could never be sure the quietest creature would not shoot out a claw suddenly. Getting more and more mixed up in the stuff, I dodged among plesiosauri and waded through brown paper and straw – until, as in a dream, I wriggled through a small hole into the open air and saw across more central mud a mass of white minarets in the later Mogul style.

But how noble and severe was the nearer landscape! Almost overwhelmingly so, had it been complete. Gravely flowed a canal, Mr Kipling was going to name the streets, every street-lamp represented the terrestrial globe together with its axis, and two vast white buildings occupied the middle slopes of a hill, one of which now negotiated the approach of a super-colossal horse. The horse was strapped upon a lorry; it lay upon its side, its stomach gleaming pallidly, and its hoofs sticking out like tureens. Bomph, squelch went the lorry, but the horse kept all of a piece. Did it propose to enter the building, like the stuffed animals, or to perch on its roof like a bird? I could not tell, nor waited to see, for neither the horse nor the building was then looking its best. No doubt both will gain in dignity when they come to terms; but they were ill at ease for the moment, so I passed on, aware that the building must be Australia, and the horse one of the Horses of the Sun. So the other building must be Canada, which lays more stress upon the tranquil afterglow. And the stern circular mass towering above them both, and executed in the loftiest Round-Tabular style of architecture – this must be the Stadium, aspiration's summit. Some advertisements of beer and biscuits topped the Stadium, and filled me with furtive relief, and I learn with regret that the public opinion of the Empire will have none of them and insists on their removal. I am sorry. Beer at tenpence the glass is surely the stuff to give them now and then, and, anyhow, the price I paid for the stuff at lunch. However, one must not become the least vulgar at Wembley, for there is a Petty Court inside it, where you can be had up in front of a couple of beaks if you enjoy yourself in the wrong way; that is said to be ready, anyhow. Pull the advertisements down. The Bishop of London has been prevailed upon to consecrate a small, aisleless church. The postage stamps have been admired by the King. In fact, with the exception of a cemetery, a seriously minded man will find through these turnstiles practically everything that he can require.

Walking along a duckboard, we reach India; some packing-cases in the entrance, labelled East Africa, prove it. Building better than they knew, the Native States appear in a most realistic and convincing state of confusion. It is impossible to settle their boundaries, to adumbrate their constitutions, to grasp their policy. I wriggled from cubicle to cubicle. In one of them, surrounded by parcels, a young lady smoked a cigarette. Asked where I was, she said Patiala. Asked what was in her parcels, she said she thought tigers, but was not sure, Indeed, no one did know what was in their parcels, and the East was unfastened amid cries of surprise and joy. 'Hilda, I had a topping time this morning . . .'; a stream of girls ran, leapt, and dived, swinging their attaché cases. Where had Hilda's friend come from, and what had she been up to? Other ladies followed, with dusty hair and bright eyes. Shrieks of 'We shall never be ready; I'm simply frantic, but they're worse; Oh, have you seen the little lacquer things?' Indians smiled charmingly, and gave incorrect information. It was all delightful; indeed, nothing was wanting except a few more exhibits.

I did come across one – a model of the Mosque of Wazir Khan at Lahore – and this was so lovely and stood so incidentally and accidentally upon a table, that it had all the magic of a real building, met by chance among squalid or pretentious streets. When I see it next, it will probably be glassed, docketed, and have lost its preternatural charm. The students of the Mayo College of Arts had made it, I was told, and perhaps have made models of the other Lahore buildings as well, but no one could be sure what the packing-cases would reveal. This mosque, and a peep-show of the Assuan dam, are the prettiest objects I hit at Wembley; there is plenty that is ludicrous, and all too much that is elevating, but little so far that is delicate, touching. Of course, beauty always does have a rough time in these shows – even rougher than in the actual world. The moment you put a picture into a Palace of Art it wilts like a cut flower, whereas a machine jibs for joy as soon as it gets into a Palace of Machinery. How triumphant the machines are! How imposing are the Horses of the Sun, and the stuffed necks and faces of the various wild animals, and cherries in bottles, and corn in shucks! They are the true denizens of Wembley, they flourish in its rich soil. The Mosque of Wazir Khan and its little friends have a very different summer before them, and I wish them happily through it, and a safe return to their homes.

Well, it is a show that will suit all tastes. Millions will spend money there, hundreds will make money, and a few highbrows will make fun. I belong to the latter class. Rule me out; go, think your own thoughts, don't forget your spats, and don't expect an Empire to be born too punctually.

[1924]

3. *The Doll Souse*

We were none of us invited to contribute, so that our thoughts are tainted by detachment, and do not dance as they ought. How differently I should feel – how differently must those feel who were permitted to throw themselves into the Queen's Dolls' House heart and soul, to paint a picture or write a book for its walls, to deposit with proud humility a celluloid cat in its kitchen or a box of real chocolates in the basement! To them it must seem what perhaps it is – a Hindenburg Statuette into which every creative artist has driven his pin; while to the uninvited eye of envy gaps are visible between the pins, bald patches, inter-atomic intervals which the insertion of one's own masterpiece might have sanctified. It is too late now. The scroll of Faerydom has been shut for ever. Wembley (as Lord Leverhulme recently reminded us) is the centre of an Empire entirely composed of opportunities, and we have failed to profit by ours. All we can do now is to pay one and sixpence in order to pay sixpence in order to pay sixpence in order to inspect the whimsicalities of others. Let us do this.

Drilled by boy scouts, let us extend through room after room in the Palace of Art, right across Canada and far into New Zealand. Most of us are ladies, but gentlemen occur, also soldiers, sailors, and other national oddments. The general public hangs on the flanks, pretending to study Colonial art, but really trying to slip into the queue out of its turn. Commissionaires stop it. 'Hi! behind for the Doll Souse,' they shout, and the general public is ashamed and obeys. Once again Colonial art has failed to obtain recognition. Just as it was about to triumph, a counter attraction has done it in. We cannot admire in passing the masterpieces of mart and prairie, however hard we try, because we cannot be still, and as we toddle and turn, so must they. Kept on the move, they too become a queue, their frames melt, schools are crumpled, tendencies crack, the portraits are swimming in landscape sauce. Who, except a bad fairy, could have foreseen such a disaster to the Empire? What but a Dolls' House could have caused it? While far away in a corner, with a shawl over its head, crouches a Gordon Craig peepshow, equally indignant with all parties. The storm from *King Lear* is not going to have any truck with any tosh, no indeed; and wraps itself up more proudly and tragically in its black and gold though not without hopes of being visited in the long run.

Gordon Craig and the colonies must wait together until we are through that final turnstile. The moment approaches, the clicks grow louder, and people who have actually seen the Dolls' House can now be discerned coming out of it in little spouts, like steam from an exhaust. They look dazed, they wipe their lips. 'What's it like?' asks someone, but she cannot reply, for she has caught her reticule in the screws of the exit-apparatus, and as she is forced outward it stretches. 'Oh, dear,' she sighs, 'that might have been one's finger, still it is wonderfully thought out.' What has impressed her so? We shall know in a moment. Neither joyous nor sorrowful, she has certainly been impressed, and she looks at the queue of which she is now the dismembered head, as if she had never belonged either to it or to her reticule, and did not recollect their meaning.

We enter, and all becomes plain. It has indeed been thought out wonderfully. The arrangements for seeing that which has to be seen are colossal. There is no confusion, no emulation, and, of course, no turning back. We find ourselves in a lofty room with a skylight-roof and mansards and cornices of purple. The light pours down exactly as it should, abundant, cold. The floor is divided by railing into terraces, and shelves towards the centre in the style of Dante or an empty swimming bath, and in the centre itself, fully exposed yet somehow or other invisible, rises a most enormous and extraordinary object. What is it? What is it like? Why is it so difficult to apprehend? A blot forms on the vision each time the effort is made. Everything must be like something, so what is this like? The carcass of a bullock? Yes, a little like a carcass, and the pallid skin has been peeled off, and is suspended high in air above the complicated interior. These are lungs, those veins, that hole might fit over the horns. But even this simile must not be pressed too far, for bullocks can be observed, whereas Queen Mary's Dolls' House cannot, it is even more elusive than Colonial art, it is the apotheosis of non-being. The ear rather than the eye finds occupation. 'Keep moving,' now says a one-armed Commissionaire who stands on a high place at the edge – a brave young man, but inclined to be noisy. 'Keep moving, keep moving,' he shouts whenever he detects us glancing towards the central mystery – such a gesture excites and dismays him to the highest degree; 'Keep moving, three times round, you'll have plenty pertunity.' We obey, still unable to look. Three times round we go; the carcass (if such it is) revolves and unwinds thrice, slowly the first time, quicker and closer and higher up afterwards. 'Keep moving, keep moving.' Some item in the deep recesses catches the eye and dominates the mind. The celluloid cat was my fate. Each time it passed me I said, 'Look, a cat,' and between whiles I waited for it to reappear. I had no other memory or expectation. My neighbour chanted 'Chocolates'. Had there been dolls, we might have concentrated on them, but the apotheosis seemed untenanted, and no doubt it is undesirable to present Royalty in doll-form, a jarring note would be struck at once. With the exception of sentries on guard, who do not count, I retain no glimpse of any human being. Pussy one, pussy two, pussy three – that was all I observed, and then I had to go out.

As we neared the exit, the young man with one arm changed his gear into a lower register and sighed, 'Souvenir,

Doll Souse, one penny buys one single copper coin.' But we were far too dazed and numb to chaffer, we could not even dawdle, so excellently had everything been arranged. Collecting into vapour, we were liberated back into the Palace of Art sharply, to observe with bewilderment that a fresh queue had formed in our absence, and that spirits from the uttermost ends of the Seven Seas were slowly toddling onwards for ever with sixpences in their hands.

[1924]

4. *Mickey and Minnie*

I am a film-fanned rather than a film-fan, and oh the things I have had to see and hear because other people wanted to! About once a fortnight a puff of wind raises me from the seat where I am meditating upon life or art, and wafts me in amiability's name towards a very different receptacle. Call it a fauteuil. Here art is not, life not. Not happy, not unhappy, I sit in an up-to-date stupor, while the international effort unrolls. American women shoot the hippopotamus with eyebrows made of platinum. British ladies and gentlemen turn the movies into the stickies for old Elstree's sake. Overrated children salute me from Germany and France, steam-tractors drone across the lengths and breadths of unholy Russia, with the monotony of wedding chimes. All around me, I have reason to believe, sit many fellow film-fanneds, chaff from the winnowing like myself, but we do not communicate with one another, and are indistinguishable from ecstasy in the gloom. Stunned by the howls of the Wurlitzer organ, choked by the fumes of the cigars – and here I break off again, in a style not unsuited to the subject. Why do cigars and cigarettes in a cinema function like syringes? Why do they squirt smoke with unerring aim down my distant throat and into my averted eyes? Where are they coming from? Where are we going to?

Before I can decide, the greatest super-novelty of all time has commenced, Ping Pong, and the toy counter at Gamage's is exhibited as a prehistoric island. Or mayn't I have a good augh? Why certainly, why sure, that's what we take your money for, a good laugh, so here's a guy who can't swim and finds he can racing a guy who can swim and pretends he can't, and the guy who can't get a laugh out of that had better —

But now the attendant beckons, a wraith in beach pyjamas, waving her electric wand. She wants someone, and can it be me? No – she wants no one, it is just a habit she has got into, poor girlie, she cannot stop herself, wave she must, it is a cinema. And when she is off duty she still cannot stop herself, but fanned by she knows not what sits skirted and bloused in the audience she lately patrolled. I do think though – for it is time for optimism to enter – I do think that she will choose a performance which bills a Mickey Mouse. And I do hope that Mickey, on his side, will observe her fidelity and will introduce her into his next Silly Symphony, half-glow-worm and half-newt, waving, waving. . . .

What fun it would be, a performance in which Mickey produced the audience as well as the film! Perhaps Mr Walt Disney will suggest it to him, and I will provide the title gratis: 'Plastic Pools.' We should see some gay sights in his semi-darkness, and more would get squirted about than smoke. Siphons that pour zig-zag, chocolates exploding into fleas – there are rich possibilities in the refreshments alone, and when it comes to Miss Cow's hatpins and fauteuils for the dachshund sisters, why should there be any limits? Yet I don't know. Perhaps not. 'Plastic Pools' is withdrawn. For much as I admire Mickey as a producer, I like him as a lover most, and rather regret these later and more elaborate efforts, for the reason that they keep him too much from Minnie. Minnie is his all, his meinie, his moon. Perhaps even the introduction of Pluto was a mistake. Have you forgotten that day when he and she strolled with their Kodaks through an oriental bazaar, snapping this and that, while their camel drank beer and galloped off on both its humps across the desert? Have you forgotten Wild Waves? Mickey's great moments are moments of heroism, and when he carries Minnie out of the harem as a pot-plant or rescues her as she falls in foam, herself its fairest flower, he reaches heights impossible for the *entrepreneur*. I would not even have the couple sing. The duets in which they increasingly indulge are distracting. Let them confine themselves to raptures for mice, and let them play their piano less.

But is Mickey a mouse? Well, I am hard put to it at moments certainly, and have had to do some thinking back. Certainly one would not recognize him in a trap. It is his character rather than his species that signifies, which one could surely recognize anywhere. He is energetic without being elevating, and although he is assuredly one of the world's great lovers he must be placed at some distance from Charlie Chaplin or Sir Philip Sidney. No one has ever been softened after seeing Mickey or has wanted to give away an extra glass of water to the poor. He is never sentimental, indeed there is a scandalous element in him which I find most restful. Why does he not pick up one of the coins thrown to him in that Texas bar? Why does one of the pillows in *Mickey's Nightmare* knock him down? Why does Pluto – Or there is that moment in *Wild Waves* when Minnie through some miscalculation on her part is drowning, and he rushes for a boat. As he heaves it out of the sand two little blobs are revealed beneath it, creatures too tiny to be anything but love-items, and they scuttle away into a world which will scarcely be as severe on them as ours. There are said to be 'privately shown' Mickeys, and though I do not want to see one, imagination being its own kingdom, I can well believe that anyone who goes so far goes further.

About Minnie too little has been said, and her name at the

top of this article is an act of homage which ought to have been paid long ago. Nor do we know anything about her family. When discovered alone, she appears to be of independent means, and to own a small house in the midst of unattractive scenery, where, with no servant and little furniture, she busies herself about trifles until Mickey comes. For he is her Rajah, her Sun. Without him, her character shines not. As he enters she expands, she becomes simple, tender, brave, and strong, and her coquetterie is of the delightful type which never conceals its object. Ah, that squeak of greeting! As you will have guessed from it, her only fault is hysteria. Minnie does not always judge justly, and she was ill advised, in *Puppy Love*, to make all that fuss over a bone. She ought to have known it belonged to the dogs. It is possible that, like most of us, she is deteriorating. To be approached so often by Mickey, and always for the first time, must make any mouse mechanical. Perhaps sometimes she worries whether she has ever been married or not, and her doubts are not easy to allay, and the wedding chimes in *Mickey's Nightmare* are no guide or a sinister one. Still, it seems likely that they have married one another, since it is unlikely that they have married anyone else, since there is nobody else for them to marry.

What of their future? At present Mickey is everybody's god, so that even members of the Film Society cease despising their fellow members when he appears. But gods are not immortal. There was an Egyptian called Bes, who was once quite as gay, and Brer Rabbit and Felix the Cat have been forgotten too, and Ganesh is being forgotten. Perhaps he and Minnie will follow them into oblivion. I do not care two hoots. I am all for the human race. But how fortunate that it should have been accompanied, down the ages, by so many cheerful animals, and how lucky that the cinema has managed to catch the last of them in its questionable reels!

[1934]

5. Chess at Cracow

WHITE	BLACK
P—K4.	P—K4.
P—KB4.	P × P.
B—B4.	Q—R5 (check).
K—B. sq.	

That is to say, White advanced his king's pawn two squares, Black did the same, White did the same with another pawn and Black took it—traditional, but risky. White's next move, bringing out the bishop, will strike the experts as odd. It is usual to bring out the knight. But why talk of oddness when the pawns were eight feet high, and the bishops ten, and the queen twelve? At Cracow, in the courtyard of the Wawel, how can anything be odd? The great renaissance arcades, the gay soldierly music, the black-and-white squares on the gravel, the soft black sky, the cathedral close by, the Vistula below, made a universe in which only human beings seemed out of place, and chessmen became real.

Chess, that inestimable possession, that precious game made and moulded by history, and by our desire for intellectual happiness, that game which the experts have not yet ruined and which has drawn together different races and classes for centuries, that man's game, if I may say so (for even the queen was a prime minister once, and even the bishop an elephant) – chess took new beauty and strength that evening in Poland, in that magic castle, the refuge of dead kings, it looked backwards triumphantly, recalled the past, adorned itself with music and light. There are moments when the world is compelled to rearrange itself, and one of these occurred when the pawns came toddling in. For a long time the courtyard had been empty, while the band played and the audience sorted themselves in the four tiers of the arcades. Then, to a special little tune, great structures of red and gold entered through a dark archway – the eight pawns of the 'White' side, suggesting Saracens, followed by eight others in green and blue, Mongolian. When they had taken their places on their squares and bowed to each other, the music became more grandiose, and the larger pieces began to emerge, culminating in the stupendous monarchs, who supported their frameworks with difficulty and sometimes had to be towed to their squares. It was a heartening sight, especially to anyone who had suffered under the fatuities of pageantry in England – Druids, Drake, the Lady Mary receiving the keys of the city in all her dowdiness. A pageant requires not only splendour, but a touch of the grotesque, which should lurk like onion in a salad. One ought to feel 'Oh, how splendid!' then smile, and so realize the splendour better than before, and there are smiles which cannot be raised by Friar Tuck. There are smiles which never interrupt beauty. How charmingly, on this occasion, was the stupidity of the castles indicated by some low, eye-shaped windows in the neighbourhood of their knees! I had never before understood why castles are so difficult to manage. What a settled despair lurked in the beards of the kings! The knights rocked to and fro on their squares, even more indifferent than usual to their immediate neighbours, and the pawns were like overgrown children, defenceless yet dangerous.

But I must describe how the game was played.

When the thirty-two pieces were in position, a mannikin in red and gold appeared, attended by two torch bearers. He inspected the 'White' pieces with all the aplomb characteristic of the human race; he was, as a matter of fact, a man, and, immensely tiny, he ascended a little dais when he had finished and gazed over the board, simulating now intelligence and now emotion, as he touched his turbaned forehead or waved his draped arms. He was followed by a mannikin in green and blue, the player of 'Black'. The band played wildly and was silent. Then, to a new tune, the red and white mannikin leapt from his dais with a Japanese lantern in his hand. What was he going to do? He seemed not to know; he had the air of never having walked on a chessboard before. But he gravitated, like many a previous player, towards his king's pawn. Finally, he approached the expectant infant and waved his lantern at its stomach. The pawn stumbled forward and, dancing before it, he caused it to advance two squares, then he went back to the dais. The second player adopted the prowling style. With the air of one who walks by night, he stole to his pawn and beckoned with his lantern stealthily. The game went on as shown at the beginning of this article, and those who do not play chess had better be told that the blue and green mannikin was, with his second move, faced with a crisis. Should he or should he not take the pawn offered by the other fellow? To take it would not be rank folly – generations of previous players had taken it – but experts are now in favour of resisting the temptation and doing something else instead. Long did he meditate. Then, his sombre decision taken, he summoned his two torch bearers, and they led the pawn away into outer darkness, to the sound of cymbals and drums. This interruption in the music always occurred when a capture was made. It was very effective, and I wished that there could be a special sound for 'check', too – the moaning of an oboe, perhaps. Check occurred as early as the third move, and by then I was already puzzled over the quality of the game. It was either too good for me or too bad.

Cracow is a strange place. What other town has threaded a golden crown on the spire of its church, or has installed a trumpeter to play every hour and to end his tune with a gasp because, centuries ago, a trumpeter was shot through the throat by the Mongols? And the strangest thing in Cracow is the royal enclosure of the Wawel, with its conflicting hints of Russia and of Rome. Self-contained, it dominates the city and the river from its height like a Kremlin, but it is all Catholicism within, and Italian artists have worked there among builders from the East. It is being repaired, and there are no more funds; and the game of Living Chess had been organized in the hope of bringing in a little money. I had paid sixpence and watched with sympathy, and I was soon engrossed by the difficulties surrounding the black queen. She had never liked being moved out so early, she had a haggard, offended look, as of a matron compelled to join in a party too soon, and was fain to rest on the hem of her mighty crinoline. By the eighth move, pawns were closing her in. I suspected collusion, and withdrew. The cathedral outside was dark and silent, and great blocks of buildings extended in various directions to the edges of the plateau, which were diversified by various towers. While I hesitated in which direction to go, there was a sound of cymbals and drums from the interior of the castle. The queen had fallen.

[1932]

6. *The Game of Life*

O Life, what art thou? Life seldom answers this question. But her silence is of little consequence, for schoolmasters and other men of goodwill are well qualified to answer for her. She is, they inform us, a game. Which game? Bagatelle? No, life is serious, so not bagatelle, but any game that ... er ... is not a game of mere chance; not Baccarat, but Chess; or, in moderation, Bridge; yes, or better still, Football with its goals and healthy open-air atmosphere and its *esprit de corps*; Fate is the umpire and Hope is the ball: hie to the football ground all, all, all.— Thus far and even further the men of goodwill. Once started on the subject of Life they lose all diffidence, because to them it is ethical. They love discussing what we ought to be instead of what we have to face – reams about conduct and nothing about those agitating apparitions that

69

rise from the ground or fall from the sky. When they say that Life is a game they only mean that some games develop certain qualities, such as heartiness, which they appreciate.

Still, they may have used the right phrase. There are some curious features about games, moments of piercing reality when an unknown process is suddenly reflected like a star. Upon the simple little universes that have been created by the device of rules and by the convention of a beginning and an end, there sometimes descends an endorsement, as it were, from the actual universe. Similar endorsements descend upon works of art. But there their effect upon us is different. They gratify. They make us feel we could be artists too. Whereas the game, when it becomes real, becomes disquieting. A win always seems shallow: it is the lose that is so profound and suggests nasty infinities. Games of mere chance must, it is true, be excluded from this charge. They have abandoned any pretence of Free Will, and consequently their irony is too mechanical to be endorsed by Life's: Life may also be mere chance, but she has evolved the imposing doctrine of effort and reward to obscure her purposelessness, and any game that mirrors her must do the same. Let us therefore turn to games of skill, and in the first place to Chess.

I play the Evans.

The invention of a naval officer, the Evans Gambit is noted for its liquidity. A heavy current rapidly sets in from the south-west and laps against the foundations of Black's King's Bishop's Pawn. The whole surface of the board breaks into whirlpools. But sooner or later out of this marine display there rises a familiar corpse. It is mine. Oh, what have I been doing, what have I been doing? The usual thing. Premature attack, followed by timidity. Oh, why didn't I move out my Rook's Pawn? Because as always I was misled by superficial emotions. No, not as always. It must be that the Evans doesn't suit my style. Henceforward I play Old Stodge.

I do so. There is nothing liquid about Old Stodge. He smacks of the soil. On either side runs a dreary ridge of Knights and Bishops. Between them is a plain (whence the term of Giuoco Piano) where the Pawns butt one another like rams. The powers of earth move slowly to the shock, then topple over with alternate and uninspiring thuds. It's supposed to be an exchange. But when the lines of the new landscape emerge from the dust, what familiar corpse is disclosed? Mine. Oh, what have I been doing? The usual thing. My character has come out. If I go down to the depths of the sea, it is there; if I seek the heart of the hills it is there also. Chess, which severely eliminates accident, is a forcing house where the fruits of character can ripen more fully than in Life. In Life we can always blame the unknowable for our failures, wave the hand to some horizon, shake the fist at some star. But surely when we make the same mistakes in the Evans, Old Stodge, the choice of a tie, a row in the office and a love affair, the same defect must be to blame – character; for which, the men of goodwill hasten to remind us, we are entirely and eternally responsible.

Since there are these two elements in life, the uncontrollable and that which we are supposed to control; and since games of chance exaggerate the former and Chess the latter – what game reflects their actual proportion?

Piquet.

Those who reply Bridge or Football introduce the incalculable element of partners and sides. One complexity cannot interpret another, and though Life may be Bridge, it is so only to the eye of faith: the resemblance cannot be grasped by an intellectual effort. But think for a moment about Piquet. It is in the first place obviously and overwhelmingly unfair. Fate is dealt, despite skill in discarding, and neither in the rules of play nor in the marking is there the least attempt to redress misfortune or to give the sufferer a fresh chance. The bias is all the other way. Disaster is an additional reason for disaster – culminating in the crowning butchery of Rubicon, where the very bones of the victim are gathered up by the conqueror and flung like sticks upon his bonfire. Yet this savage pastime admits the element of Free Will. It is possible to retard or accelerate Fate. Play, subtle and vigorous play, goes on all the time, though the player is being swept to disaster or victory by causes beyond his control, and it is in the play, rather than the result, that the real interest of the game resides. Another affair, in which all the living and possibly all the dead are engaged, runs on similar lines. Failure or success seem to have been allotted to men by their stars. But they retain the power of wriggling, of fighting with their star or against it, and in the whole universe the only really interesting movement is this wriggle. O Life, thou art Piquet, in fact. A grim relaxation. Still, she might have been Golf.

[1919]

7. *My Own Centenary*
(From *The Times* of A.D. 2027)

It is a hundred years ago today since Forster died; we celebrate his centenary indeed within a few months of the bicentenary of Beethoven, within a few weeks of that of Blake. What special tribute shall we bring him? The question is not easy to answer, and were he himself still alive he would no doubt reply, 'My work is my truest memorial.' It is the reply that a great artist can always be trusted to make. Conscious of his lofty mission, endowed with the divine gift of self-expression, he may rest content, he is at peace, doubly at peace. But we, we who are not great artists, only the recipients of their bounty – what shall we say about Forster? What can we say that has not already been said about Beethoven, about Blake? Whatever shall we say?

The Dean of Dulborough, preaching last Sunday in his own beautiful cathedral, struck perhaps the truest note. Taking as his text that profound verse in Ecclesiasticus, 'Let us now praise famous men,' he took it word by word, paused when he came to the word 'famous', and, slowly raising his voice, said: 'He whose hundredth anniversary we celebrate on Thursday next is famous, and why?' No answer was needed, none came. The lofty Gothic nave, the great western windows, the silent congregation – they gave answer sufficient, and passing on to the final word of his text, 'men', the Dean expatiated upon what is perhaps the most mysterious characteristic of genius, its tendency to appear among members of the human race. Why this is, why, since it is, it is not accompanied by some definite outward sign through which it might be recognized easily, are questions not lightly to be raised. There can be no doubt that his contemporaries did not recognize the greatness of Forster. Immersed in their own little affairs, they either ignored him, or forgot him, or confused him, or, strangest of all, discussed him as if he was their equal. We may smile at their blindness, but for him it can have been no laughing matter, he must have had much to bear, and indeed he could scarcely have endured to put forth masterpiece after masterpiece had he not felt assured of the verdict of posterity.

Sir Vincent Edwards, when broadcasting last night, voiced that verdict not uncertainly, and was fortunately able to employ more wealth of illustration than had been appropriate in Dulborough Minster for the Dean. The point he very properly stressed was our writer's loftiness of aim. 'It would be impossible,' he said, 'to quote a single sentence that was not written from the very loftiest motive,' and he drew from this a sharp and salutary lesson for the so-called writers of today. As permanent head of the Ministry of Edification, Sir Vincent has, we believe, frequently come into contact with the younger generation, and has checked with the kindliness of which he

is a pastmaster their self-styled individualism – an individualism which is the precise antithesis of true genius. They confuse
violence with strength, cynicism with open-mindedness, frivolity with joyousness – mistakes never made by Forster who
was never gay until he had earned the right to be so, and only
criticized the religious and social institutions of his time because they were notoriously corrupt. We know what the
twentieth century was. We know the sort of men who were
in power under George V. We know what the State was, what
were the churches. We can as easily conceive of Beethoven as
a Privy Councillor or of Blake as, forsooth, an Archbishop as
of this burning and sensitive soul acquiescing in the deadening
conditions of his age. What he worked for – what all great
men work for – was for a New Jerusalem, a vitalized State, a
purified Church; and the offertory at Dulborough last Sunday,
like the success of Sir Edward's appeal for voluntary workers
under the Ministry, shows that he did not labour in vain.

The official ceremony is for this morning. This afternoon
Lady Turton will unveil Mr Boston Jack's charming statue in
Kensington Gardens, and so illustrate another aspect of our
national hero: his love of little children. It had originally been
Mr Boston Jack's intention to represent him as pursuing an
ideal. Since, however, the Gardens are largely frequented by
the young and their immediate supervisors, it was felt that
something more whimsical would be in place, and a butterfly
was substituted. The change is certainly for the better. It is true
that we cannot have too many ideals. On the other hand, we
must not have too much of them too soon, nor, attached as it
will be to a long copper wire, can the butterfly be confused
with any existing species and regarded as an incentive to im-
mature collectors. Lady Turton will couple her remarks with
an appeal for the Imperial Daisy Chain, of which she is the
energetic Vice-President, and simultaneously there will be a
flag collection throughout the provinces.

Dulborough, the Ministry of Edification, the official ceremony, Kensington Gardens! What more could be said? Not a
little. Yet enough has been said to remind the public of its
heritage, and to emphasize and define the central essence of
these immortal works. And what is that essence? Need we
say? Not their greatness – they are obviously great. Not their
profundity – they are admittedly profound. It is something
more precious than either: their nobility. Noble works, nobly
conceived, nobly executed, nobler than the Ninth Symphony
or the Songs of Innocence. Here is no small praise, yet it can
be given, we are in the presence of the very loftiest, we need
not spare or mince our words, nay, we will add one more
word, a word that has been implicit in all that have gone
before: like Beethoven, like Blake, Forster was essentially
English, and in commemorating him we can yet again celebrate what is best and most permanent in ourselves.

LIBERTY IN ENGLAND

*(An address delivered at the Congrès International des Ecrivains at Paris
on 21 June 1935.)*

WHEN this committee honoured me with an invitation to
speak and asked me to choose a subject, I replied that I would
speak either on liberty of expression or on cultural tradition,
as they preferred, but that in either case I should make the
same speech. Coming from an Englishman, this is not an
epigram. In England, our traditions and our liberties are
closely connected, and so it should be possible to treat the two
at once. Freedom has been praised in my country for several
hundred years. Duty and self-abnegation have been praised
too, but freedom has won the larger chorus. And if we writers

today could carry this tradition on, if we could assert, under modern conditions, what has been asserted by Milton in his century and by Shelley and by Dickens in theirs, we should have no fear for our liberties.

I know very well how limited, and how open to criticism, English freedom is. It is race-bound and it's class-bound. It means freedom for the Englishman, but not for the subject-races of his Empire. If you invite the average Englishman to share his liberties with the inhabitants of India or Kenya, he will reply, 'Never,' if he is a Tory, and 'Not until I consider them worthy' if he is a Liberal. Last year, General Smuts made a magnificent speech about freedom to the students of the University of St Andrews. With every word that he said, I agreed. But there was one thing he didn't say. He never suggested that the blessings he praised so eloquently might be applicable to the coloured peoples of South Africa. He was not even thinking about them. And this omission made his eulogy a mockery.

Then as to class. Freedom in England is only enjoyed by people who are fairly well off. For the down and out – unless he is very exceptional – it does not signify a plate of fish and chips. There is nothing to interest an average man on the dole in the right to express oneself, which we authors think so important. He regards liberty as a fad of the upper classes, which they take up because they have enough to eat, and enjoy breaking regulations. I have friends who are not down and out, but are near the border-line and have relatives over the border, and they are cynical about our congress and its possibilities. And I think that anyone who, like myself, believes in freedom yet keeps his ears open will catch at moments this irritable snarl. The hungry and the homeless don't care about liberty any more than they care about cultural heritage. To pretend that they do care is cant.

I've tried to be honest about these two limitations, the racial and the social, because in spite of them I do believe in liberty, and think that the particular type that has been developed in Great Britain may still be of use both to us and to the world. As for my politics, you will have guessed that I am not a Fascist – Fascism does evil that evil may come. And you may have guessed that I am not a Communist, though perhaps I might be one if I was a younger and a braver man, for in Communism I can see hope. It does many things which I think evil, but I know that it intends good. I am actually what my age and my upbringing have made me – a bourgeois who adheres to the British constitution, adheres to it rather than supports it, and the fact that this isn't dignified doesn't worry me. I do care about the past. I do care about the preservation and the extension of freedom. And I have come to this congress mainly to listen to what is being done and suffered in other lands. My own land – we're in for a bad time, too, I've no doubt about it, but the fact that our rulers have to *pretend* to like freedom is an advantage. Shakespeare, whatever his personal opinions were – Shakespeare appreciated hypocrisy, and the words which Hamlet addresses to his erring mother might equally be addressed by us to the mother of Parliaments: –

> Good night; but go not to mine uncle's bed;
> Assume a virtue, if you have it not.
> That monster, custom, who all sense doth eat,
> Of habits devil, is angel yet in this,
> That to the use of actions fair and good
> He likewise gives a frock or livery,
> That aptly is put on.

If Britannia goes a-whoring, she can be the more easily found out because of her professions of monogamy in the past. That is why, with us, the *forms* of government and the *forms* of justice are so important, and need watching so zealously.

'Mine uncle's bed' lies all too close to the benches of the Houses of Parliament, and has its carnal attractions, even when the uncle is Sir Oswald Mosley. It is something that in England dictatorship is still supposed to be ungentlemanly, and massacres of Jews in bad form, and private armies figures of fun.

Our danger from Fascism – unless a war starts, when anything may happen – is negligible. We're menaced by something more much insidious – by what I might call 'Fabio-Fascism', by the dictator-spirit working quietly away behind the façade of constitutional forms, passing a little law (like the Sedition Act) here, endorsing a departmental tyranny there, emphasizing the national need of secrecy elsewhere, and whispering and cooing the so-called 'news' every evening over the wireless, until opposition is tamed and gulled. Fabio-Fascism is what I am afraid of, for it is the traditional method by which liberty has been attacked in England. It was the method of King Charles I – a gentleman if ever there was one – the method of our enlightened authoritarian gentleman today. This Fabio-Fascism is our old enemy, the tyrant:

> He shall mark our goings, question whence we came,
> Set his guards about us, as in Freedom's name.
> He shall peep and mutter, and the night shall bring
> Watchers 'neath our window, lest we mock the King.

'As in Freedom's name.' How well Rudyard Kipling puts it – though he will scarcely thank me for quoting him.

The most open blow that has been struck lately against freedom of expression in England is the Sedition Act which I have just mentioned. Its official title is the Incitement to Dis-affection Act, and it was passed last year by our so-called National Government by the large majority which is always at its command. This act restores the right of General Search (condemned as illegal for the last 170 years), it impedes the moral and political education of the soldier, it encourages the informer, and it can be employed against pacifists. There were strong protests against it, which were scarcely reported either by the daily Press or by the B.B.C. The protests were not without effect, and some of the more dangerous clauses in the original Bill were withdrawn while it was in committee. It is the sort of a measure which a government passes in order to have up its sleeve, in the event of emergency, and does not intend to use at once. Nevertheless, it had an immediate effect; I know of a case in which some printers refused to print a pacifist children's story, on the ground that the story might fall into the hands of a soldier, and be held to have seduced him from his allegiance! The printers were over-timid. Yet this is what always happens and is intended to happen when a law of this type is passed. The public is vaguely intimidated, and determines to be on the safe side, and do less, say less, and think less than usual. That, rather than the actual exercise of the law, is the real evil. A psychological censorship gets set up, and the human heritage is impaired.

Much more might be said about the Sedition Act, but it must be left to experts. I am more concerned with the blows which are being struck against freedom in my country secretly and quietly, either by the illegitimate action of the police or by the unwarrantable if legal application of the law. I have in my mind a recent case in which the law has been used to crush a book, a novel of much literary merit, and since this is a congress of authors the case is apposite and I will deal with it faithfully.

The book in question is *Boy*, by James Hanley. *Boy* was published nearly four years ago, and went into no less than four editions before it attracted the wrath of the authorities. It had been discussed, praised, blamed, and generally accepted as a serious and painful piece of work, whose moral, if it had one, was definitely on the side of chastity and of virtue. Its contemporary backing was considerable – for instance, I have seen quoted a testimony from the late Colonel Lawrence, whom respectable society is at present canonizing. One assumed that *Boy* had, so to speak, passed into our literary heritage, where it would remain for posterity to consider and finally to assess. Then, like a bolt from the blue, the publishers were summoned by the Lancashire police, because they had 'published an obscene libel'.

Why Lancashire, when it had been published in London? Why in 1934, when it had been published in 1930? The answer to these questions is only to be found in the mysteries of the English law. The publishers were advised to plead guilty, for technical reasons; they did so, and at the Manchester Assizes they were heavily fined to the extent of £400. The author, I am glad to say, has not been attacked in the matter. But his publishers, a small and very decent firm who only handle reputable work, have nearly been ruined. Nor is this all. Although they have withdrawn *Boy* from circulation they are advised that they are still liable legally to be summoned in respect of every copy which had been sold before withdrawal. That is to say, they might be fined another £400 in Cheshire, another £400 in Devonshire, and so on, and this might go on for years and years. I am not telling you a fairy tale out of Swift or Voltaire. I am telling you what can happen in England, the home of free speech. What can happen when the law is put into action unwarrantably.

Boy is the sort of case where protests are useful – not as regards the past, which they cannot remedy, but as regards the future. Public opinion still counts, and if public opinion declares that the case ought never to have been brought and that the fine was excessive, the authorities concerned are likely to be more cautious. We have had, of course, ridiculous cases in the past – the suppression of *The Well of Loneliness*, and of the original edition of D. H. Lawrence's *Rainbow*, and the solemn burning of *Ulysses* in the Folkestone Custom House. But none of them have been so fantastic as *Boy*, which asserts the right of Authority to prosecute after any lapse of time and at the initiative of any policeman in any provincial town. The publishers have been selected for punishment this time. Next time it will be the author, unless authors make their voices heard.

But to turn from these details to the possibility of a general campaign – that, I suppose, is the main reason of our congress. I fear that I have little to contribute. I know what I *want* and will epitomize it. I want greater freedom for writers, both as creators and as critics. In England, more than elsewhere, their creative work is hampered because they can't write freely about sex, and I want it recognized that sex is a subject for serious treatment and also for comic treatment; this latter aspect of it is usually ignored by speakers when they get on to platforms, so I don't wish to miss it out. As for criticism, I want to maintain the right of public comment – in England here we are fortunate, because we possess it still, whereas from some of you it has been withdrawn. But public comment is negative, if nobody hears it, and so I want publicity for all sorts of comment – and that in England as elsewhere is being lost, chiefly owing to the governmental control of broadcasting. And I want the maintenance of culture.

How would I bring this about? By an attempt in my own country to utilize the existing apparatus, and to extend to all classes and races what has hitherto been confined to a few wealthy and white-coloured people. And by bringing English writers into closer touch with their Continental colleagues. We are terribly isolated and ignorant as to what is going on.

Before I conclude my remarks, I must make clear that they are composed independently and do not represent the general opinion of the English delegation. My colleagues probably agree with my account of the situation in our country, but they may disagree with my old-fashioned attitude over it, and may feel that it is waste of time to talk about freedom and tradition when the economic structure of society is unsatisfactory. They may say that if there is another war writers of the individualistic and liberalizing type, like myself and Mr Aldous Huxley, will be swept away. I am sure that we shall be swept away, and I think furthermore that there may be another war. It seems to me that if nations keep on amassing armaments, they can no more help discharging their filth than an animal which keeps on eating can stop itself from excreting. This being so, my job, and the job of those who feel with me, is an interim job. We have just to go on tinkering as well as we can with our old tools until the crash comes. When the crash comes, nothing is any good. After it – if there is an after – the task of civilization will be carried on by people whose training has been different from my own.

I am worried by thoughts of a war oftener than by thoughts of my own death, yet the line to be adopted over both these nuisances is the same. One must behave as if one is immortal, and as if civilization is eternal. Both statements are false – I shall not survive, no more will the great globe itself – both of them must be assumed to be true if we are to go on eating and working and travelling, and keep open a few breathing holes for the human spirit. Although I am not a public speaker, I wanted to come to Paris to say this. Whatever our various remedies for the present evils – and we are sure to differ – we all believe in courage. If a writer is courageous and sensitive he has to my mind fulfilled his public calling. He has helped to rally humanity in the presence of catastrophe. And the courage that I shall find here among colleagues from so many nations – it will reinforce my own.

PART II

BOOKS

A NOTE ON THE WAY

AFTER letting myself go lately on the depressing subject of military tattooes and tainted investments, I thought, as I often do, of a line of Matthew Arnold's: 'Who prop, thou ask'st, in these bad days, my mind?' It is a line that rather makes me smile. For one thing the difficulty of pronouncing 'skst' is almost insuperable, for another Matthew Arnold's 'bad days' are Halcyon when compared with our own. He belonged to an age which was concerned with problems of faith, doubt, and personal survival; he was worried by these, but the collapse of all civilization, so realistic for us, sounded in his ears like a distant and harmonious cataract, plunging from Alpine snows into the eternal bosom of the Lake of Geneva. We are passing through a much rougher time, perhaps the roughest time that has ever been. And if we look back into the past for comfort, we see upon the faces of its great men a curious mixture of comprehension and of blankness. They seem at the same time to understand us and not to understand. If public violences increase and Geneva itself disappears – who is going to prop our minds? They? The great minds of the past? They, who imagined, at the worst, a local or a philosophic catastrophe?

Yes. They are going to do something. If we have read them, or have listened to good music, it is going to be some use. The individual who has been rendered sensitive by education will not be deserted by it in his hour of need. But the help won't be given as directly, as crudely, as Matthew Arnold thought. An educationist as well as a poet, he believed one could 'turn' to writers – to Homer, Epictetus, and Sophocles in his own case – and by quoting their beauties or remembering their thoughts could steel oneself against injustice or cruelty. I don't think they are going to bring their help that way. Their gifts are received less consciously and often provoke no thanks. But it is a great mistake to assume that nothing is going on, and a great blunder to close one's mind to the past because the present is so large and so frightening. The past, through its very detachment, can re-interpret.

It is easier to catch it failing than succeeding, and a little experience of my own not long ago, when Beethoven failed to do his job, will, anyhow, indicate the area where the job lies. I was going to a Busch Quartet and much looking forward to it, but just before starting I heard a decent and straightforward story of misfortune – quite unprintable, even in these advanced columns. Much of what one hears and says can never be printed; that is why newspapers are so unreal. This particular story involved procreation, marriage, birth. I got to the Wigmore Hall so occupied and worried over it, that I could not listen to the music at all, and yet I heard the whole of the music. I could not be caught up to meet my Lord in the air, yet there Beethoven was, working away all the time, and seeming to be actually a few feet above my head, where I could not reach him. It is, perhaps, creditable to my heart that I couldn't, but exactly the same thing happened in the Queen's Hall a few years ago when I had received a notice that my evidence would be wanted in the *Well of Loneliness* case. Here my thoughts were purely selfish. I was so fidgeting as to what figure I should cut in the witness-box that again nothing came through. The arts are not drugs. They are not guaranteed to act when taken. Something as mysterious and as capricious as the creative impulse has to be released before they can prop our minds. Siegfried Sassoon calls them 'lamps for our gloom, hands guiding where we stumble', which quiet personal image suits them very well.

The propping quality in books, music, etc., is only a by-product of another quality in them; their power to give pleasure. Consequently, it is impossible to advise one's friends what to read in 'these bad days', and even more impossible to advise people whom one doesn't know. All I can suggest is that where the fire was thence will the light come; where there was intense enjoyment, grave or gay, thence will proceed the help which every individual needs. And I don't want to exaggerate that help. Art is not enough, any more than love is enough, and thought isn't stronger than artillery parks now, whatever it may have been in the days of Carlyle. But art, love, and thought can all do something, and art, the most nervous of the three, mustn't be brushed aside like a butterfly. It is not all gossamer, what we have delighted in, it has become part of our armour, and we can gird it on, although there is no armour against fate.

> Fair as unshaded light, or as the day
> In its first birth, when all the year was May;
> Sweet as the altar's smoke, or as the new
> Unfolded bud, swelled by the early dew;
> Smooth as the face of waters first appeared,
> Ere tides began to strive or winds were heard —

I quote these lines, not because they are great poetry (it is only Sir William Davenant addressing Queen Henrietta Maria), nor because they bear on the matter in hand (he is only welcoming her to an evening at the Countess of Anglesey's), but because they have happened to deposit a grain of strength in my mind. They are so lovely in their little way, and they have helped towards that general belief in loveliness which is part of our outfit against brutality. And I thought I would try to bring this out in my present note rather than deal with 'actualities'. These lines of Davenant – not 'ready when wanted', yet serviceable somehow – have gone down to a region in me which Matthew Arnold and Beethoven have also reached.

In the 'great' war, books helped me enormously, they even helped men in the trenches. My own position was easy. I was comfortable in Egypt, yet could I have come through without those 'lamps for my gloom'? I did not seek help consciously – except on one occasion: from Browning, a poet whom I don't much admire, and Browning, knowing this, gave the help in a hard hygienic way, for the occasion only, and at the price of my reading his *Flight of the Duchess*. The people I really clung to were those who had nothing tangible to offer: Blake, William Morris, the early T. S. Eliot, J. K. Huysmans, Yeats. They took me into a country where the will is not everything, and the braying patriots of the moment made no sound. They were personal guides, and if I mention their names and add César Franck's, it is not to give a tip to 1934, only to suggest some parallel. We are all harder and more disillusioned now than we were then, the League of Nations lies behind us instead of before, and no political creed except communism offers an intelligent man any hope. And those who are, like myself, too old for communism or too conscious of the blood to be shed before its problematic victory, turn to literature, because it is disinterested. Action? Yes, no objection to action if it tinkers in the right direction, stops tattoos for instance. But not action the Fascist anodyne:

> Not milder is the general lot
> Because our spirits have forgot,
> In action's dizzying eddy whirl'd
> The something that infects the world.

Matthew Arnold, the poet, felt and knew much more than Matthew Arnold, the prose-writer, succeeded in saying. His poetry stands up in the middle of the nineteenth century as a beacon to the twentieth, it is both an armoury and an enchanted garden. Literature as a retreat is rightly discredited; it is both selfish and foolish to bury one's head in the flowers. But herbs grow in the garden, too, and share in its magics, and from them is distilled the stoicism which we badly need today. Uneducated people have a quantity of valuable resources which are denied to people like ourselves, on whom much money has been spent, but that is no reason why we should despise our proper stock in trade. If we are accustomed to enjoy poetry Matthew Arnold may come in useful, and if I am on the right track it is not the didactic poems, like the great *Empedocles*, which will help, but the allusive wisdom of his lyrics. Anyone who cares to make an experiment might re-read the *Switzerland* series, which professes only to describe the parting between two lovers. Like Davenant, and more obviously, Arnold will deposit grains of strength. I have not the least wish to see him, or to put before him our troubles about tariff walls and aeroplanes. I know that he would be unhelpful, departmental. And I would no more consult him about conduct that I would a great poet who is actually alive: Professor A. E. Housman. Yet he props my mind. He writes to us because he is not writing about us, he can give us calm.

[1934]

FORREST REID

BELFAST, as all men of affairs know, stands no nonsense and lies at the head of Belfast Lough. One slides up to it at dawn through mists and past the clangor of shipyards. Unreal yet squalid, its streets lack either picturesqueness or plan, and manage to exclude all prospect of the mountains that neighbour them. A clammy ooze clings to the pavements, to the dark red bricks, the air is full of the rawness though not of the freshness of the sea, and the numerous Protestant places of worship stand sentinel over huddled slums and over dour little residences whose staircases are covered with linoleum and whose windows seem always to face the east. Foursquare amid the confusion, like a wardrobe in a warehouse, rises the immense City Hall. It is a costly Renaissance pile, which shouts 'Dublin can't beat me' from all its pediments and domes, but it does not succeed in saying anything else. Near the City Hall, at the junction of three small thoroughfares, is 'The Junction', where all life congregates and where a motor-car containing Mr Winston Churchill was once nearly tipped over. Here, too, are the principal shops. The bookshops of Belfast are instructive. They are not only small, but incredibly provincial, and breathe Samuel Smiles when they are respectable and 'Aristotle' when they are not, 'Aristotle' being in these parts the compiler of a pornographic manual who is bound in red and gold and usually tied up with string. Yes; in all our far-flung Empire one could scarcely find a city which stood nonsense less. And yet she is haunted by a ghost, by some exile from the realms of the ideal who has slipped into her common-sense, much as the sea and the dispossessed fields, avenging nature, have re-emerged as dampness and as weeds in her streets.

Close outside her is some beautiful country, which has ghosts also. The exquisite valley of the Lagan disentangles itself with a sigh, and losing its slimy foreshores winds among solemn beech-trees, beside parks, and between round green hills. The river is crossed by small bridges, and is flanked by backwaters overshadowed by alders; here and there a house, inexpressibly sad even in sunshine, looks down a slope or across a meadow, and seems the home of some mysterious secret which will awake when the intruder has passed, and stealing forth without lifting a bolt will seek the grey surface of the water or the disk of the moon. Should one indulge in such a fancy, local legends are prompt to confirm it; stories about fairies, told with every degree of affectation, can be collected in the vicinity – fairy rings, fairy thorns, fairies ninety miles high – proving, if nothing else, that the Irish mind turns easily to the supernatural when it feels hospitable or tired. The charm of the valley – that needs no proof. And as with the Lagan, so with other places in the district; the Glens of Antrim, the cliffs near Ballycastle, the dark Mourne Mountains to the south – all, despite the variety of their scenery, have the sadness and the sense of unreality that we associate with an indwelling power. It is only the ordinary Celtic atmosphere which may be breathed more fully elsewhere, but it gains a peculiar quality when near to a great city and to such a city as Belfast.

To call Mr Forrest Reid the novelist of this region would give a false idea of his art, for he is only concerned incidentally with topography. But it does so happen that most of his scenes take place in or near Belfast and that his art itself contains the two elements indicated above: there is squalor and there is beauty, and both of them are haunted. Haunted by what? It would take some time to answer the question. Certainly not by fairies ninety miles high. But in nearly every chapter, if we look closely, there are hints of that indwelling power seen, sometimes clearly, sometimes remotely. Despite the realism of his method and the prevalence of football matches, razor-strops, and all that, we are conscious of an underlying note that is sometimes sinister and always sad, so that we might say of his best work what he himself so beautifully says of the poetry of Poe:

Delicate and unsubstantial as the grey dew upon the grass before the sun has risen, it appeals to us in some dim region of the mind where the laws of logic and of reason have no meaning. It acts upon our emotions or nervous sensibility very much as the sound of wind on a dreary winter's night may act upon it, creating a mood of sadness, of foreboding, or of terror. The world that is called up is some dark nameless star swimming in a black remote sky, and the creatures that inhabit it are phantoms, misty beings without flesh and blood, but knowing all the grim secrets of the grave.

He approaches the supernatural along two lines, and his method here is well illustrated in *The Bracknels*, the first of his mature works. There is the business of Amy Bracknel's love-potion (which has its counterpart in the mediumistic scenes of later books) – a squalid business and evil so far as it is not silly. And there is the delicate and rare divinity of the moon, slowly waxing until the grey of the chronicle is touched with silver. Yet the two lines are not unconnected, and the connexion is typical of Mr Reid. As Denis Bracknel, the young moon-worshipper, increases in initiation, he sacrifices living flesh upon the Druidical stone that lies in his father's shrubbery, and, finally, he sees a hideous and vile vision that kills him. He has reached squalor through beauty. It is as if, in the world beyond daily life, there was no moral full-stop: it is as if the scale of ecstasy might there rise until it has traversed the entire circle of its dial, and, passing the zero, indicate a state far lower than that from which it started. Or – to put the point in the language of psychology, and it can be so put if preferred – it is that those who are most sensitive to good are also most sensitive to evil, and that stolid people, like Hubert Rusk, are likely to lead the happier lives. What is the final answer to Denis's search? Are squalor and beauty, Belfast and country – are 'Hades and Dionysus the same'? We are never told, and it is the uncertainty that gives the books their grave charm. Behind vulgarity, as behind rarity, there is a presence – of what kind and blending into what Mr Reid does not choose to say.

Over this profound and equivocal background is stretched a world that bears sufficient resemblance to the present to solace a novel-reading public. It is not the present world, if only for the preponderance given in it to youth. Few of the protagonists have seen eighteen summers, while their elders exist mainly as sympathizers, tyrants, and choruses. The actors in *Pirates of the Spring* are schoolboys; in *Spring Song* children; in *At the Door of the Gate*, though the hero marries he never seems to grow up; though *The Gentle Lover* steps forward at forty-seven it is only to be shelved. The author believes that a man's great decisions and experiences occur in boyhood, and that his subsequent career is little more than recollection – a belief which, as we shall see, has significance in his own literary development. Here one must note that the belief necessarily restricts his canvas as a novelist and that, regarded as a transcript of human activities, his novels are a failure. They cover too small a field. They see so few types, just as they see so little of the globe. All the characters have, or are thinking of, youth, and all the scenery is, or is trying to be, some twilit spot in the north of Ireland. Modern fiction, many-sided and well informed, is strong exactly where they are weak, and amid its promiscuous but uninspired utterances the voice of such a masterpiece as *Following Darkness* is apt to be lost. They must be classed not as transcripts but as visions before they can be appreciated, and their vision is that of the hierophant who sees what lies behind objects rather than what lies between them, and who is not interested in the pageants of society or history.

Some realism lies in the foreground – for these are visions of the Western, not of the Oriental type, and proceed not directly to the illimitable inane. The sketches of middle-class Belfast are amusing and satirical enough, its Aristotelianism is not omitted, and the savagery of its croquet is duly noted. And more important than the realism is the strong ethical tendency. Questions of loyalty, courage, chastity, and personal decency, are always occurring; indeed, the author tells us that the highest beauty he knows is 'a kind of moral fragrance'. Such a fragrance is rooted, however remotely, in Christianity and the books approach nearer to the Gospel spirit than appears on the first reading. Complementary to moral fragrance is the odour of sin, and here (perhaps one is stupid or callous) one feels that Mr Reid makes too much fuss; he is almost as much upset by sin as Nathaniel Hawthorne. He never preaches, he is never puritanical. But he is always a puritan, and he regards it of absolute and eternal importance that youth should reach maturity unscathed. Peter Waring, in *Following Darkness*, fails, and so loses the love and friendship of Katherine Dale. But this couldn't have happened if Katherine had been worth her salt, surely. However, be this as it may, the ethical tendency is, from the artistic point of view, quite sound. The moral 'fragrance' and the odour of sin both connect the foreground with the background. Working by natural processes they lead the characters towards the supernatural, so that the world of spirits is invoked not by magic arts, but through conduct, through habits, just as Henry James invoked it in *The Turn of the Screw*.

Vision is only one of the instruments that the imagination provides, and those artists who select it develop on different lines from their empirical brethren. They do not, like Shakespeare or Goethe, pick up something and then something more. Everything comes to them in a rush, their arms are filled at once with material for a life's work, and their task is to sort and re-sort what they have rather than to seek fresh experiences. Wordsworth was an artist of this type. He had some vision in the Lakes when young, and the whole of his subsequent career was but a recollection of it and a continual effort to restate. Mr Reid also belongs to this type. His two best novels, *The Bracknels* and *Following Darkness*, probably neighbour some spiritual experience into which the 'supernatural', as we crudely call it, entered. They are intensely passionate beneath their surface calm. The book on Yeats, despite its difference of content, derives from the same experience, but it is more conscious: the writer not only feels but understands, and so can understand another writer and can produce one of the subtlest and profoundest literary studies of our day. As for the later novels, they are reminiscences, or rather reconsiderations, of what is past. A vision may only yield its inmost meaning to the touch of memory, and there is no reason to suppose that Mr Reid's best work is not still to come.* But we must not expect anything 'new' from him in the sense that we may expect it from more inquisitive writers. He does not care for fresh people or problems; it is not thus that his mind works. He is always harking back to some lonely garden or sombre grove, to some deserted house whose entrance is indeed narrow but whose passages stretch to infinity, and when his genius gains the recognition that has so strangely been withheld from it, he will be ranked with the artists who have preferred to see life steadily rather than to see it whole, and who have concentrated their regard upon a single point, a point which, when rightly focused, may perhaps make all the surrounding landscape intelligible.

[1919]

IBSEN THE ROMANTIC

'My book *is* poetry, and if it is not poetry, then it will be.' – Ibsen to Björnson.

IBSEN was a poet during the earlier part of his life. He began as a lyricist, and his first plays are either in verse or are inspired by an imaginative contemplation of the past. When he was

* Written twelve years before the publication of his masterpiece, *Uncle Stephen*.

about forty, a change occurred, the importance of which has been differently estimated. Certain critics, both friendly and hostile, regard it as a fundamental change. They argue that with *The League of Youth* the real or realistic Ibsen begins to emerge, the singer dies, the social castigator is born, the scene clarifies and darkens, and ideas come to the front which do not necessarily contradict previous ideas, but which are given a prominence that entirely alters the dramatic emphasis. We pass from the epic to the domestic. Peer Gynt becomes Hialmar Ekdal, and Brand as Gregers Werle tears the spectacles of illusion from his eyes, and they work out their tragedy not among forests and fjords, but in a photographic studio opening into a sort of aviary. The aviary contains a few dead Christmas trees, also a water trough, some rabbits but no bears, one wild duck and that a damaged one. We could not be further from romance, the critics say, and turn, if we are friendly, to the character drawing, the technique, and the moral and social issues; if they are hostile, to the squalor. 'Somewhere in the course of the battle of his life Ibsen had a lyric Pegasus killed under him,' writes Brandes. 'Novel and perilous nonsense,' wrote the *Daily Telegraph*. The critics agree in thinking that the poetry, if ever there was any, has gone.

Has it gone? Can the habits of forty years be set aside? Of twenty years – yes; most people are romantic at twenty, owing to lack of experience. As they grow older life offers various alternatives, such as worldliness or philosophy or the sense of humour, and they usually accept one of these. If, in spite of more solid temptations, they still cling to poetry, it is because a deep preference has to be satisfied. Ibsen was a poet at forty because he had that preference. He was a poet at sixty also. His continued interest in avalanches, water, trees, fire, mines, high places, travelling, was not accidental. Not only was he born a poet – he died one, and as soon as we try to understand him instead of asking him to teach us, the point becomes clearer.

He is, of course, not easy to understand. Two obstacles may be noted. In the first place although he is not a teacher he has the air of being one, there is something in his method that implies a message, though the message really rested on passing irritabilities, and not on any permanent view of conduct or the universe. In the second place, he further throws us off the scent by taking a harsh or a depressing view of human relationships. As a rule, if a writer has a romantic temperament, he will find human relationships beautiful. His characters may hate one another or be unhappy together, but they will generate nobility or charm, they will never be squalid, whatever their other defects. And the crux in Ibsen is that, though he had the romantic temperament, he found personal intercourse sordid. Sooner or later his characters draw their little knives, they rip up the present and the past, and the closer their intimacy the better their opportunities for exchanging pain. Oswald Alving knows how to hurt his mother, Rosmer: his mistress, and married couples are even more favourably placed. The Helmers, the Tesmans, the Wangels, Solnesses, Allmers, Borkmans, Rubeks – what a procession, equally incapable of comradeship and ecstasy! If they were heroic or happy once, it was before the curtain rose, and only survives as decay. And if they attain reconciliation, like the Rentheim sisters, the curtain has to fall. Their intercourse is worse than unfriendly, it is petty; moral ugliness trespasses into the aesthetic. And when a play is full of such characters and evolves round their fortunes, how can it possibly be a romantic play? Poetry might perhaps be achieved if Ibsen's indignation was of the straight-hitting sort, like Dante's. But for all its sincerity there is something automatic about it, he reminds us too often of father at the breakfast table after a bad night, sensitive to the defects of society as revealed by a chance glance at the newspaper, and apt to blame all parties for them indiscriminately.

Now it is the position of women that upsets father, now the lies people tell, now their inability to lie, now the drains, now the newspaper itself, which he crumples up, but his helpers and servers have to retrieve it, for bad as are all political parties he must really see who got in at Rosmersholm. Seldom can a great genius have had so large a dose of domestic irritability. He was cross with his enemies and friends, with theatre-managers, professors, and students, and so cross with his countrymen for not volunteering to help the Danes in 1864 that he had to go to Italy to say so. He might have volunteered in person – he was in the prime of life at the time – but this did not occur to him, he preferred instead to write a scathing little satire about a Norwegian mother whose son was safe at the front. And it is (if one may adopt the phrase) precisely the volunteer spirit that is absent from his conception of human relationships. He put everything into them except the strength of his arm.

'Not a great writer . . . almost great, but marred by this lack of generosity.' How readily the phrases rise to the lips! How false they are! For this nagging quality, this habitual bitterness – they are essential in his greatness, because they beckon to the poetry in him, and carry it with them under the ground. Underground. Into the depths of the sea, the depths of the sea. Had he been of heroic build and turned to the light and the sun, his gifts would have evaporated. But he was – thank heaven – subterranean, he loved narrow passages and darkness, and his later plays have a romantic intensity which not only rivals the romantic expansion of their predecessors, but is absolutely unique in literature. The trees in old Ekdal's aviary are as numerous as a forest because they are countless, the water in the chickens' trough includes all the waves on which the Vikings could sail. To his impassioned vision dead and damaged things, however contemptible socially, dwell for ever in the land of romance, and this is the secret of his so-called symbolism: a connexion is found between objects that lead different types of existence; they reinforce one another and each lives more intensely than before. Consequently his stage throbs with a mysteriousness for which no obvious preparation has been made, with beckonings, tremblings, sudden compressions of the air, and his characters as they wrangle among the oval tables and stoves are watched by an unseen power which slips between their words.

A weaker dramatist who had this peculiar gift would try to get his effect by patches of fine writing, but with Ibsen as with Beethoven the beauty comes not from the tunes, but from the way they are used and are worked into the joints of the action. *The Master Builder* contains superb examples of this. The plot unfolds logically, the diction is flat and austere, the scene is a villa close to which another villa is being erected, the chief characters are an elderly couple and a young woman who is determined to get a thrill out of her visit, even if it entails breaking her host's neck. Hilda is a minx, and though her restlessness is not as vulgar as Hedda Gabler's it is quite as pernicious and lacks the saving gesture of suicide. That is one side of Hilda. But on the other side she touches Gerd and the Rat Wife and the Button Moulder, she is a lure and an assessor, she comes from the non-human and asks for her kingdom and for castles in the air that shall rest on solid masonry, and from the moment she knocks at the door poetry filters into the play. Solness, when he listened to her, was neither a dead man nor an old fool. No prose memorial can be raised to him, and consequently Ibsen himself can say nothing when he falls from the scaffolding, and Bernard Shaw does not know that there is anything to say. But Hilda hears harps and voices in the air, and though her own voice may be that of a sadistic schoolgirl the sound has nevertheless gone out into the dramatist's universe, the avalanches in *Brand* and *When We Dead Awaken* echo it, so does the metal in John Gabriel Borkman's mine. And it has all been done so competently. The symbolism never holds up the action, because it is part of the action, and because Ibsen was a poet, to whom creation and craftsmanship were one. It is the same with the white horse in *Rosmersholm*, the fire of life in *Ghosts*, the gnawing pains in *Little Eyolf*, the sea in *The Lady from the Sea*, where Hilda's own stepmother voices more openly than usual the malaise that connects the forces of nature and the fortunes of men. Everything rings true and echoes far because it is in the exact place which its surroundings require.

The source of Ibsen's poetry is indefinable; presumably it comes from the same place as his view of human nature, otherwise they would not harmonize as they do in his art. The vehicle in which poetry reached him – that can easily be defined; it was, of course, the scenery of western and southwestern Norway. At some date previous to his Italian journey he must have had experiences of passionate intensity among the mountains, comparable to the early experiences of Wordsworth in the English lakes. All his life they kept returning to him, clothed in streams, trees, precipices, and hallowing his characters while they recriminated. In *Brand* and *Peer Gynt* they filled the stage; subsequently they shrank and concentrated; in the two last plays they again fill the stage and hasten the catastrophes by a shroud of snow. To compare Ibsen with Wordsworth is to scandalize the faithful in either camp, yet they had one important point in common: they were both of them haunted until the end of their lives by the romantic possibilities of scenery. Wordsworth fell into the residential fallacy; he continued to look at his gods direct, and to pin with decreasing success his precepts to the flanks of Helvellyn. Ibsen, wiser and greater, sank and smashed the Dovrëfjeld in the depths of the sea, the depths of the sea. He knew that he should find it again. Neither his satire nor his character drawing dwelt as deep; neither the problems he found in human conduct nor the tentative solutions he propounded lay at the roots of his extraordinary heart. There, in that strange gnarled region, a primeval romanticism lurked, frozen or twisted or exuding slime, there was the nest of the great Boyg. The Great Boyg did not strive, did not die, lay beneath good and evil, did not say one thing more than another:

> Forward or back, and it's just as far;
> Out or in, and it's just as strait.

What do the words mean, and, apart from their meaning, are they meant to be right? And if right, are the prayers of Solveig, which silence them for a moment, wrong? It is proper that we should ask such questions as these when focusing on the moral and social aspect of his work, and they have been brilliantly asked and answered by Bernard Shaw. But as soon as we shift the focus the questions go dim, the reformer becomes a dramatist, we shift again and the dramatist becomes a lyric poet, listening from first to last for the movements of the trolls. Ibsen is at bottom Peer Gynt. Side whiskers and all, he is a boy bewitched:

> The boy has been sitting on his mother's lap
> They two have been playing all the life-day long.

And though the brow that bends over him can scarcely be described as maternal, it will assuredly preserve him from the melting ladle as long as books are read or plays seen.

[1928]

T. S. ELIOT

IT was during the war that I first came across Mr Eliot's work. It was Egypt, no danger or discomfort; still it was the war, and while waiting for a tram in Cairo I sprained my ankle upon the asphalt pavement and was carried into the garden of a friend. Literature was available. I lay for two or three weeks among the oleanders and bananas, watched from over the wall by a friendly and rakish minaret, and reading whatever was least likely to be bracing. Huysmans's *A Rebours* is the book of that blessed period that I remember best. Oh, the relief of a world which lived for its sensations and ignored the will – the world of des Esseintes! Was it decadent? Yes, and thank God. Yes; here again was a human being who had time to feel and experiment with his feelings, to taste and smell and arrange books and fabricate flowers, and be selfish and himself. The waves of edifying bilge rolled off me, the newspapers ebbed; Professor Cramb, that profound philosopher, and Raemaekers, that inspired artist, floated out into an oblivion which, thank God, has since become permanent, and something resembling reality took their place. Perhaps it was not real, but it was not helpful, and in 1917 that was enough to make me repeat after the muezzin on my minaret 'Thank God.' And in the hasty uncritical fashion of those days I tacked on to Huysmans some poems which had come out in a sort of paperish volume from England: *Prufrock*, *The Portrait of a Lady*, and a few more.

The poems were not epicurean; still they were innocent of public-spiritness: they sang of private disgust and diffidence, and of people who seemed genuine because they were unattractive or weak. The author was irritated by tea-parties, and not afraid to say so, with the result that his occasional 'might-have-beens' rang out with the precision of a gong.

> I should have been a pair of ragged claws,
> Scuttling across the floors of silent seas.

Here was a protest, and a feeble one, and the more congenial for being feeble. For what, in that world of gigantic horror, was tolerable except the slighter gestures of dissent? He who measured himself against the war, who drew himself to his full height, as it were, and said to Armadillo-Armageddon 'Avaunt!' collapsed at once into a pinch of dust. But he who could turn aside to complain of ladies and drawing-rooms preserved a tiny drop of our self-respect, he carried on the human heritage. And in all the years that have followed, years in which Mr Eliot has gone both beyond me and behind, this early fragmentary sympathy has remained, so that still when I read him it is for the witty resentment followed by the pinch of glory.

> Yet there the nightingale
> Filled all the desert with inviolable voice
> And still she cried, and still the world pursues,
> 'Jug-jug' to dirty ears.

This simple reaction of mine was not unsound. But it was too facile. There was much more in his work than black followed by white. Even the early poems, when studied, revealed crossing shadows, and in time one discerned blends, or it might be confusions, of colours. Here was a poet whose gesture, whatever its ultimate intention, certainly was not a handshake, and here was a critic who held that a poet does not possess a personality, but is 'only a medium, in which impressions and experiences combine in peculiar and unexpected ways'. Here was a character habitually urbane, but liable to sudden spleen, which was vented on Milton or Hobbes or Mr Bernard Shaw so as rather to take the breath away. Here, in a word, was a difficult writer. And it is my aim now to sort the difficulties presented by him into two heaps. For though I cannot solve them, into two heaps I am convinced they will go.

One heap – and it is a large one – will contain all those difficulties that are due to our own incompetence or inattention. Mr Eliot does not write for the lazy, the stupid, or the gross. Literature is to him a serious affair, and criticism not less serious than creation, though severely to be distinguished from it. A reader who cannot rise to his level, and who opens a book as he would open a cigarette case, cannot expect to get very far. There is abundance of beauty and even of amusement awaiting us, there is all the treasure of a richly-stored and active mind, but we are expected to do our share, and if (to take a concrete test) we cannot do it over the little essay in *The Sacred Wood* entitled *Hamlet and his Problems*, it means that we are not up to his standard, and must keep to ready-made stuff. I instance the Hamlet essay because it is both sensitive and lucid (two of Mr Eliot's great merits), because it handles with amazing skill problems both of historical criticism and of psychology, and because it never attempts to mystify. If we find difficulties here, the fault is ours.

But is the fault always ours? Are there not cases where we turn away because there was no way in? And if our check is due to the writer, why is it that, having set out to address us, he should change his intention, and mislead?

It is natural, at this point of our inquiry, to ask help of the young. For Mr Eliot's work, particularly *The Waste Land*, has made a profound impression on them, and given them precisely the food they needed. And by 'the young' I mean those men and women between the ages of eighteen and thirty whose opinions one most respects and whose reactions one most admires. He is the most important author of their day, his influence is enormous, they are inside his idiom as the young of 1900 were inside George Meredith's, they are far better qualified than their elders to expound him, and in certain directions they do expound him. But they are averse to answering leading questions. 'What is *The Waste Land* about?' provokes no enthusiastic reply. Yet it is, to my mind, a pertinent question, and to be told that the poem is simply a poem or just a work of art is unsatisfying. Who is the drowned sailor in it? What does the scrap-heap of quotations at the end signify? Is it helpful, here and elsewhere, to know where the quotations come from? or to read Miss Weston's *From Ritual to Romance*, or the other authorities recommended in the notes? No answer comes, or perhaps a sly rejoinder that questions as to Mr Eliot's meaning are only asked by those who will never understand it, and that his notes are intended for those whom they will lead deeper into confusion. It is implied that if he sees a reader floundering he might amuse himself by setting an additional trap. And I am afraid there is a little truth in this.

There is no reason why a writer should not play tricks on his audience; Samuel Butler and André Gide have done it with success. But it denotes a divided purpose, a shifting of energy, and in Mr Eliot's case pure love of fun will scarcely be the cause. His is rather the love of the cryptogrammatic. 'I hope,' he says, in his *Homage to John Dryden*, 'that these three papers may, in spite of and partly because of their defects, preserve in cryptogram certain notions which, if expressed directly, would be destined to immediate obloquy, followed by per-petual oblivion.' What is he trying to put across us here? Something which we should dislike and forget. Why, if he believes in it, can he not say it out straight and face the conse-quences – the very trivial consequences? And not only here, but again and again we have the sense of being outwitted, which is agreeable to the young, who always take a sell in good part, but which nevertheless needs analysing. Whose fault has it been? Into which heap is the difficulty to be thrown? The verse always sounds beautiful, but often conveys nothing. The prose always conveys something, but is often occupied in tracing the boundaries of the unsaid. The more we look into the fabrics, the more intellectual and emotional reservations do we find.

Mr Eliot is quite frank about this. He admits to the

reservations, and he offers an apology for them which we must now examine. Tradition is the keynote of it. An English writer, to be great, must create in the English tradition. He will not, of course, be imitative, and he need not be erudite, but he will acquire the sense of the past, that is to say he will feel the past of Europe present in him while he composes, and within it he will feel the past of England. Such a feeling can only be gained at a price. To acquire tradition, the writer must give up all personal idiosyncrasies, he must not indulge in private mythologies like Blake or facile reactions like Mr Arthur Symons; even as a critic he must submit to discipline, while as a creative artist he will engage in 'a continual self-sacrifice, a continual extinction of personality'. And it will be readily understood that with so much in his bones he cannot speak to the reader as man to man; indeed, while he creates he has ceased to be a man in the hand-shaking sense, he has dissociated himself for the reception of something else, something timeless. Reticence, mental and emotional, is to be expected, and the reader who has likewise the sense of the past will appreciate this, while the reader who has not got it must expect to feel baffled and slighted. This argument, adumbrated in *The Sacred Wood*, has been underlined in *For Lancelot Andrewes*, where it is shown to entail classicism in literature, royalism in politics, and Anglo-Catholicism in religion – none of these three ideals being quite what, in our haste, we might suppose them to be. And the 'uncommon reader' who is further interested is referred to three small volumes which Mr Eliot has in preparation.

The argument draws no clear line between literary and social tradition, and one has a feeling at moments that the Muses are connected not so much with Apollo as with the oldest county families. One feels, moreover, that there is never all this talk about tradition until it has ceased to exist, and that Mr Eliot, like Henry James, is romanticizing the land of his adoption. However, criticisms such as these are beside the point. They do not affect the apology, which is a serious one, and which does explain his work. The poems – so novel, startling, subtle, coarse – are not offered as the product of a private whim. They belong to the succession of Ben Jonson, Marvell, and Donne; they are a protest against the personal raptures of the Lake School. And when they are evasive and when the prose evades, it is because the writer is following an inner rule – some canon of wit, elegance, taste, or Divine Grace, the working of which is not apparent to the indisciplined reader. That is the explanation. When there are difficulties, the fault is always ours.

It is not an explanation under which I propose to sit down. Let me go straight to the heart of the matter, fling my poor little hand on the table, and say what I think *The Waste Land* is about. It is about the fertilizing waters that arrived too late. It is a poem of horror. The earth is barren, the sea salt, the fertilizing thunderstorm broke too late. And the horror is so intense that the poet has an inhibition and is unable to state it openly.

> What are the roots that clutch, what branches grow
> Out of this stony rubbish? Son of man,
> You cannot say, or guess, for you know only
> A heap of broken images.

He cannot say 'Avaunt!' to the horror, or he would crumble into dust. Consequently, there are outworks and blind alleys all over the poem – obstacles which are due to the nature of the central emotion, and are not to be charged to the reader. *The Waste Land* is Mr Eliot's greatest achievement. It intensifies the drawing-room premonitions of the earlier poems, and it is the key to what is puzzling in the prose. But, if I have its hang, it has nothing to do with the English tradition in literature, or law or order, nor, except incidentally, has the rest of his work anything to do with them either. It is just a personal comment on the universe, as individual and as isolated as Shelley's *Prometheus*.

In respect to the horror that they find in life, men can be divided into three classes. In the first class are those who have not suffered often or acutely; in the second, those who have escaped through horror into a further vision; in the third, those who continue to suffer. Most of us belong to the first class, and to the elect outside it our comments must sound shallow; they may feel that we have no right to comment at all. The mystics, such as Dostoievsky and Blake, belong to the second class. Mr Eliot, their equal in sensitiveness, distinct from them in fate, belongs to the third. He is not a mystic. *For Lancelot Andrewes* contains several well-turned compliments to religion and Divine Grace, but no trace of religious emotion. Is he relegating it to another place? No; if it exists, it cannot be relegated. He has not got it; what he seeks is not revelation, but stability.* Hence his approval of institutions deeply rooted in the State, such as the Anglican Church, hence the high premium he places upon statesmanship. 'These fragments I have shored against my ruins.' Hence the attempted impersonality and (if one can use the word here) the inhospitality of his writing. Most writers sound, somewhere or other in their scale, a note of invitation. They ask the reader in, to cooperate or to look. Gerard Manley Hopkins is a case in point – a poet as difficult as Mr Eliot, and far more specialized ecclesiastically, yet however twisted his diction and pietistic his emotion, there is always a hint to the layman to come in if he can, and participate. Mr Eliot does not want us in. He feels we shall increase the barrenness. To say he is wrong would be rash, and to pity him would be the height of impertinence, but it does seem proper to emphasize the real as opposed to the

* In view of Mr Eliot's later work (not here considered) I would modify these remarks.

apparent difficulty of his work. He is difficult because he has seen something terrible, and (underestimating, I think, the general decency of his audience) has declined to say so plainly.

I have called that terrible thing Armadillo-Armageddon, and perhaps another personal reminiscence may conclude this very personal approach. It is of a bright August morning in 1914. I am lying in bed. The milkman below calls as usual with the milk, and through the clink of the handle I hear him say: 'We've gone in.' This, in its small way, is the kind of experience that must have beset Mr Eliot, and rooted itself in the soil of his mind. Most of us forget such an experience, or do not feel it acutely. Only here and there does it expand and contort into

> The circles of the stormy moon
> Slide westward toward the River Plate,
> Death and the Raven drift above
> And Sweeney guards the horned gate.

[1928]

PROUST

MR SCOTT MONCRIEFF's monumental translation of Proust's *À la recherche du temps perdu* is both sensitive and accurate; it has been unreservedly praised by the best judges, and if I do not altogether concur it is because I was hoping to find Proust easier in English than in French, and do not. All the difficulties of the original are here faithfully reproduced. A sentence begins quite simply, then it undulates and expands, parentheses intervene like quickset hedges, the flowers of comparison bloom, and three fields off, like a wounded partridge, crouches the principal verb, making one wonder as one picks it up, poor little thing, whether after all it was worth such a tramp, so many guns, and such expensive dogs, and what, after all, is its relation to the main subject, potted so gaily half a page back, and proving finally to have been in the accusative case. These, however, are the disciplines of Proust. No earnest sportsman would forgo them. And perhaps Mr Scott Moncrieff is right in insisting that the English audience shall also participate, and shall train, through the ardours of each single sentence, for the mastery of the work as a whole.

The work as a whole! Ten times as long as an ordinary novel! And as baffling as life itself – life when apprehended by the modern cultivated man. 'Life' and 'Proust' are not identical, it is true; as we shall see, there are notable differences between them, all in life's favour. But the main features correspond, and it is possible to say that the work, more than any other, expresses the spirit of our age. As a contemporary document, it is invaluable. Just as the historian of the early Roman Empire turns to Virgil and finds in his sensitive verse not the exploits of Aeneas but the semi-content and the half-expressed regrets of a generation that had escaped the republican storms and abandoned the risks of liberty: just as the historian of the late Middle Ages turns to Dante and finds there described not a personal fantasy but the last and the greatest of the crusades that were supposed to end in heaven; so, reading Proust, the historian of the early twentieth century will see not the dallyings of the insignificant hero, not the local snobberies of the Faubourg Saint Germain, but – you and me! He will say, 'This work, whatever its qualities as art, is an epic, for it expresses the spirit of its age.' And he will add (perhaps rather to our surprise if we still take notice of the remarks of wise men): 'It was pre-eminently an age of adventure.'

There is, of course, nothing of the swashbuckler about Proust, me, or you. There is no question of adventure of that sort; the laurels of the House of Guermantes have faded long before the action starts; the martial ardours of Saint Loup are slightly *démodé* and absurd, like the caperings of a heraldic lion; there is no true summons to battle when the bugles of Doncières blow and its fortifications take shape in the mists. And when the Great War does come it is a monster, indecent and imbecile, shaggy with dispatches, in whose foetid darkness M. de Charlus waddles about seeking pleasure and Madame Verdurin personates Joan of Arc. Of adventure in the chivalrous or romantic sense there is nothing, nothing. But the characters want to live, the author wants to write about them, and when we ask why, in a world so obviously unsatisfactory, we get an answer which will be echoed in our own private diary, namely, 'We want to know what will happen tomorrow.' Tomorrow may not be better than today, and may well be worse, but it has one unique attraction: it has not yet come. Proust, though introspective, and unhappy, was full of vitality – he could not have written a million words if he was not – he was inquisitive about tomorrow, he and his characters cling to existence though logic indicates suicide, and though disease drags them down still keep one eye open, half an eye, and scan the bitter unremunerative levels of the sea. *À la recherche du temps perdu* is an epic of curiosity and of despair. It is an adventure in the modern mode where the nerves and brain as well as the blood take part, and the whole man moves forward to encounter he does not know what; certainly not to any goal.

His despair is fundamental. It is not a theory in him, but an assumption, so that the wreckage of his creation evolves as naturally as the music of the spheres. Consider his insistence on illness. Disease and death await every individual, but it is only when we are ill ourselves, or are nursing a friend or passing through a hospital ward that we realize this vividly. To Proust it was always vivid, at garden parties and dinners the germs continue to work and disintegrate the bodies of the guests, Swann trails about with dotlets of prussian blue on his face, a cuirass of diamonds heaves above Princesse d'Orvillers's cancer, the grandmother poses coquettishly for her photograph after a stroke. The cumulative effect (and this is an important point) is *not* macabre. He was too great an artist to indulge in the facile jiggle of a Dance of Death. They are living beings, not masked skeletons or physiological transparencies who climb the height of La Raspelière or talk against the music of Vinteuil. But they are doomed more obviously than ourselves to decay. Avoiding tragic horror, which perhaps he mistrusted, and pity, which he could seldom supply, he has achieved a new view of the impermanence of the human race, and it is instructive to compare him here for a moment with Tolstoy.

The epilogue at the close of *War and Peace* is disheartening enough; it is sad to see what time has done to Nicolay and Natasha. But there the rhythmic rise, fall, rise, of the generations offers an alternative vision, whereas Proust, at the close of *Le Temps retrouvé*, is tethered to his selected personages, and cannot supply their wastage by new births. He introduces a new generation it is true; Madame de Saint-Euverte is a girl instead of the anxious harridan whom we have hitherto connected with the title. But he only introduces it to slap the old in the face. The upwelling of fresh lives did not interest him, and as to babies, they were quite outside his imaginative scope. His vision of humanity is (in this sense) limited, and perhaps he was assisted in it by his unusual conception of time. Tolstoy conceived of time as something regular, against which a chronicle could be stretched; to Proust it is almost as intermittent as memory and affection, and it is easier in such a cosmogony to picture the human race as always decaying and never being renovated. But his actual belief in decay – that lies deeper than any fancy or theory, that rests direct upon his equipment of despair.

Despair underlies all his view of personal relationships. How he emphasizes the element of gratuitous cruelty that exists in us, shows Françoise, apparently such a dear old family servant, torturing the scullery-maid with the unexpected weapon of asparagus, and inserts at the very end of the epic, like a full-stop of blood, the virtual murder of Berma! And – apart from cruelty – what repulsive defects he discovers in us! The worst of them is our inability to love or be loved. Let A and B be two people (for one can put his view in algebraic form) who do not love one another, but have some slight social relationship. They get on quite well. Then let A fall in love with B. Instantly their understanding vanishes, because A's affection has transformed B into a non-existing quantity called X. B has never heard of X, cannot behave like X, is accused of inconsistency and duplicity, retorts with similar charges, and it ends in a quarrel. And if love happens to be mutual the situation is even worse, for now not one mind but two are engaged on the falsification, and while A transforms B into X, B transforms A into Y. The charges of cruelty and deceit are now doubled, nay, quadrupled, for in their mutual excitement the lovers, like two flawed mirrors, reflect and distort each other's misunderstandings into infinity. Mutual love, fortunately for the human race, is uncommon, but when it comes such tortures arise that love unrequited seems like heaven.

Thus Proust's general theory of human intercourse is that the fonder we are of people the less we understand them – the theory of the complete pessimist. Dante took a different view. And it is worth while stopping a moment in this maelstrom of the modern and, looking back six hundred years, reminding ourselves what that other view of love was, and why Dante took it. Dante believed that the fonder we are of people the better we understand them – the theory of the complete optimist. To him, knowledge was love, love knowledge, and Beatrice not Beatrice until he could meet her in heaven. On earth, an imperfect place, he, too, had made the mistake of turning her into X and of expecting a response from her that she could no more supply than Odette could supply it to

Swann. But in the empyrean these illusions fade, the fact of love is disengaged from the accidents of loving, and by the time the triple rainbow is reached the mind and the heart are completely reconciled and begin their real existence. His view is the complete antithesis of Proust's, not because of a different temperament, but because he lived in the age of Faith.

To myself, a child of unbelief, Proust seems more likely to be right, yet does he make enough allowance for a certain good sense that persists in the human organism even when it is heated by passion? Does he not lay too much stress on jealousy? He regards it as the very food of love. When the hero is tired of Albertine and about to leave her, the suspicion that she loves another renders her suddenly desirable, there is nothing he will not do to own her, no lengths of tyranny, self-abnegation, or ridiculousness, and the same idea runs through the other two big affairs in the book, and makes his world more uncomfortable than our own. We, too, are jealous, but not all of us, all the time, partly because we have our livings to get, whereas Proust's people taste the sweets and attendant bitternesses of leisure. He and 'life' are not identical here, life being the more amiable of the two, and future historians will find that his epic of curiosity and despair almost sums up you and me, but not quite.

A word in conclusion on his curiosity. It was indefatigable. Never looking upward, and seldom down, it advances like some rare insect across the floors of France, waving its antennae and exploring both the realm of social conduct and the realm of art. He is not sure which realm is the more tolerable, he varies, as every sensitive creature must. But on the whole he votes for art. Bergotte, Elstir, Vinteuil, Berma, even the dilettante Swann, are superior to the smart hostesses, the politicians, the lift-boys, the lovers; they, too, will die, their work will be misunderstood, . . . but on the whole . . . one cannot put it more strongly than that; on the whole art is best, and at the close we leave the hero starting out to be an author, rummaging in his part, disinterring forgotten facts, facts which exist again for an instant before they crumble and are lost for ever. That instant is the artist's instant; he must simultaneously recollect and create, and Mr Clive Bell, in an interesting essay, gives us an account of Proust's method here, and of the memory-snatching habits that have produced a masterpiece. His book is the product of a double curiosity. The initial curiosity was social; he went to all those awful parties and had those barren relationships and expensive illnesses, and knew in his own person what it is to be a snob, a jealous lover, an orphan, and an invalid with a red nose. And then came the second curiosity, the artistic. He recollected the parties, and robbed them of their stings; they hurt him no longer, and were for the first time useful. Even love, that most distressing of all illusions, can be useful, and A and B, subjected to analysis, can be seen functioning like bacteria in a test-tube, innocuous at last, and suitable as characters for a book. The curiosity of Proust was not quite the same as yours and mine, but then he was not as nice as you and me and he was also infinitely more sensitive and intelligent. His curiosity belongs to our age; we can say that of it, just as his despair is akin to ours, although we sometimes hope. Almost, though not entirely, does he represent us; to the historian the similarity will be sufficient, and the epic quality of the work will be acknowledged.

[1929]

WORD-MAKING AND SOUND-TAKING

WAS William de Morgan a good novelist? No one speaks of him today, I have not read him for twenty years and know he is full of lapses. But one of the lapses was so congenial to me

that it has found refuge in that rabbit-warren, my mind, and
bred progeny there. It is a sentimental lapse, on the subject of
music. Perhaps in *Joseph Vance*, perhaps in *Alice for Short*, a
little tune is introduced, and words are put to it, a tune by
Beethoven. The tune floats out of upper windows and is
heard by Mr de Morgan's characters when they are feeling
depressed. They are cheered by the sound of the piano; they
pull themselves together as the pianist's left hand passes over
her right, and as she hits the upper G successfully they leap
towards the happy ending which their kindly creator has destined for them. Happy universe! Happy tune! Nice words:

> No, no, no, you're quite mistaken.
> No, no, no, you must be wrong.

For that is how it goes.

How Proust, in his far from happy universe, would wince
at this! Proust also has a little tune, the *petite phrase* of the
Vinteuil sonata which presents facet after facet to the varying
sensitiveness of his characters. It would be impossible for
Proust to label a tune. He understands too much about music,
and also about people, to suppose that the relationship between
them could be bottled up in words. The author of *Somehow
Good* knew no such scruples, and I don't know all of them
myself. I feel bound to put words to a classical tune every
now and then, and this is an example of what I can do:

> Áh nò, áh nò,
> The world will yet be saved, bé sàved.
>
> Áh, nò, áh nò,
> The world will yet be saved,
> Bé sáved.

Thus, to my ear, sings the second theme of the march-move-
ment of Schumann's piano quintet; deserting the march-
rhythm, the lovely liar sings to me of Geneva Triumphant and

of a clean sweep of all our troubles, and lulls me into a sort of sleep. As soon as the theme starts, the associations I have had when listening to it previously take charge, and they are of a humanitarian character. Schumann is nowhere, his five instruments are nothing, and the five performers are nobodies unless they happen to hit badly wrong notes, when an aesthetic sensation returns.

If this habit of mine was constant, music would disappear and be replaced by a series of remarks, but it is luckily intermittent, and I am more inclined to thank William de Morgan than to censure him. He felt, as I do, that the pot of art gets cracked here and there, and sheds a few drops into life, and he is supported by the respectable authority of Beethoven. Once or twice – as in the Absence and Farewell sonata or in the posthumous F major quartet – Beethoven turns coarse and introduces a few words, and the Ninth Symphony itself may be regarded as an essay in coarseness. That awkward moment of transition from the orchestral to the vocal; that nervous entry of the soloist when he tries to look as much like a double-bass as he can, and invites his 'friends' in a stomachy voice to rise in their shirt-fronts and shout; the rising of the friends and of the lady-friends, the clearing of pastilled throats, the concerted human breathing, the glint of pince-nez, the dubious numbers of Schiller – it is all vaguely disquieting after three great movements of music, where nothing seemed tethered to the earth. And yet without it there could be no Ninth Symphony. This rickety bridge has to be crossed before the army can enter heaven:

> No, no, no, you're quite mistaken,
> No, no, no, I'm sure you're wrong

if you deny to Beethoven or even to his auditors the right to stick on an occasional label, 'Liberty', 'Joy', 'Peace'.

The labels I have in mind are emotional. One, so to speak,

finds them in the hand. Intellectual labels can also be applied, but they tend to take the form of jokes. Here are two – not made by me:

> There was a bee
> Upon a wall,
> And it said buzz and that was all;
> And it said buzz and that was all.

This is a fugue by Brahms. It occurs at the end of his Handel variations for piano. And this is a fugue by Bach:

> O Ebenezer Prout,
> You're a very funny man,
> You have set Bach's tunes
> To a lot of silly words.

I don't know Prout's settings: no doubt they were full of demure gaiety. No doubt he was a very funny man, and entertainment may be gained by such carpentry. I am more interested by the workings of the unconscious, and here is another of my own efforts in that direction, my handling of the slow movement of Beethoven's G major piano concerto.

This famous little movement consists of a dialogue between orchestra and piano, the orchestra rough, the piano plaintive, the orchestra gradually calmer. It is very easy music; it strikes or strokes immediately, and elderly gentlemen before myself have called it 'Beauty and the Beast'. What about Orpheus and the Furies, though? That is the idea that has slipped into my mind to the detriment of the actual musical sounds, and when the movement begins I always repair to the entrance of Hell and descend under the guidance of Gluck through diminishing opposition to the Elysian Fields. There has been no word-making, to be sure, but there has been a big operatic import, and not even the moment in the *Meistersinger* where a bit of *Tristan* comes in so changes the scene. The piano turns into Orpheus and *via* him into Miss Marie Brema, whom I best remember in that role, and the strings and wind, waving less and less their snaky locks, sink at last into acquiescence with true love. Then the third movement starts. The parallel breaks, and I am back in a world which seems four-square and self-contained, the world of the opening.

These capricious insertions of words, parallels, images, jokes, ideas, make listening to music a rocky and romantic affair, and I am very glad that there are also times when I seem to be alone with the sounds. It would not be worth while to pay for tickets or records, or to muddle at scores, if the release of one's fancy were the sole result. There is such a thing as the composer's intention, or if even that seems too colourful, there are such things as lines and marks upon pieces of paper which indicate the Goldberg Variations. In the spirit of William de Morgan himself, I smile on both sides of my face at once over this. I praise music because it gives access to two worlds:

> Oh, no, no, you're quite mistaken,
> No, no, no, you're quite, quite wrong

if you limit yourself to one type of optimism here, and if you forbid the hearer either to verbalize or to deverbalize the final movement of the Waldstein.

[1935]

THE EARLY NOVELS OF VIRGINIA WOOLF

I

IT is profoundly characteristic of the art of Virginia Woolf that when I decided to write about it and had planned a suitable opening paragraph, my fountain pen should disappear.

Tiresome creature! It slipped through a pocket into a seam. I could pinch it, chivy it about, make holes in the coat lining, but a layer of tailor's stuffing prevented recovery. So near, and yet so far! Which is what one feels about her art. The pen is extricated in time, but during the struggle the opening paragraph has escaped; the words are here but the birds have flown; 'opals and emeralds, they lie about the roots of turnips.' It is far more difficult to catch her than it is for her to catch what she calls life – 'life; London; this moment in June.' Again and again she eludes, until the pen, getting restive, sets to work on its own and grinds out something like this, something totally false such as: 'Mrs Woolf is a talented but impressionistic writer, with little feeling for form and none for actuality.' Rubbish. She has, among other achievements, made a definite contribution to the novelist's art. But how is this contribution to be stated? And how does she handle the ingredients of fiction – human beings, time, and space? Let us glance at her novels in the order of their composition.

The Voyage Out was published in 1915. It is a strange, tragic, inspired book whose scene is a South America not found on any map and reached by a boat which would not float on any sea, an America whose spiritual boundaries touch Xanadu and Atlantis. Hither, to a hotel, various English tourists repair, and the sketches of them are so lively and 'lifelike' that we expect a comedy of manners to result. Gradually a current sets in, a deep unrest. What are all these people doing – talking, eating, kissing, reading, being kind or unkind? What do they understand of each other or of themselves? What relations are possible between them? Two young men, bleak and honest intellectuals from Cambridge, ask the question; Rachel, an undeveloped girl, answers it. The uneasiness of society and its occasional panics take hold of her, and nothing can exorcize them, because it is her own desire to face the truth; nothing, not even love.

They stood together in front of the looking-glass, and with a brush tried to make themselves look as if they had been feeling nothing all the morning, neither pain nor happiness. But it chilled them to see themselves in the glass, for instead of being vast and indivisible they were really very small and separate, the size of the glass leaving a large space for the reflection of other things.

Wedded bliss is promised her, but the voyage continues, the current deepens, carrying her between green banks of the jungle into disease and death. The closing chapters of the book are as poignant as anything in modern fiction, yet they arise naturally out of what has gone before. They are not an interruption but a fulfilment. Rachel has lost everything – for there is no hint of compensation beyond the grave – but she has not swerved from the course honesty marked out, she has not jabbered or pretended that human relationships are satisfactory. It is a noble book, so noble that a word of warning must be added: like all Virginia Woolf's work, it is not romantic, not mystic, not explanatory of the universe. By using a wrong tone of voice – over-stressing 'South America' for instance – the critic might easily make it appear to be all these things, and perhaps waft it towards popular success! His honesty must equal the writer's; he is offered no ultimate good, but 'life; London; this moment in June'; and it is his job to find out what the promise entails.

Will *Night and Day* help him? It is the simplest novel she has written, and to my mind the least successful. Very long, very careful, it condescends to many of the devices she so gaily derides in her essay on *Mr Bennett and Mrs Brown*. The two principal characters are equipped with houses and relatives which document their reality, they are screwed into Chelsea and Highgate as the case may be, and move from their bases to meet in the rooms and streets of a topographical metropolis. After misunderstandings, they marry, they are promised happiness. In view of what preceded it and of what is to follow,

Night and Day seems to me a deliberate exercise in classicism. It contains all that has characterized English fiction for good or evil during the last hundred and fifty years – faith in personal relations, recourse to humorous sideshows, insistence on petty social differences. Even the style has been normalized, and though the machinery is modern, the resultant form is as traditional as *Emma*. Surely the writer is using tools that don't belong to her. At all events she has never touched them again.

For, contemporary with this full-length book, she made a very different experiment, published two little – stories, sketches, what is one to call them? – which show the direction in which her genius has since moved. At last her sensitiveness finds full play, and she is able to describe what she sees in her own words. In *The Mark on the Wall* she sees a mark on the wall, wonders what it is . . . and that is the entire story. In *Kew Gardens* she sees men, sometimes looking at flowers, and flowers never looking at men. And, in either case, she reports her vision impartially; she strays forward, murmuring, wandering, falling asleep. Her style trails after her, catching up grass and dust in its folds, and instead of the precision of the earlier writing we have something more elusive than has yet been achieved in English. If a drowsy and desultory person could also be a great artist he would talk like this:

Yellow and black, pink and snow white, shapes of all these colours, men, women and children were spotted for a second upon the horizon, and then, seeing the breadth of yellow that lay upon the grass, they wavered and sought shade beneath the trees, dissolving like drops of water in the yellow and green atmosphere, staining it faintly with red and blue. It seemed as if all gross and heavy bodies had sunk down in the heat motionless and lay huddled upon the ground, but their voices went wavering from them as if they were flames lolling from the thick waxen bodies of candles. Voices. Yes, voices. Wordless voices, breaking the silence suddenly with such depth of contentment, such passion of desire; or, in the voices of children, such freshness of surprise: breaking the silence? But there was no silence; all the time the motor omnibuses were turning their wheels and changing their gear: like a vast nest of Chinese boxes all of wrought steel turning ceaselessly one within another the city murmured; on the top of which the voices cried aloud and the petals of myriads of flowers flashed their colours in the air.

The objection (or apparent objection) to this sort of writing is that it cannot say much or be sure of saying anything. It is an inspired breathlessness, a beautiful droning or gasping which trusts to luck, and can never express human relationships or the structure of society. So at least one would suppose, and that is why the novel of *Jacob's Room* (1922) comes as a tremendous surprise. The impossible has occurred. The style closely resembles that of *Kew Gardens*. The blobs of colour continue to drift past; but in their midst, interrupting their course like a closely sealed jar, rises the solid figure of a young man. In what sense Jacob is alive – in what sense any of Virginia Woolf's characters live – we have yet to determine. But that he exists, that he stands as does a monument is certain, and wherever he stands we recognize him for the same and are touched by his outline. The coherence of the book is even more amazing than its beauty. In the stream of glittering similes, unfinished sentences, hectic catalogues, unanchored proper names, we seem to be going nowhere. Yet the goal comes, the method and the matter prove to have been one, and looking back from the pathos of the closing scene we see for a moment the airy drifting atoms piled into a colonnade. The break with *Night and Day* and even with *The Voyage Out* is complete. A new type of fiction has swum into view, and it is none the less new because it has had a few predecessors – laborious, well-meaning, still-born books by up-to-date authors, which worked the gasp and the drone for all they were worth, and are unreadable.

Three years after *Jacob's Room* comes another novel in the same style, or slight modification of the style: *Mrs Dalloway*. It is perhaps her masterpiece,* but difficult, and I am not altogether sure about every detail, except when my fountain pen is in my hand. Here is London at all events – so much is certain, London chorusing with all its clocks and shops and sunlit parks, and writing texts with an aeroplane across God's heaven. Here is Clarissa Dalloway, elderly, kind, graceful, rather hard and superficial, and a terrible snob. How she loves London! And there is Septimus Warren Smith – she never meets him – a case of shell shock – very sad – who hears behind the chorus the voices of the dead singing, and sees his own apotheosis or damnation in the sky. That dreadful war! Sir William Bradshaw of Harley Street, himself in perfect health, very properly arranges for Septimus Warren Smith to go to a lunatic asylum. Septimus is ungrateful and throws himself out of the window. 'Coward,' cries the doctor, but is too late. News of which comes to Clarissa as she is giving an evening party. Does she likewise commit suicide? I thought she did the first time I read the book; not at my second reading, nor is the physical act important, for she is certainly left with the full knowledge – inside knowledge – of what suicide is. The societified lady and the obscure maniac are in a sense the same person. His foot has slipped through the gay surface on which she still stands – that is all the difference between them. She returns (it would seem) to her party and to the man she loves, and a hint of her new knowledge comes through to him as the London clock strikes three. Such apparently is the outline of this exquisite and superbly constructed book, and having made the outline one must rub it out at once. For emphasis is fatal to the understanding of this author's work. If we dared not overstress 'South America' in *The Voyage Out*,

* *The Waves* (published 1931) lies outside the scope of this article.

still lighter must fall our touch on London here, still more disastrous would be the application to its shimmering fabric of mysticism, unity beneath multiplicity, twin souls. . . .

Why creeds and prayers and mackintoshes? when, thought Clarissa, that's the miracle, that's the mystery; that old lady, she meant, whom she could see going from chest of drawers to dressing-table. She could still see her. And the supreme mystery which Kilman might say she had solved, or Peter might say he had solved, but Clarissa didn't believe either of them had the ghost of an idea of solving, was simply this: here is one room: there another. Did religion solve that, or love?

As far as her work has a message, it seems to be contained in the above paragraph. Here is one room, there another. Required like most writers to choose between the surface and the depths as the basis of her operations, she chooses the surface and then burrows in as far as she can.

2

After this glance we can better understand her equipment, and realize that visual sensitiveness – in itself so slight a tool for a novelist – becomes in her case a productive force. How beautifully she sees! Look at 'those churches, like shapes of grey paper, breasting the stream of the Strand,' for instance. Or at 'The flames were struggling through the wood and roaring up when, goodness knows where from, pails flung water in beautiful hollow shapes as of polished tortoiseshell; flung again and again; until the hiss was like a swarm of bees; and all the faces went out.' How beautiful! Yet vision is only the frontier of her kingdom. Behind it lie other treasures; in particular the mind.

Her remarkable intellectual powers have nothing to do with common sense – masses of roses can be gathered at Christmas for instance, and the characters in one book need bear no resemblance to their namesakes in another. Nor is she much occupied in presenting clever men and women. What thrills her – for it starts as a thrill – is the actual working of a brain, especially of a youthful brain, and there are passages in *Jacob's Room* where the process becomes as physical as the raising of a hand. Moreover she reverences learning; it gives her disinterested pleasure, increases the natural nobility of her work.

Stone lies solid over the British Museum, as bone lies cool over the visions and heats of the brain. Only here the brain is Plato's brain and Shakespeare's; the brain has made pots and statues, great bulls and little jewels, and crossed the river of death this way and that incessantly, seeking some landing, now wrapping the body well for its long sleep; now laying a penny piece on the eyes; now turning the toes scrupulously to the East. Meanwhile Plato continues his dialogue; in spite of the rain; in spite of the cab whistles; in spite of the woman in the mews behind Great Ormond Street who has come home drunk and cries all night long 'Let me in, let me in.'

The *Phaedrus* is very difficult. And so, when at length one reads straight ahead, falling into step, marching on becoming (so it seems) momentarily part of this rolling, imperturbable energy, which has driven darkness before it since Plato walked the Acropolis, it is impossible to see to the fire.

The dialogue draws to its close. Plato's argument is done. Plato's argument is stowed away in Jacob's mind, and for five minutes Jacob's mind continues alone, onwards, into the darkness. Then, getting up, he parted the curtains, and saw, with astonishing clearness, how the Springetts opposite had gone to bed; how it rained; how the Jews and the foreign woman, at the end of the street, stood by the pillar-box, arguing.

It is easy for a novelist to describe what a character thinks of; look at Mrs Humphry Ward. But to convey the actual process of thinking is a creative feat, and I know of no one except Virginia Woolf who has accomplished it. Here at last thought, and the learning that is the result of thought, take their own high place upon the dais, exposed no longer to the patronage of the hostess or the jeers of the buffoon. Here Cambridge, with all its dons, is raised into the upper air and becomes a light for ships at sea, and Rachel, playing Bach upon an hotel piano, builds a momentary palace for the human mind.

But what of the subject that she regards as of the highest importance: human beings as a whole and as wholes? She tells us (in her essays) that human beings are the permanent material of fiction, that it is only the method of presenting them which changes and ought to change, that to capture their inner life presents a different problem to each generation of novelists; the great Victorians solved it in their way; the Edwardians shelved it by looking outwards at relatives and houses; the Georgians must solve it anew, and if they succeed a new age of fiction will begin. Has she herself succeeded? Do her own characters live?

I feel that they do live, but not continuously, whereas the characters of Tolstoy (let us say) live continuously. With her, the reader is in a state of constant approval. 'Yes, that is right,' he says, each time she implies something more about Jacob or Peter: 'yes, that would be so: yes.' Whereas in the case of Tolstoy approval is absent. We sink into André, into Nicolay Rostoff during the moments they come forth, and no more endorse the correctness of their functioning than we endorse our own. And the problem before her – the problem that she has set herself, and that certainly would inaugurate a new literature if solved – is to retain her own wonderful new method and form, and yet allow her readers to inhabit each character with Victorian thoroughness. Think how difficult this is. If you work in a storm of atoms and seconds, if your highest joy is 'life; London; this moment in June' and your deepest mystery 'here is one room; there another,' then how can you construct your human beings so that each shall be not a movable monument but an abiding home, how can you build between them any permanent roads of love and hate?

There was continuous life in the little hotel people of *The Voyage Out* because there was no innovation in the method. But Jacob in *Jacob's Room* is discontinuous, demanding – and obtaining – separate approval for everything he feels or does. And *Mrs Dalloway*? There seems a slight change here, an approach towards character-construction in the Tolstoyan sense; Sir William Bradshaw, for instance, is uninterruptedly and embracingly evil. Any approach is significant, for it suggests that in future books she may solve the problem as a whole. She herself believes it can be done, and, with the exception of Joyce, she is the only writer of genius who is trying. All the other so-called innovators are (if not pretentious bunglers) merely innovators in subject matter and the praise we give them is of the kind we should accord to scientists. Their novels admit aeroplanes or bigamy, or give some fresh interpretation of the spirit of Norfolk or Persia, or at the most reveal some slight discovery about human nature. They do good work, because everything is subject matter for the novel, nothing ought to be ruled out on the ground that it is remote or indecent. But they do not advance the novelist's art. Virginia Woolf has already done that a little, and if she succeeds in her problem of rendering character, she will advance it enormously.

For English fiction, despite the variety of its content, has made little innovation in form between the days of Fielding and those of Arnold Bennett. It might be compared to a picture gallery, lit by windows placed at suitable intervals between the pictures. First come some portraits, then a window with a view say of Norfolk, then some more portraits and perhaps a still life, followed by a window with a view of Persia, then more portraits and perhaps a fancy piece, followed by a view of the universe. The pictures and the windows are infinite in number, so that every variety of experience seems assured, and yet there is one factor that never varies: namely the gallery itself; the gallery is always the same, and the reader always has the feeling that he is pacing along it, under the conditions of time and space that regulate his daily life. Virginia Woolf would do away with the sense of pacing. The pictures and windows may remain if they can – indeed the portraits must remain – but she wants to destroy the gallery in which they are embedded and in its place build – build what? Something more rhythmical. *Jacob's Room* suggests a spiral whirling down to a point, *Mrs Dalloway* a cathedral.

[1925]

RONALD FIRBANK

To break a butterfly, or even a beetle, upon a wheel is a delicate task. Lovers of nature disapprove, moreover the victim is apt to reappear each time the wheel revolves, still alive, and with a reproachful expression upon its squashed face to address its tormentor in some such words as the following: 'Critic! What do you? Neither my pleasure nor your knowledge has been increased. I was flying or crawling, and that is all that there was to be learnt about me. Impossible to anatomize and find what breeds about my heart. Dissect the higher animals if you like, such as the frog, the cow, or the goose – no doubt they are full of helpful secrets. By all means write articles on George Eliot. Review from every point of view Lord Morley of Borley's autobiography. Estimate Addison. But leave me in peace. I only exist in my surroundings, and become meaningless as soon as you stretch me on this rack.'

The insect plaint is unanswerable, and if critics had not their living to get they would seldom handle any literary fantasy. It makes them look so foolish. Their state of mind is the exact antithesis of that of the author whom they propose to interpret.

With quiet eyes and cool fingers they pass from point to point, they define fantasy as 'the unserious treatment of the unusual' – an impeccable definition, the only objection to it being that it defines. A gulf between the critical and creative states exists in all cases, but in the case of a fantastical creation it is so wide as to be grotesque. And in saying a few words about our butterflies and beetles we must not be unmindful of the remarks which, if they felt it worth while, they might pass upon us.

Butterflies and beetles are not always identical, and are sometimes dragon-flies, etc., too. For instance, in the paragraph above, when the phrase 'Lord Morley of Borley' slipped in, a beetle was speaking. No butterfly would probe so far. And when a Mrs Shamefoot says, in one of Ronald Firbank's novels, 'The world is disgracefully managed, one hardly knows to whom to complain,' she, again, is a beetle. But when she says 'I adore the end of summer, when a new haystack appears on every hill,' she has hovered from wittiness to charm. And: 'Nearer, hither and thither, appeared a few sleepy spires of churches, too sensible to compete with the Cathedral, but possibly more personal, like the minor characters in repertoire that support the star' – well here we get both, the coloured glint, the naughty tweak. And when a gentleman who is married to a fox dreams all night of public schools for the children, and cannot think why Eton will not quite do, nor Harrow, nor Winchester, nor even Rugby, and then wakes up and thinks 'Ah! a private tutor is the solution,' yet still feels dissatisfied, and finally remembers, and bursts into tears – here, again, we get something different, something downy and mothlike brushing the cheek, something at once countrified and sophisticated which pervades all the work of another fantast, Mr David Garnett. It is indeed impossible to decide where one insect stops and another starts; they are metamorphosed behind a rafter or in full flight, or in the calyx of a single flower, even on the very wheel of criticism, and there is only one quality that they all share in common: the absence of a soul.

With the soul we reach solid ground. As soon as it enters literature, whether in full radiance or behind a cloud, two great side-scenes accompany it, the mountains of Right and Wrong, and we get a complete change of *décor*, adapted for writers who likewise treat the unusual, but who treat it mystically or humanistically. Butterflies and beetles may survive the soul's arrival, but they serve another purpose: they bear some relationship to Salvation. Think of all they go through in *Water Babies* or Sir James Barrie! Even the Three Mulla Mulgars are not completely on their own. Whereas in the creatures considered today there is nothing to be saved or damned, their modish ecclesiasticism and rural magic bear no relation to philosophic truth, the miracles that transform them, the earthquakes that shatter, have no deeper implication than a conjuring trick. As soon as we realize that we cannot save them we shall enjoy them. But it is not easy for an Anglo-Saxon to realize so little. He requires a book to be serious unless it is comic, and when it is neither is apt to ring for the police.

In his masterly introduction to Firbank's collected works, Mr Arthur Waley put us on the proper track. He remarked of Firbank that he 'seems as though endowed with a kind of inverted X-ray, which enabled him, not to penetrate the unseen, but, on the contrary, continually to hover, as it were, an inch or two above the surface of things'. The remark applies to this literature generally, which omits not merely the soul but many material actualities, and, if taken in large quantities, is unsatisfying. The writer who hovers two inches off everything may fascinate for a time, but finally he gives one the fidgets, and the reader will be both kind and wise to imitate him, and to repair to some other book at the first hint of boredom. So, like a swarm of summer insects, feeling perfectly free and disclaiming any vested interests in the soul, let us continue to flit. . . .

Ronald Firbank died a few years ago, still young. But there is nothing up to date in him. He is *fin de siècle*, as it used to be called; he belongs to the nineties and the *Yellow Book*; his mind inherits the furniture and his prose the cadences of Aubrey Beardsley's *Under the Hill*. To the historian he is an interesting example of literary conservatism; to his fellow insects a radiance and a joy. Is he affected? Yes, always. Is he self-conscious? No; he wants to mop and mow, and put on birettas and stays, and he does it as naturally as healthy Englishmen light their pipes. Is he himself healthy? Perish the thought! Is he passionate, compassionate, dispassionate? Next question! Is he intelligent? Not particularly, if we compare him with another writer whom he occasionally resembles – Max. Has he genius? Yes, in his flit-about fashion he has, but genius is a critic's word, and one insect should not fasten it wantonly upon another. What charms us in him is his taste, his choice of words, the rhythm both of his narrative and of his conversations, his wit, and – in his later work – an opulence as of gathered fruit and enamelled skies. His very monsignor-ishness is acceptable. It is *chic*, it is *risqué*, to titter in sacristies and peep through grilles at ecclesiastical Thesmophoriazusae, and if he becomes petulant, and lets a convent or a pipkin crash, it does not signify, for likely enough we have thrown down the book ourselves a page before. Yes, he has genius, for we are certain to take up the book again, and to come across Reggie, whose voice was rather like cheap scent, or Cardinal Pirelli baptizing a dog, or Miss Sinquier, daughter to a dean, who gave up all for the drama, and was killed by a mouse-trap, or Mrs Cresswell, who would have been canon-ized but for her unfortunate mot: 'If we are all a part of God, then God must, indeed, be horrible,' or Princess Elsie of England, or St Laura de Nazianzi her rival, or the Mouth family leaving their negro nakedness for the lures of Cuna-Cuna, or a hundred other sentences or people (the two classes are not separable) which have been evoked by his gaiety and exoticism. It is tempting to conclude the catalogue with the words 'He was a perfect artist'; tempting but unwise, for the words have something of the heavenly extinguisher about them, and we may discover that after all he was a glow-worm, and that now we cannot see him any more.

Vainglory is a good example of his earlier manner, and *Prancing Nigger* (first called *Sorrow in Sunlight*) of his later. *Vainglory* is all tweaks and skips. It professes to describe the attempts of Mrs Shamefoot to insert herself into Ashringford Cathedral in the form of a stained-glass window. Bishop Pantry is reluctant. Meanwhile she runs a florist's shop; indeed, *Meanwhile* would do admirably as a sub-title for the book. On we read, confusing the characters with the incidents and neglecting the outcome, but tickled by the images and the turns of the talk. It is frivolous stuff, and how rare, how precious is frivolity! How few writers can prostitute all their powers! They are always implying 'I am capable of higher things'. Firbank is completely absorbed in his own nonsense; he has nothing to hide, he is not showing off, he is not (or is very seldom) polemical. When he attempts satire, or wistfulness (as in *Santal*), he fails at once, he was incapable of totting up life. But there are no attempts in *Vainglory*, it is an untainted series of absurdities, and most delightful although Mrs Shamefoot's efforts have not even a comic coherency.

It is strange that such a writer should have developed, but *Prancing Nigger* offers quite another pair of wings. The butterfly has come out, and has demanded, with such severity as it can master, a temperature and even a cage. The temperature is tropical; we are on an exquisite island which travesties Haiti. The cage is the fortunes of the Mouth family; we are bounded by them, and it is the first time we have been bounded by anything, we are approaching the semblance of a novel. Is colour, after a certain point, only to be increased by a judicious mixture of human interest? Perhaps the question presented itself to him. Certainly one comes nearer to 'minding' about Edna Miami and Charlie than about any of his previous characters – Charlie, the glorified symbol of the writer himself, the happy black boy, passing through the customs at Cuna-Cuna with a butterfly net and nothing to declare.

The English novel, to Mr Waley's distress, is at present cluttered up with realistic lumber, and he draws a comparison between it and English painting. Fiction is mostly 'still in the Chantrey Bequest stage', and Firbank was an Impressionist, who broke away from academic naturalism by the method of selection and choice. Another reaction besides the Impressionistic is possible, namely the pre-Raphaelite, where the writer or painter throws himself into a state of mind more simple than his own, and thus raises his work from the anecdotic to the lyrical. This, Mr Waley points out, is the reaction of Mr David Garnett, who is deliberately naïve; and has found in fantasy a serviceable ally rather than a fairy queen. Unlike Firbank, he wants to do something, he wants to write a story, and we are here in the presence of a much more sophisticated mind, a sophistication all the greater because it is so carefully controlled, and always kept out of doors. His art is a hybrid. It blends in a new relationship the stocks of fantasy and commonsense. It is a successful experiment – unlike the art of Firbank, which contains no experiments at all. All that the two share in common is an omission: they do not introduce the soul nor its attendant scenery of Right and Wrong, they are fundamentally unserious. This disconcerts the Anglo-Saxon reader, who approves of playfulness, but likes it to have a holiday air. In the absence of regular office hours 'to sport would be as tedious as to work,' says Prince Henry the prig, and the butterflies and their kindred neither contradict him nor agree – they merely go away, and allow him to ruin Falstaff and save England. Play is their business. If for an instant they swerve from it they are swept into the nets of allegory. They may or may not possess will-power, may or may not desire to hover over a certain hedge, but the will is a trifle in the realm of the lower air which they inhabit and invite us to share.

[1929]

HOWARD OVERING STURGIS

How many people have read *Belchamber* today? Of the few who have read it, how many, besides myself, have carried about scraps of its wisdom and wit, its tact and its bitterness, for the last thirty years? The description in it of the converted Jew 'who instead of not attending the synagogue now stayed away from church'; Cissy Eccleston and her mother 'squashed sideways by the open drawers of their respective writing-tables, like people playing a perpetual duet on two organs with all the stops pulled out'; Sainty's grandmother, the duchess: 'the little of her grace's dress that was visible above the line of the tablecloth was of a delicate peach-colour'; the cameo of Edwardian gaiety preserved in, 'Lor! we did have fun, though, how was the poor piano this morning after those boys pouring the champagne into it?'; Cissy's row with her mother-in-law and the baleful, 'Oh, in the matter of a baby, take care I don't astonish some of you yet,' with which she concludes it; the kindly, vulgar note from Lady Arthur which concludes the book itself and puts the last polish on its irony – all these scraps have lain about in my mind among scraps from accredited authors like George Meredith and Thackeray, they have borne the test of time, and the novel from which they are taken has become, so far as one reader is concerned, a classic. Here is *Belchamber* reprinted. Re-read, it exercises its old power. Perhaps it is a classic after all. Anyhow, let me empty yesterday's champagne out of the poor piano, and cautiously try a few notes. The instrument cost a good deal to begin with – that is indisputable.

Howard Sturgis was born in 1855, in London, of American stock. He grew up in affluence, he was educated at Eton and Cambridge, adopted no profession, and was well placed for observing the airs and graces of the great – a foreigner in a front seat. His friend Henry James, equally well placed, fidgets in the seat slightly, and registers at moments a gratified awe as the procession passes, but Sturgis sits very quiet; socially he was always at his ease, he had nothing of the flustered immigrant about him, and he could mock at the 'errors in the Fourth Dimension' often made by his less fortunate compatriots. His father, Russell Sturgis, was for many years head of a great banking-house in this country, and this naturally brought him into contact with the eminent. After his father's death he remained in attendance on his mother, and after her death he settled close to Windsor in a smallish house, Queen's Acre, which he wrote 'Qu'Acre' and pronounced 'Quaker'. Here he completed a change which to us in our storm-tossed age may not seem a dramatic one, but it appeared significant enough at the time: the change from fashionableness to bookishness. There had always been a strong literary bent in him – and indeed in his family, for his brother Julian was a prolific novelist – and now that he was independent he lived more exactly according to his desires. He took to writing himself and he produced three novels, *Tim* (1891), *All that was Possible* (1895), and *Belchamber* (1904). His friends liked *Tim*, but some of them disapproved of *All that was Possible*. *Belchamber* pleased neither them nor the world at large. Sturgis was a domestic author, of the type of Cowper – he wrote to please his friends, and deterred by his failure to do so he gave up the practice of literature and devoted himself instead to embroidery, of which he had always been fond. His life wore away in quiet occupations, and in hospitality to interesting people and to the young, family servants looked after him or grew old in his service, invalid dogs tottered about, he lost much of his money, he became ill, and at the age of sixty-five he died in his own house. Not a thrilling life, nor according to some theorists an admirable one. A life that was only possible at a particular epoch in our civilization.

The most authoritative account of him is to be found in Mr Percy Lubbock's sketch of their mutual friend Mary Cholmondeley. There is also a chapter in Mrs Edith Wharton's reminiscences, some reference in A. C. Benson's Diary, and some further detail in the preface contributed by Mr Gerard Hopkins to this new edition of *Belchamber*. I went once to Qu'Acre myself – years ago – I don't remember much. A novel of my own had just been published, and Howard Sturgis's urbanity about it rather disconcerted me. He praised very neatly, and conscious of their own crudity the young are not always reassured by neatness. He was neat in everything. He has been compared to a clean, plump, extremely kind yet distinctly formidable old lady, the sort of old lady who seems all benignity and knitting but who follows everything that is said and much that isn't, and pounces and scratches before you know where you are – pounces on the present company and scratches the absent. After lunch I made a little slip. My host led me up to the fireplace, to show me a finished specimen of his embroidery. Unluckily there were two fabrics near the fireplace, and my eye hesitated for an instant between them. There was a demi-semiquaver of a pause. Then graciously did he indicate which his embroidery was, and then did I see that the rival fabric was a cloth kettle-holder, which could only have been mistaken for embroidery by a lout. Simultaneously

I received the impression that my novels contained me rather than I them. He was very kind and courteous, but we did not meet again.

His friends called him 'Howdie'. He was of medium height and rather heavily built, and he gave a general impression of softness though not of timidity. His most remarkable feature was the strong growth of brilliantly white hair. The forehead was tall and narrow, the eyes soft and rather prominent, the moustache heavy and well trimmed, the complexion delicate, the voice grave and low. As to the character, kindness and malice, tenderness and courage appear to have blended, as they occasionally do with the highly cultivated. He was a bit of a muff and far, far, far from a fool. He was at the mercy of life, yet never afraid of it, and almost his last words were 'I am enjoying dying very much'. He loved his friends. Piety towards the past and the departed was very strong in him – the sort of piety which Henry James has illuminated in *The Altar of the Dead*. Finally – but need this be underlined? – he was most intelligent and probably quite unshockable. One gets at moments an impression from his books that he is waiting for people to catch him up, and that they have not done so yet.

Tim is an Etonian meditation rather than a novel. The hero, a delicate, sensitive, skinny little boy, falls in love with a friend four years older than himself, and his devotion only ends with death. Tim is well drawn, and of the nature of a first sketch for the finished portrait of Sainty in *Belchamber*. Carol is a wish-fulfilment rather than a living youth, and too blue and gold and pink to be real. Both boys go to Eton – for Sturgis was in the thrall of his own school and class, and could no more imagine a gentleman not going to Eton than a servant not dropping an 'h'. More interesting than the main relationship is the reaction of the other characters towards it: their irritability and jealousy over an emotion which they do not share or direct and cannot understand. Tim's father is

admirably done in this respect, so is Carol's fiancée, and Sturgis
already shows himself expert in the less amiable detours of the
human heart. Death – which in his later work was to be less
accommodating – comes in here as a god, at the suitable moment, to explain and to reconcile. It is a wistful, 'pretty' book,
unlikely to find favour in this hard-boiled age, but it can still
be read with pleasure if read indulgently, and it was written
to please.

If *Tim* is a meditation, *All that was Possible* is a *tour de force*.
It records 'a summer in the life of Mrs Sybil Crofts, comedian,
extracted from her correspondence'. She has been the mistress
of a man who has discarded her, as generously as his circumstances permit, and now she has come to a remote valley in
Wales, to shut herself up from the world. The neighbours
suspect her of immorality, and the Henshaws, the chief family
of the district, cut her. She writes about it all to a friend in a
civilized, amusing way. Then, among her indifferent comments and pleasant accounts of the scenery, a new emotion
enters: she is falling in love with Robert Henshaw and he with
her. The situation is handled by Sturgis with great subtlety: he
is already a competent novelist who knows what he wants to
do and how not to overdo it, and he works up step by step to
his rather conventional *dénouement*. Sibyl had supposed that
Henshaw wished to marry her – surely to a man of his strict
morality no other relation could be possible – and all her
delicacy was bent on preventing him, since it would hinder
his career. But she might have saved herself the trouble: he
had never thought of her for a wife! 'I had looked on him as
an angel – a redeemer – and he had regarded me as something
pleasant but wrong, a temptation of St Anthony, to be resisted
if possible; and when resistance became irksome, to be yielded
to, and enjoyed in secret. . . . There was no thought of lifting
me; he would come down to me in the mud, and we would
lie there contentedly together.' She is not angry with him and

being intelligent she realizes that a secret liaison is all that is possible from his point of view. But she loves him too much to explain her own, and slips away one night, when he thinks he is coming to her arms.

> O that 'twere possible
> After long grief and pain.

These lines from *Maud* provide the emotional undertone to all three books. The heart is never appeased. Perhaps Sturgis was not quite free from self-pity, and, when he comes to draw the character of Sainty, he seems tempted to load the dice against him, in order to demonstrate how badly the game of life goes. He may have had happy relationships himself, but he never allows them to persist between his characters. However, happiness is a very difficult thing to do in art, and what novelists have put it across convincingly? It only arrives through music.

He must have learnt much when writing *All that was Possible*. A novel told through letters is a severe exercise; monotony threatens on the one hand, inconsistency on the other, and here both are avoided. There are no positive faults in the book, and many technical merits: that it is profoundly moving or interesting cannot be claimed. It is unlikely ever to be read again, and for this reason some account of it seemed desirable.

Fortunately there is no need to give an account of *Belchamber*. Thanks to this reprint, the reader can judge for himself, and all I need do is indicate the world which he may expect to enter. It is a long novel. Sturgis, having learnt his craft and consorted with other practitioners, is about to employ it for a double purpose: he will display his matured view of life, and he will depict the aristocracy. The aristocracy are a favourite subject for writers today; in our general break-up they have become museum-pieces. But this American approached them with no awe, he used them because he had observed them with his parents as a young man. As a result, his lords and ladies are easy and convincing: he seems to have got the hang of them externally, and he has animated them within by his experience of human nature. Even Sainty, the misfit, remains an aristocrat; he is bored by his class yet never ceases to belong to it. And his painted grandmother, his grim mother, his cad of a cousin, his manly uncle, his rotter of a brother – they belong to it too, swimming round and round in an aquarium whose glass seems unbreakable. (The action takes place in the early nineties, before the death-duties have done their work.)

As at a charity bazaar, the aristocracy is supported by some side-shows, such as dear Alice Meakins the governess, a Thackerayan dear, who marries rich and reminds us of the existence and the ineffectiveness of virtue. And there are the Ecclestons, spongers, who provide the fatal alliance. And there is Gerald Newby, the young Cambridge don. Gerald is the most highly finished product of the author's observant malice; he comes before us as a being not indeed perfect, not immune from faults, yet not unworthy to be mentor and hero to the Marquis of Belchamber. Alas, Gerald's faults increase, and by the time of the coming-of-age party, he is focused as a snob and a prig. His subsequent appearances are a nightmare, one dreads to see his name on the page, and this is all that fate has offered poor Sainty by way of a friend.

Sainty himself is the crux. He is on the stage the whole time. Does he hold it? Believing that he does, I rank *Belchamber* high. Henry James complained to A. C. Benson in the Athenaeum one evening that Sainty was a 'poor rat' and the book a 'mere ante-chamber', but James was a poor critic of any work not composed according to his own recipes, and he was particularly severe on novels by his friends. Sainty is not a rat. He can be dignified and even stern. His tragedy is only partly due to his own defects: he really fails because he lives among people who cannot understand what delicacy is; at the best they are dictators, like his mother, and miss it that way; at the worst they are bitches, like his wife. As a scholar and quiet bachelor he would have made a success of his career. And Sturgis, writing away at Qu'Acre, must have enjoyed precipitating himself into perilous surroundings and returning in safety to dedicate the results to a friend. 'The world,' he says, 'is like a huge theatrical company in which half the actors and actresses have been cast for the wrong parts.' He himself had not been cast ill, but there is a fascination in imagining misfortunes, which he did not forgo, and which helped him to create his hero.

At the appointed time Sainty found himself planted by a great bank of palms and heavy-scented white flowers that made him feel sick. From where he stood the whole great church was visible. Dimly, as through a mist, he could decry his mother, straight and stern, in puritanical drab, beside the huddled white chuddah and nodding plumes of his grandmother, the duchess strapped into a petunia velvet with a silver bonnet whose aigrette seemed to sweep the skies, his Aunt Eva in a Gainsborough hat, taking rapid notes for the *Looking Glass*, and Claude, slim, cool, and elegant, his beautifully gloved, pearl grey hands crossed upon his cane, which he had rested on the seat beside him as he stood sideways looking for the bride. Behind them a sea of faces, mostly unknown, of light colours and black coats, of feathers, flowers and laces, stretched back to where, in a cloud of pink and white, the bridesmaids clustered round the door, holding the great bouquets of roses he had so nearly forgotten to order for them.

The organ boomed, and the knowing-looking little choristers in their stiff surplices went clattering down the aisle, followed by a perfect procession of smug ecclesiastics, among whom Sainty caught a fleeting glimpse of dear old Meakins from Great Charmington. Lady Eccleston, emotional, devotional, and gorgeous as the morning, rustled hastily to her place in the front pew where George and Randolph were already nudging each other and giggling. Then the little white-robed boys began to come back, shrilly, chanting, and as the choir separated to right and left Sainty could see Tommy, very solemn and as red as the carnation in his buttonhole, and on his arm a vision of soft shrouded loveliness, coming slowly towards him. All the riddle of the future was hid in that veiled figure. How little he really knew what was in the little head and heart under all that whiteness; was it happiness or misery she was bringing him? an honoured, dignified married life, an equal share of joys and sorrows, 'his children like the olive-branches round about their table'? or a loveless existence, the straining bonds of those unequally yoked? Its little sordid daily squabbles that eat the heart, perhaps even shame, dishonour . . .? What thoughts for a bridegroom stepping forward to meet his bride at the altar! But who is master of his thoughts?

The above extract will give some idea of the documentary value of *Belchamber*, of its pictorial quality, and also of its method: the paragraphs of narrative with psychological stings in their tails are typical. It is a melancholy and disastrous story, and yet it exhilarates, for the disasters grow out of one another so naturally that the reader is delighted as by the spectacle of some rare if monstrous growth. When Sainty's brother marries a chorus-girl he thinks that the depths of family shame have been reached, but his own marriage, necessitated by the misalliance, has yet to come, and then the consequences of that marriage . . . until he actually gets to feel that Lady Arthur is not so bad a sort, after all, whereupon the book closes. No prizes have been handed out, no palms, no butter, and doubtless it is this refusal to compromise which has damaged *Belchamber* with the general public. If it had portrayed a good woman, or her spiritual equivalent a moral victory, the sales would have been higher.

On some such note as the above – a note of hardness – it seems most courteous to take leave of this brilliant, sensitive, and neglected writer. He did not care for the applause of outsiders. He wrote and he lived for his personal friends.

[1935]

SINCLAIR LEWIS

'I WOULD like to see Gopher Prairie,' says the heroine of Mr Sinclair Lewis's *Main Street*, and her husband promptly replies: 'Trust me. Here she is. Brought some snapshots down to show you.' That, in substance, is what Mr Lewis has done himself. He has brought down some snapshots to show us and posterity. The collection is as vivid and stimulating as any writer who adopts this particular method can offer. Let us examine it; let us consider the method in general. And let us at once dismiss the notion that any fool can use a camera. Photography is a great gift, whether or no we rank it as an art. If we have not been to Gopher Prairie we cry: 'So that's it!' on seeing the snap. If we have been we either cry: 'How like it!' or 'How perfectly disgraceful, not the least like it!' and in all three cases our vehemence shows that we are in the presence of something alive.

I have never been to Gopher Prairie, Nautilus, Zenith, or any of their big brothers and sisters, and my exclamations throughout are those of a non-American, and worthless as a comment on the facts. Nevertheless, I persist in exclaiming, for what Mr Lewis has done for myself and thousands of others is to lodge a piece of a continent in our imagination. America, for many of us, used to mean a very large apron, covered with a pattern of lozenges, edged by a frill, and chastely suspended by a boundary tape round the ample waist of Canada. The frill, like the tape, we visualized slightly; on the New York side it puckered up into sky-scrapers, on the farther side it was a blend of cinemas and cowboys, and more or less down the middle of the preposterous garment we discerned a pleat associated with the humour of Mark Twain.

But the apron proper, the lozenges of pale pink and pale green – they meant nothing at all: they were only something through which railways went and dividends occasionally came from, and which had been arbitrarily spattered with familiar names, like a lunar landscape. As we murmured 'Syracuse, Cairo, London even, Macon, Memphis, Rochester, Plymouth,' the titles, so charged with meaning in their old settings, cancelled each other out in their new, and helped to make the apron more unreal. And then Sinclair Lewis strode along, developed his films, and stopped our havering. The lozenges lived. We saw that they were composed of mud, dust, grass, crops, shops, clubs, hotels, railway stations, churches, universities, etc., which were sufficiently like their familiar counterparts to be real, and sufficiently unlike them to be extremely exciting. We saw men and women who were not quite ourselves, but ourselves modified by new surroundings, and we heard them talk a language which we could usually, but not always, understand. We enjoyed at once the thrills of intimacy and discovery, and for that and much else we are grateful, and posterity will echo our gratitude. Whether he has 'got' the Middle West, only the Middle West can say, but he has made thousands of people all over the globe alive to its existence, and anxious for further news. Ought a statue of him, camera in hand, to be erected in every little town? This, again, is a question for the Middle West.

Let us watch the camera at work:

In the flesh, Mrs Opal Emerson Mudge fell somewhat short of a prophetic aspect. She was pony-built and plump, with the face of a haughty Pekinese, a button of a nose, and arms so short that, despite her most indignant endeavours, she could not clasp her hands in front of her as she sat on the platform waiting.

Angus Duer came by, disdainful as a greyhound, and pushing on white gloves (which are the whitest and the most superciliously white objects on earth) . . . .

At the counter of the Greek Confectionery Parlour, while they [i.e. the local youths] ate dreadful messes of decayed bananas, acid cherries, whipped cream, and gelatinous ice cream, they screamed to one another: 'Hey, lemme 'lone,' 'Quit doggone you, looka what you went and done, you almost spilled my glass swater,' 'Like hell I did,' 'Hey, gol darn your hide, don't you go sticking your coffin nail in my i-scream.'

She saw that his hands were not in keeping with a Hellenic face. They were thick, roughened with needle and hot iron and plough handle. Even in the shop he persisted in his finery. He wore a silk shirt, a topaz scarf, thin tan shoes.

The drain pipe was dripping, a dulcet and lively song: drippety-drip-drip-dribble; drippety-drip-drip-drip.

The method throughout is the photographic. Click, and the picture's ours. A less spontaneous or more fastidious writer would have tinkered at all of the above extracts, and ruined everything. The freshness and vigour would have gone, and nothing been put in their places. For all his knowingness about life, and commercially-travelled airs, Mr Lewis is a novelist of the instinctive sort, he goes to his point direct. There is detachment, but not of the panoramic type: we are never lifted above the lozenges, Thomas Hardy fashion, to see the townlets seething beneath, never even given as wide a view as Arnold Bennett accords us of his Five Towns. It is rather the detachment of the close observer, of the man who stands half a dozen yards off his subject, or at any rate within easy speaking distance of it, and the absence of superiority and swank (which so pleasantly characterizes the books) is connected with this. Always in the same house or street as his characters, eating their foodstuffs, breathing their air, Mr Lewis claims no special advantages; though frequently annoyed with them, he is never contemptuous, and though he can be ironic and even denunciatory, he has nothing of the aseptic awfulness of the seer. Neither for good nor evil is he lifted above his theme; he is neither a poet nor a preacher, but a fellow with a camera a few yards away.

Even a fellow with a camera has his favourite subjects, as we can see by looking through the Kodak-albums of our friends. One amateur prefers the family group, another bathing-scenes, another his own house taken from every possible point of view, another cows upon an alp, or kittens held upside down in the arms of a black-faced child. This tendency to choose one subject rather than another indicates the photographer's temperament. Nevertheless, his passion is for photography rather than for selection, a kitten will serve when no cows are present, and, if I interpret Mr Lewis correctly, we must not lay too much stress on his attitude to life. He has an attitude; he is against dullness, heartiness, and intolerance, a trinity of evils most closely entwined; he mistrusts Y.M.C.A. helpfulness and rotarian idealism; while as for a positive creed (if we can accept *Martin Arrowsmith* as an unaided confession of faith) he believes in scientific research. 'So many men, Martin, have been kind and helpful, so few have added to knowledge,' complains the old bacteriologist. One can safely class him with writers termed 'advanced', with people who prefer truth to comfort, passion to stability, prevention to cure. But the classification lets what is most vital in him escape; his attitude, though it exists, does not dwell in the depths of his being. His likes and dislikes mean less to him than the quickness of his eye, and though he tends to snapshot muscular Christians when they are attacked with cramp, he would sooner snap them amid clouds of angels than not at all. His commentary on society is constant, coherent, sincere; yet the reader's eye follows the author's eye rather than his voice, and when Main Street is quitted it is not its narrowness, but its existence that remains as a permanent possession.

His method of book-building is unaffected and appropriate. In a sense (a very faint sense) his novels are tales of unrest. He takes a character who is not quite at ease in his or her surroundings, contrives episodes that urge this way or that, and a final issue of revolt or acquiescence. In his earlier work both character and episodes are clearcut; in his later – but let us postpone for a moment the painful problem of a photographer's old age. Carrol Endicott, the heroine of his first important book, is a perfect medium, and also a living being. Her walks down Main Street are overwhelming; we see the houses, we see her against them, and when the dinginess breaks and Erik Valborg arises with his gallant clothes and poet's face, we, too, are seduced, and feel that such a world might well be lost for love. Never again is Mr Lewis to be so poignant or to arrange his simple impressions so nearly in the order of high tragedy; 'I may not have fought the good fight, but I have kept the faith' are Carrol's final words, and how completely are they justified by all she has suffered and done! Babbitt follows her – of grosser clay, and a native while she was an exile, but even Babbitt sees that there is something better in life than graft and goodfellowship, though he acquiesces in them at the close. Martin Arrowsmith succeeds where Carrol and Babbitt failed, because he is built strongly and prepared to sacrifice a home, but, regarded as a medium, he is identical with them, he can register their doubts and difficulties. And the same is true of Elmer Gantry; his heavy feet are turned to acquiescence from the first, but he, too, has moments of uneasiness, and hypocrisy; religious eroticism and superstition can be focused through him. And so with Samuel Dodsworth in *Dodsworth*. He reacts this way and that among the main streets of Europe, and many pictures of them can be taken before he decides that they will not do.

Now, in the earlier books this method was a complete success, but with *Elmer Gantry* doubts begin; the theme is interesting, but the snapshots less remarkable. And in *Dodsworth* doubt becomes dismay. Dodsworth is a decent citizen of

Zenith who retires early and goes to Europe with his wife. She is cultivated and snobby – a *rechauffée* of the second Mrs Arrowsmith, but served upon an enormous dish. She talks, talks, flirts, patronizes, talks, and he, humble and observant, gradually realizes her inadequacies, but all the time he talks, talks, talks. The talk is rhetoric, the slang tired, the pictures blurred. The English country church, palace at Venice, restaurant at Paris, journey in an aeroplane, Bernese Oberland, back in New York, the right sort of American tourist, the wrong sort, is there a right sort, is it wrong to think there is a right sort? . . . on the story trundles, unprofitably broad-minded and with unlucky thematic parallels to Henry James. The method remains, but something has died. The following quotation will show us what:

He found that in certain French bathrooms one can have hot water without waiting for a geyser. He found that he needn't have brought two dozen tubes of his favourite (and very smelly) toothpaste from America—one actually could buy toothpaste, corn-plaster, New York Sunday papers, Bromo-Seltzer, Lucky Strikes, safety razor blades, and ice cream almost as easily in Paris as in the United States; and a man he met in Luigi's bar insisted that if one quested earnestly enough he could find B.D.V.s.

What has happened? What has changed the Greek Confectionery Parlour at Gopher Prairie, where every decaying banana mattered, to this spiritless general catalogue? The explanation is all too plain: photography is a pursuit for the young. So long as a writer has the freshness of youth on him, he can work the snapshot method, but when it passes he has nothing to fall back upon. It is here that he differs from the artist. The artist has the power of retaining and digesting experiences, which, years later, he may bring forth in a different form; to the end of life he is accompanied by a secret store.

The artist may not be good. He may be very bad. He generally is. And it is not to celebrate him and to decry the photographer that I draw this distinction between them. But it does explain, I think, why quick spontaneous writers (the kind that give me more pleasure than any) are apt, when they lose their spontaneity, to have nothing left, and to be condemned by critics as superficial. They are not superficial, they are merely not artistic; they are members of a different profession, the photographic, and the historian of our future will cease to worry over this, will pick up the earlier and brighter volumes in which their genius is enshrined, and will find there not only that genius, but a record of our age.

Mr Lewis is not our sole photographer. There is always Mr H. G. Wells. They have just the same gift of hitting off a person or place in a few quick words; moreover, they share the same indifference to poetry and pass much the same judgements on conduct. Consequently, one might have expected that their literary careers would be similar, that the authors of *Love and Mr Lewisham* and *Main Street* would develop in the same way and at the same rate. They have diverged, and for an instructive reason. Wells is still kicking because photography was only one of his resources. When his early freshness wore off, he could bring into play his restless curiosity about the universe, and thus galvanize his later novels into life. In Mr Lewis, curiosity about the universe has never been very strong. Only occasionally has he thought of the past, the future, international relationships, science, labour, the salvation or damnation of the globe. The people in the room and the houses across the street are what really interest him, and, when the power to reproduce them sharply fails, he has nothing to do except to reproduce them dimly. If this view of his development is correct, the later stages of it are bound to be disappointing. However, there the early books are, done, safe, mankind's for ever; also, the longer one lives, the less important does 'development' appear.

[1929]

JOSEPH CONRAD: A NOTE

In his *Notes on Life and Letters*, Mr Conrad takes the public for the second time into the severe little apartment that must, for want of a better word, be called his confidence. It greeted us, first, in *A Personal Record*, where he was interesting, stimulating, profound, beautiful – but confiding? Scarcely; nor is he in these 'Notes'. He guards himself by ironies and politenesses; he says, 'Here is my little interior, which it is your weakness to see and perhaps mine to show; I will tell you what I think about Poland, and luxury-ships and Henry James. That will satisfy your curiosity, will it not? Good morning. Do not feel obliged to praise what you have seen; indeed, I should almost prefer it if you didn't.' And he bows us out.

A proud and formidable character appears rather more clearly here than in the novels; that is all we can say. The character will never be really clear, for one of two reasons. The first reason has already been indicated; the writer's dread of intimacy. He has a rigid conception as to where the rights of the public stop, he has determined we shall not be 'all over' him, and has half contemptuously thrown open this vestibule and invited us to mistake it for the private apartments if we choose. We may not see such a character clearly because he does not wish us to see. But we also may not see it clearly because it is essentially unclear. This possibility must be considered. Behind the smoke screen of his reticence there may be another obscurity, connected with the foreground by wisps of vapour, yet proceeding from another source, from the central chasm of his tremendous genius. This isn't an aesthetic criticism, nor a moral one. Just a suggestion that our

difficulties with Mr Conrad may proceed in part from difficulties of his own.

What is so elusive about him is that he is always promising
to make some general philosophic statement about the universe, and then refraining with a gruff disclaimer. Dealing
even in the slightest of these essays with vast and eternal
issues, he won't say whether such issues lead or don't lead to a
goal. 'For which may I put you down, Mr Conrad, for the
One or the None?' At such a question Mr Conrad roughens
into a shrewd sailorman promptly. He implies that the One
and the None are highly interesting, but that it is more important to distinguish a bulwark from a bollard. Can the
reader do that much? If he cannot, may not the interview
cease? 'I see, Mr Conrad. You are a cynic.' By no means:

From a charge of cynicism I have always shrunk instinctively. It is
like a charge of being blind in one eye, a moral disablement, a sort of
disgraceful calamity that must be carried off with a jaunty bearing – a
sort of thing I am not capable of.

And the disclaimers continue each time a general point is
raised. He never gives himself away. Our impertinence is
rebuked; sentence after sentence discharges its smoke screen
into our abashed eyes, yet the problem isn't settled really. Is
there not also a central obscurity, something noble, heroic,
beautiful, inspiring half a dozen great books; but obscure,
obscure? While reading the half-dozen books one doesn't or
shouldn't ask such a question, but it occurs, not improperly,
when the author professes to be personal, and to take us into
that confidence of his. These essays do suggest that he is misty
in the middle as well as at the edges, that the secret casket of
his genius contains a vapour rather than a jewel; and that we
need not try to write him down philosophically, because there
is, in this particular direction, nothing to write. No creed, in
fact. Only opinions, and the right to throw them overboard

when facts make them look absurd. Opinions held under the semblance of eternity, girt with the sea, crowned with the stars, and therefore easily mistaken for a creed.

As the simple sailorman, concerned only with his job, and resenting interference, he is not difficult to understand, and it is this side of him that has given what is most solid, though not what is most splendid, to his books. Nor is he mysterious as a Pole. Seven of these Essays deal with the sea – or rather with ships – for only landsmen would sentimentalize about the sea and think it beautiful or lovable, or a field for adventure. He has no respect for adventure, unless it comes incidentally. If pursued for its own sake it leads to 'red noses and watery eyes', and 'lays a man under no obligation of faithfulness to an idea'. Work filled the life of the men whom he admired and imitated and whom, more articulate than they, he would express. They had no thoughts of the One or None. And (passing from his profession to his nationality) we find the same quality in his five Essays on Poland, where he voices an oppressed and leaderless people, to whom Russia and Germany are equally loathsome and who can hope for nothing but disaster from the war.

The British Merchant Service and Poland are the local accidents of his life, and his character permits their vehement defence. We need not take him as our guide through the *Titanic disaster*, still less to the Eastern imbroglio. The passions are intelligible and frank: having lived thus, thus he feels, and it is as idle to regret his account of Russians as it would be to regret Dostoievsky's account of Poles in *The Brothers Kara-mazov*. A philosopher would moderate his transports, or attempt to correlate them. Conrad isn't that type, he claims the right to be unreasonable when he or those whom he respects have suffered.

He does not respect all humanity. Indeed, were he less self-conscious, he would probably be a misanthrope. He has to pull himself up with a reminder that misanthropy wouldn't be quite fair – on himself. Observe (in the quotation given above) why he objected to being charged with cynicism. Cynicism may be undeserved by the poor victims, but that didn't occur to him. He objected because 'it is like a charge of being blind in one eye, a moral disablement, a sort of disgraceful calamity,' because he was touched in his pride. It becomes a point of honour not to be misanthropic, so that even when he hits out there is a fierce restraint that wounds more deeply than the blows. He will not despise men, yet cannot respect them, and consequently our careers seem to him important and unimportant at the same time, and our fates like those of the characters of Alphonse Daudet, 'poignant, intensely interesting, and not of the slightest consequence.'

Now, together with these loyalties and prejudices and personal scruples, he holds another ideal, a universal, the love of Truth. But Truth is a flower in whose neighbourhood others must wither, and Mr Conrad has no intention that the blossoms he has culled with such pains and in so many lands should suffer and be thrown aside. So there are constant discrepancies between his nearer and his further vision, and here would seem to be the cause of his central obscurity. If he lived only in his experiences, never lifting his eyes to what lies beyond them: or if, having seen what lies beyond, he would subordinate his experiences to it – then in either case he would be easier to read. But he is in neither case. He is too much of a seer to restrain his spirit; he is too much Joseph Conrad, too jealous of personal honour, to give any but the fullest value to deeds and dangers he has known. Thus, 'in the whole record of human transactions there have never been performances so brazen and so vile as the manifestoes of the German Emperor and the Grand Duke Nicholas of Russia' to Poland at the beginning of the war; while psychical research, which he affects to examine, is rejected not on the ground that it is false, but because it will not benefit humanity. Anatole France, on the other hand, who runs counter to no prejudice or loyalty, can be judged by the light of Truth alone, by the absolute value of what he has written, and can be given philosophic approval.

Were these essays from a smaller writer, they would not set us worrying. But they are like the snow man that Michelangelo made for young Piero de' Medici at Florence. Every line in them is important because the material differs from the imperishable marble that we know, and may help to interpret the lines of that. Grave historians deplore the snow man, as derogatory to artistic majesty, and Mr Conrad himself, in his preface, rather doubts whether he has been wise either to write or republish these fugitive articles. Perhaps he has been unwise, but that is his look-out; his readers have an extra volume to treasure. One realizes, more definitely, what a noble artist is here, what an austere character, by whose side most of our contemporary writers appear obsequious. One would like to offer him not only praise but friendship, which cannot, however, be done; witness the fate of the unlucky reviewer who, hoping to be friendly, characterized the crew of one of his earlier works as 'a lot of engaging ruffians'. Most other novelists, pleased with the compliment, would have pardoned the indiscretion. Mr Conrad takes the opportunity to growl.

What on earth is an 'engaging ruffian'. He must be a creature of literary imagination, I thought, for the two words don't match in my personal experience. It has happened to me to meet a few ruffians here and there, but I never found one of them 'engaging'. I consoled myself, however, by reflecting that the friendly reviewer must have been talking like a parrot, which so often seems to understand what it says.

The castigation is merited, yet few writers, great or small, would have inflicted it, because they have a hankering for friendship. Neither explicitly nor implicitly does Mr Conrad demand friendship: he desires no good wishes from his readers: the anonymous intimacy, so dear to most, is only an annoyance and a hindrance to him.

[1920]

T. E. LAWRENCE

THE little fellow who is labelled for posterity as Lawrence of Arabia detested the title. He often asked people to call him T.E., and perhaps it is fitting to respect that wish when writing about him now. T.E. did not think very well of the *Seven Pillars of Wisdom*. 'Not good enough, but as good, apparently, as I can do' was inscribed in my own copy of it. He compared the thing to a builder's yard, he called the style gummy, and he advised beer to be spilt freely upon the binding. A public edition of the sacred volume now appears. It is a noble and a scrupulous reprint, and the multitudes who are expecting it will not go empty away. Layout, presentation, editing by Mr A. W. Lawrence; new maps and indexes, choice of illustrations – all are very, very good. So are the contents, but if the public falls down and worships them it will do so without the author's approval. T.E. hated deference. He hated to feel respectable, respected, exempted, safe, in a world full of disreputables. At the bottom of our social ladder lie not only the failures, who are at all events printable, but the unprintable scamps who enjoy degradation. He had sympathy with both sorts, and any attempt to canonize him because he has written a book as big as a bible would make him jeer in his grave.

The text of the work is already a joy for experts. Things begin well with the losing of the original MS. in a bag on the platform of Reading station. A later MS. forms the basis of the so-called 'Oxford' edition of 1922. I have read through this edition twice. One always tends to overpraise a long book, because one has got through it; still the 'Oxford' is in the judgement of several critics even superior to the version offered now, and it is good news that a reprint of it may eventually be made. Only about half a dozen copies exist. It contains nearly 330,000 words, and was printed by the *Oxford Times* in double column on one side of the paper. Fearful of prolixity, the author set to work to cut it down by 50,000 words. He removed, among other passages, the entire opening chapter, which seems a pity, for it was a helpful piece of writing and propelled the reader easily into the action. (One sentence in that cancelled chapter always stays in my memory: 'All the subject provinces of the Empire to me were not worth one dead English boy'; a sentence to be weighed against 'The sword also means cleanness and death', which is stamped on the cover of the present volume.) From the cut-down 'Oxford' the famous 'subscribers' edition of 1926 was made; it was adorned with magnificent and sometimes arbitrary illustrations, and with an ornamental initial at the top of each page when possible. *Revolt in the Desert*, for public consumption, appeared at the same time. This is, of course, a drastic abridgement, though T.E. once remarked that he had added one unpublished item to it, in order to tease the subscribers. He loved teasing people who thought themselves It. The present edition reprints the 'subscribers' – with three minute omissions, carefully indicated in the text. Here the matter rests, unless the lost handbag is discovered and its contents revealed, when there may be the dickens to pay.

What is this long book about?

It describes the revolt in Arabia against the Turks, as it appeared to an Englishman who took part in it; he would not allow us to write 'the leading part'. It opens with his preliminary visit to Rabegh and understanding with Feisul; then comes the new idea: shifting north to Wejh and harrying thence the Medina railway. The idea works, and he leaves Feisul for a time and moves against Akaba with Auda, another great figure of the revolt. A second success: Akaba falls. The war then ceases to be in the Hejaz and becomes Syrian. Henceforward he cooperates with the British Army under his hero Allenby, and his main work is in Trans-Jordania; it leads up to the cutting of the three railways round Deraa. Deraa isolated, the way lies clear to the third success, the capture of Damascus; the united armies enter Damascus, the revolt has triumphed.

That is what the book is about, and it could only be reviewed authoritatively by a staff officer who knows the East.

That is what the book is about, and *Moby Dick* was about catching a whale.

For round this tent-pole of a military chronicle T.E. has hung an unexampled fabric of portraits, descriptions, philosophies, emotions, adventures, dreams. He has brought to his task a fastidious scholarship, an impeccable memory, a style nicely woven out of Oxfordisms and Doughty, an eye unparalleled, a sexual frankness which would cause most authors to be run in by the police, a profound distrust of himself, a still profounder faith. The 'seven-pillared worthy house' was in his judgement never finished; the peace settlement of Versailles and some personal loss combined to shatter it and 'the little things crept out to patch themselves hovels in its shadow'. But the fabric propped by the tent-pole of the military chronicle survives, stretched taut against the sun. As we penetrate its vast interior and are bewildered by contrary effects, it is natural that we should ask for a guide, and I would suggest for that purpose not the explosions of gun-cotton and cries of dying Turks, not the cracklings of councils, not even the self-communings, but some such passage as this:

From this rock a silver runlet issued into the sunlight. I looked in to see the spout, a little thinner than my wrist, jetting out firmly from a fissure in the roof, and falling with that clean sound into a shallow,

frothing pool, behind the step which served as entrance. The walls
and roof of the crevice dripped with moisture. Thick ferns and grasses
of the finest green made it a paradise just five feet square.

Upon the water-cleansed and fragrant ledge I undressed my soiled
body, and stepped into the little basin, to taste at last a freshness of
moving air and water against my tired skin. It was deliciously cool.
I lay there quietly, letting the clear, dark red water run over me in a
ribbly stream, and rub the travel-dirt away. While I was so happy, a
grey-bearded, ragged man, with a hewn face of great power and
weariness, came slowly along the path till opposite the spring; and
there he let himself down with a sigh upon my clothes spread out
over a rock beside the path, for the sun-heat to chase out their
thronging vermin.

He heard me and leaned forward, peering with rheumy eyes at this
white thing splashing in the hollow beyond the veil of sun-mist.
After a long stare he seemed content, and closed his eyes, groaning,
'The love is from God; and of God; and towards God.'

T.E. was a very difficult person, and no one who knew him
at all well would venture to sum him up. But he certainly
possessed the three heroic virtues: courage, generosity, and
compassion. His courage and generosity he could not conceal, though he perversely tried to do so. Compassion is more
easily hidden, and this passage is valuable because it reveals it.
The little unhusked body, so happy in its baptism, the half-
witted prophet contemplating it, lift us up into a region of
tenderness and unselfish love which was probably his real
world. A world unknown to the Arabs, he thought, and the
mumblings of the old man quite upset his theories about them.

In fear of a revelation, I put an end to my bath, and advanced to
recover my clothes. He shut his eyes with his hands, and groaned
heavily. Tenderly I persuaded him to rise up and let me dress, and
then to come with me along the crazy path which the camels had
made in their climbing to and from the other water springs. He sat
down by our coffee place, where Mohammed blew up the fire while
I sought to make him utter doctrine. [Which the old man wouldn't

do.] The Howeitat told me that life-long he had wandered among them moaning strange things, not knowing day or night, not troubling himself for food or work or shelter. He was given bounty of them all, as an afflicted man; but never replied a word, or talked aloud, except when abroad by himself or alone among the sheep and goats.

If we take compassion as a lodestar, it may lead us through the psychology of the *Seven Pillars* as surely as Damascus led us northward through the geography. Here is a young man, describing himself as he was when still younger. He has discovered that he can lead an Arab army, fight, bluff, and spy, be hard and disciplinary, and this is exhilarating; but the course of his inner life runs contrary. That course is turbid, slow, weighted by remorse for victory, and by disgust against the body. Personal ill-luck and ill-health, particularly a horrible masochistic experience, emphasize this, so that when he analyses himself it is as a spiritual outcast, on the lines of Herman Melville's Ishmael. To the attentive reader, something has gone wrong here, the analysis has reached one conclusion, the text keeps implying another. Does it imply that 'the love is from God and of God and towards God'? Nothing as theological as that, but there is a latent unselfishness, a constant goodwill which are fundamental, and which the fires of his own suffering fuse into compassion.

Whatever his inner life, he yearned to create a single work of art out of that life and out of his military experiences. He was rather superstitious about works of art, and spoke of them as if they belonged to a special category. The *Seven Pillars* to him was a failure, a 'builder's yard', where wealth of material did not compensate for absence of form. The romantic evocations of Rumm and Azrak, the masterly character-sketches of Auda and other chiefs, the episode of Farraj and Daud, the gargantuan mutton-feast – he regarded them as bricks for a future and better architect. Perhaps when the subscribers' edition came out and all sorts of people thought it good, he worried less as to whether it was a work of art, but he was so modest that he never grasped its greatness, or admitted that he had given something unique to our literature.

He has also contributed to sociology, in recording what is probably the last of the picturesque wars. Camels, pennants, the blowing up of little railway trains by little charges of dynamite in the desert – it is unlikely to recur. Next time the aeroplane will blot out everything in an indifferent death, but the aeroplane in this yarn is only a visitor, which arrives in the last chapters to give special thrills. A personal note can still be struck. It is possible to pot at the fat station master as he sits drinking coffee with his friends . . . good . . I got him . . . he rolls off his deck-chair! Steal up behind the shepherds and score their feet, so that they do not carry the news! Hide under the bridge in the rain all night! This is not only agreeable to the reader, it is important to the historian. Because it was waged under archaistic conditions, the Arab revolt is likely to be remembered. It is the last effort of the war-god before he laid down his godhead, and turned chemist.

What T.E. himself thought of war it is impossible to say. He spent most of his life waging it or helping to prepare for it, but the military meditation which occupies Chapter 33 shows that he did not believe in killing people. Probably he was muddled and rattled like the rest of us, and cherished the theory that war is inevitable in order to steady himself. He was, of course, devoted to the Arab cause. Yet when it triumphed he felt that he had let down both his own countrymen and the foreigner by aping foreign ways, and became more English than ever. To regard him as 'gone native' is wrong. He belonged body and soul to our islands. And he should have been happier in olden days, when a man could feel surer that he was fighting for his own hearth, and this terrible modern mix-up had not begun.

It must be remembered, in conclusion, that the *Seven Pillars* are not his last testament. He had still several years to live, during which he was developing through methods which he himself understood, and writing things which often pleased him better. He seemed to have plenty of time. More and more people liked him. He made every sort of contact, and he could reveal only a little of himself to each person and yet not arouse distrust. One never thought of saying to him 'Tell me more'. Now that he is gone away, he has to come into the open, which he dreaded, he must be analysed, estimated, claimed. A legend will probably flourish, and, twisted from his true bearings even further than Nelson, Lawrence of Arabia may turn into a tattoo master's asset, the boy scout's hero and the girl guide's dream. Committees have already been formed by his more influential friends, directing public enthusiasm about him into suitable channels. They will protect him from the sharks, and this is a good thing, and let us hope that they will save him from the governesses also.

[1935]

JANE AUSTEN

1. *The Six Novels*

I AM a Jane Austenite, and therefore slightly imbecile about Jane Austen. My fatuous expression, and airs of personal immunity – how ill they set on the face, say, of a Stevensonian! But Jane Austen is so different. She is my favourite author! I read and re-read, the mouth open and the mind closed. Shut up in measureless content, I greet her by the name of most kind hostess, while criticism slumbers. The Jane Austenite possesses little of the brightness he ascribes so freely to his idol.

Like all regular churchgoers, he scarcely notices what is being said. For instance, the grammar of the following sentence from *Mansfield Park* does not cause him the least uneasiness:

And, alas! how always known no principle to supply as a duty what the heart was deficient in.

Nor does he notice any flatness in this dialogue from *Pride and Prejudice*:

'Kitty has no discretion in her coughs,' said her father; 'she times them ill.'
'I do not cough for my own amusement,' replied Kitty fretfully.
'When is your next ball to be, Lizzy?'

Why should Kitty ask what she must have known? And why does she say 'your' ball when she was going to it herself? Fretfulness would never carry her to such lengths. No, something is amiss in the text; but the loyal adorer will never suspect it. He reads and re-reads. And Mr R. W. Chapman's fine new edition has, among its other merits, the advantage of waking the Jane Austenite up. After reading its notes and appendixes, after a single glance at its illustrations, he will never relapse again into the primal stupor. Without violence, the spell has been broken. The six princesses remain on their sofas, but their eyelids quiver and they move their hands. Their twelve suitors do likewise, and their subordinates stir on the perches to which humour or propriety assigned them. The novels continue to live their own wonderful internal life, but it has been freshened and enriched by contact with the life of facts. To promote this contact is the chief function of an editor, and Mr Chapman fulfils it. All his erudition and taste contribute to this end – his extracts from Mrs Radcliffe and Mrs Inchbald, his disquisitions on punctuation and travel, his indexes. Even his textual criticism helps. Observe his brilliant solution of the second of the two difficulties quoted above.

He has noticed that in the original edition of *Pride and Prejudice* the words 'When is your next ball to be, Lizzy?' began a line, and he suggests that the printer failed to indent them, and, in consequence, they are not Kitty's words at all, but her father's. It is a tiny point, yet how it stirs the pools of complacency! Mr Bennet, not Kitty, is speaking, and all these years one had never known! The dialogue lights up and sends a little spark of fire into the main mass of the novel. And so, to a lesser degree, with the shapeless sentence from *Mansfield Park*. Here we emend 'how always known' into 'now all was known'; and the sentence not only makes sense but illumines its surroundings. Fanny is meditating on the character of Crawford, and, now that all is known to her, she condemns it. And finally, what a light is thrown on Jane Austen's own character by an intelligent collation of the two editions of *Sense and Sensibility*! In the 1811 edition we read:

Lady Middleton's delicacy was shocked; and in order to banish so improper a subject as the mention of a natural daughter, she actually took the trouble of saying something herself about the weather.

In the 1813 edition the sentence is omitted, in the interests of propriety: the authoress is moving away from the eighteenth century into the nineteenth, from *Love and Friendship* towards *Persuasion*.

Texts are mainly for scholars; the general attractions of Mr Chapman's work lie elsewhere. His illustrations are beyond all praise. Selected from contemporary prints, from fashion plates, manuals of dancing and gardening, tradesmen's advertisements, views, plans, etc., they have the most wonderful power of stimulating the reader and causing him to forget he is in church; incidentally, they purge his mind of the lamentable Hugh Thompson. Never again will he tolerate illustrations which illustrate nothing except the obscurity of the artist. Here is the real right thing. Here is a mezzotint of 'The Encampment at Brighton', where the desires of Lydia and Kitty mount as busbies into the ambient air. Here is the soul of Mrs Rushworth in the form of a country house with a flap across it. Here is Jane Fairfax's Broadwood, standing in the corner of a print that carries us on to Poor Isabella, for its title is 'Maternal Recreation'. Here are Matlock and Dovedale as Elizabeth hoped they would be, and Lyme Regis as Anne saw it. Here is a Mona Marble Chimneypiece, radiating heat. Mr Chapman could not have chosen such illustrations unless he, too, kindled a flame – they lie beyond the grasp of scholarship. And so with the rest of his work; again and again he achieves contact between the life of the novels and the life of facts – a timely contact, for Austen was getting just a trifle stuffy; our fault, not hers, but it was happening.

The edition is not perfect. Pedantry sometimes asserts itself; when *Persuasion* was published with *Northanger Abbey* in 1818, its title did not appear on the back of the volumes; but why should the inconvenience be perpetuated in 1923? And there is one really grave defect: *Love and Friendship*, *The Watsons*, and *Lady Susan* have all been ignored. Perhaps there may be difficulties of copyright that prevent a reprint of them, but this does not excuse their almost complete omission from the terminal essays. There are many points, both of diction and manners, that they would have illustrated. Their absence is a serious loss, both for the student and for the general reader, and it is to be hoped that Mr Chapman will be able to issue a supplementary volume containing them and all the other scraps he can lay his hands on. There exist at least two manuscript-books of Jane Austen. The amazing *Love and Friendship* volume was extracted out of one of them; what else lies hidden? It is over a hundred years since the authoress died, and all the materials for a final estimate ought to be accessible by now, and to have been included in this edition.

Yet with all the help in the world how shall we drag these shy, proud books into the centre of our minds? To be one with Jane Austen! It is a contradiction in terms, yet every Jane Austenite has made the attempt. When the humour has been absorbed and the cynicism and moral earnestness both discounted, something remains which is easily called Life, but does not thus become more approachable. It is the books rather than the author that seem to reject us – natural enough, since the books are literature and the author an aunt. As Miss Bates remarked, 'Dear Jane, how shall we ever recollect half the dishes?' – for though the banquet was not long, it has never been assimilated to our minds. Miss Bates received no answer to her most apposite question; her dear Jane was thinking of something else. The dishes were carried back into the kitchen of the Crown before she could memorize them, and Heaven knows now what they contained! – strawberries from Donwell, perhaps, or apricots from Mansfield Rectory, or sugar-plums from Barton, or hothouse grapes from Pemberley, or melted butter from Woodston, or the hazel nut that Captain Wentworth once picked for Louisa Musgrove in a double hedgerow near Uppercross. Something has flashed past the faces of the guests and brushed their hearts – something as impalpable as stardust, yet it is part of the soil of England. Miss Austen herself, though she evoked it, cannot retain it any more than we can. When *Pride and Prejudice* is finished she goes up to London and searches in vain through the picture galleries for a portrait of Elizabeth Bennet. 'I dare say she will be in yellow,' she writes to Cassandra. But not in that nor in any colour could she find her.

[1924]

2. Sanditon

The fragment known to Miss Austen's family as *Sanditon* is of small literary merit, but no one is to blame for this:

neither the authoress, who left it a fragment, nor the owner of the MS., who has rightly decided on publication, nor the editor of the text, who has done his work with care and skill. Though of small merit, it is of great interest, for it was written after *Persuasion*, and consequently may throw light on the last phase of the great novelist. In 1817 she had reached maturity, but she was also ill, and these are the two factors we must bear in mind while we read. Are there signs of new development in *Sanditon*? Or is everything overshadowed by the advance of death?

The MS. (the editor tells us) is firmly written. Nevertheless, the fragment gives the effect of weakness, if only because it is reminiscent from first to last. It opens with a Mr and Mrs Parker falling out of a carriage (cf. *Love and Friendship*), and Mr Parker, like Marianne Dashwood, sprains his ankle. A Mr Heywood rescues him. The Parkers and Heywoods both have large families, and when the former return to their seaside home they take with them Miss Charlotte Heywood, 'a very pleasing young woman of two-and-twenty', who is destined to be the heroine. Charlotte belongs to a type which has attracted Miss Austen all the way from *Sense and Sensibility* to *Persuasion*, and naturally dominates her pen when vitality is low; she is the well-scoured channel through which comment most readily flows. But whereas Eleanor Dashwood, Fanny Price, Anne Elliot, were real people whose good sense, modesty, and detachment were personal qualities, Charlotte turns these qualities into labels and can be seen from some distance as she sits observing other labels upon the sea-front. It is a procession of adjectives. Here comes Clara Brereton, talented, good-looking, dependent, and not wholly trustworthy, whom we knew in a more living state as Jane Fairfax. Here is Clara's patroness, Lady Denham, who is jolly and downright like Mrs Jennings, but domineers like Lady Catherine de Burgh. Here are the Miss Beauforts – shadows of the shadow of Isabella Thorpe, and the harp on which they perform echoes the dying echo of Mary Crawford's, even as the gruel of Mr Woodhouse mingles with the cocoa of Arthur Parker a just perceptible aroma. And here come other labels, and in their midst sits the 'very pleasing young woman' reading them out loud for our advantage and finding none of them quite to her taste. Clearly, so far as character-drawing is concerned, Jane Austen is here completely in the grip of her previous novels. She writes out of what she has written, and anyone who has himself tried to write when feeling out of sorts will realize her state. The pen always finds life difficult to record; left to itself, it records the pen. The effort of creating was too much, and the numerous alterations in the MS. are never in the direction of vitality. Even the wit is reminiscent. This is the best it can do:

> All that he understood of himself he readily told, for he was very open-hearted; and where he might be himself in the dark, his conversation was still giving information to such of the Heywoods as could observe.

It is the old flavour, but how faint! Sometimes it is even stale, and we realize with pain that we are listening to a slightly tiresome spinster, who has talked too much in the past to be silent unaided. *Sanditon* is a sad little experience from this point of view, and sentimentalists will doubtless say that it ought not to have been published lest it perform the mysterious operation known as 'harming an author'.

But meanwhile Charlotte sits on the sea-front. Why a seafront?

Since the book promises little vigour of character and incident, one is tempted to assume that atmosphere and outline will be reminiscent also, and that the scene is laid in a watering-place because the writer had recently dealt with Lyme Regis and found marine humours easiest to handle. Nevertheless, there is a queer taste in these eleven chapters which is not easily defined: a double-flavoured taste – half topography, half romance. Sanditon is not like Lyme or Highbury or Northanger or the other places that provide scenes or titles to past novels. It exists in itself and for itself. Character-drawing, incident, and wit are on the decline, but topography comes to the front, and is screwed much deeper than usual into the story. Mr Parker is an Enthusiast for Sanditon. He has invested money in the resort, so has Lady Denham; and not only their humours but their fortunes depend on its development and the filling of its lodging-houses. Isn't this new? Was there anything like it in the preceding novels which were purely social? And – now for the romantic flavour – is there not a new cadence in this prose?

Charlotte having received possession of her apartment, found amusement enough in standing at her ample Venetian window and looking over the miscellaneous foreground of unfinished Buildings, waving Linen, and tops of Houses, to the Sea, dancing and sparkling in Sunshine and Freshness.

'Found amusement enough' is typical Jane Austen, but the conclusion of the sentence belongs to someone else – to someone who had been laughed out of court but who now returns in more radiant garb. It is Mrs Radcliffe. She is creeping back attired as a Nereid, and not without hope of brandishing some day the sword Excalibur.

Poor Burns's known irregularities greatly interrupt my enjoyment of his Lines.

Very proper that they should, but why enjoy such lines at all? Why read and discuss Burns, Wordsworth, and Scott? The new literature rises over old landmarks like a tide, and not only does the sea dance in freshness, but another configuration has been given to the earth, making it at once more poetic and more definite. Sanditon gives out an atmosphere, and also exists as a geographic and economic force. It was clearly intended to influence the faded fabric of the story and govern its matrimonial weavings. Of course, Miss Austen would not have stressed this, and her book, even if conceived with vigour, would not have marked a turning-point in the English novel or overshadowed *Waverley*. The change is merely interesting because it took place in her mind – that self-contained mind which had hitherto regarded the face of the earth as a site for shrubberies and strawberry beds, and had denied it features of its own. Perhaps here, too, we can trace the influence of ill-health: the invalid looks out of her window, weary of her invaluable Cassandra, weary of civility and auntish fun, and finds an unexpected repose in the expanses of Nature:

At last, from the low French windows of the Drawing-room, which commanded the road and all the Paths across the Down, Charlotte and Sir Edward, as they sat, could not but observe Lady Denham and Miss Brereton. . . .

'The road and all the Paths across the Down.' The cadence is curious again: Henry Tilney would have pricked up his ears. After all, they have not been exorcized – those ebony cabinets and massive chests that so disquieted Catherine's sleep. The Lady of the Lake is creeping out of them, followed by her entire school.

[1925]

3. *The Letters*

Miss Austen had no idea of what awaited Jane Austen. Within certain limits she could perhaps forecast her contemporary's future: she must have known that the novels would remain before the public for some years, and she would not have been surprised by the tributes of the Austen Leighs and of Lord Brabourne, for they were relatives, and might be expected to do what they could for an aunt. But that the affair should go further, that it should reach the twentieth century and reach it in such proportions – of that she could have had no premonition. She would have been amazed at Mr Chapman's magnificent and scholarly edition of the novels, published nine years ago, and still more amazed at the interest shown over *Love and Friendship* and *Sanditon*, and the lid (for now we must be as modern as we can), the lid would have been put on by this final achievement of Mr Chapman's, this monumental and definitive edition of the letters.

What would she have thought about it all? The question is not uninteresting, though it is more important that we should think about it correctly ourselves, that we should maintain critical perspective, that we should not overwhelm by our superior awareness, and that Jane Austen, whom we know so well, should not distort or overshadow Miss Austen, whom we cannot know, because she died over a century ago at Winchester. Sitting up in our thousands and taking notice, as we shall, we had better first of all listen to the words of Cassandra, who was with her at the end:

I *have* lost such a Sister, such a friend as never can have been surpassed – she was the sun of my life, the gilder of every pleasure, the soother of every sorrow, I had not a thought concealed from her, and it is as if I had lost a part of myself.

We like these words of Cassandra's, and we had better read the words that follow, which we may not like so well:

I loved her only too well, not better than she deserved, but I am conscious that my affection for her made me sometimes unjust to & negligent of others, & I can acknowledge, more than as a general principle, the justice of the hand that struck the blow.

In that union of tenderness and sanctimoniousness, let us leave her for a moment to rest. She wrote letters. They have re-appeared exactly as she wrote them, but in a setting which makes them look strange to her, and we are part of the setting. They do not draw distant ages together, like the letters which were written at the same time by Keats. They were temporary and local in their appeal, and their essential meaning went down with her into the grave.

Now let us honour Mr Chapman's edition. It is elaborate, but, as we may expect from a scholar of his experience and taste, he makes us search for his learning. The letters are printed without comment, and at the end of each volume we find, if we choose, an abundance of notes and other apparatus, together with illustrations which evoke the facts or the spirit of the period. The text of the letters, apparently as simple as a rectory garden, covers many little secrets, some of them only known to the children and the servants, others almost peculiar to the hens; and all are here patiently disinterred by the editor, while we look on with admiration, our hands folded uselessly before us. For instance, when Miss Austen says: 'If there were but a coach from Hungerford to Chawton!' we do not guess what lay beneath her wish, and as a matter of fact there was not very much; still there was something, and we can find out what it is by referring to the terminal note:

Caroline Austen's *Reminiscences* show that Mrs James Austen and C. E. A. took Caroline to Cheltenham via Kintbury, there picking up Mary Jane Fowle. In their return they left M. J. F. at Kintbury and then diverged, Mrs J. A. returning to Steventon, C. E. A. taking Caroline to Chawton. J. A.'s sigh for a coach from Hungerford is no doubt connected with this diversion of the party.

Erudition can no further go, and we fling up our hands in amazement as far as they will go in 1932. 'How shall we ever recollect half the dishes for grandmamma?' cried Miss Bates at the Highbury Assembly Rooms; but Mr Chapman can recollect them all, and grandmamma, the world crashing about her ears, may regale herself upon no fewer than eight indexes, one of which distinguishes the various generations of the Austen family by four types of print – namely, *A U S T E N*, A U S T E N, Austen, and *Austen*.

The tact and good temper of the editing are as admirable as its learning. Naturally when one invests in a concern one comes to value it, and Mr Chapman is not exempt from this sensible rule. He has contended with the subject manfully, like St Paul at Ephesus; and would he have done so if it was not worth while? He puts his plea endearingly, he does not thrust his struggle down our throats, and he leads us with just the right combination of honesty and circumspection past a very dubious spot in the rectory garden. What's wrong in the garden? The drainage? No. The novels are good – of that there is no doubt, and they are so good that everything connected with the novelist and everything she wrote ought certainly to be published and annotated. Of that too, there is no doubt, and this elaborate edition is thoroughly justified. But – and here comes the dubious spot – are the letters themselves good? Very reluctantly, and in spite of Mr Chapman's quiet instigations to the contrary, one must answer 'No'.

Oh yes, one can safeguard oneself against the Janeites, should they attack. Oh yes, some of the letters are good, most of them contain something good, Cassandra may have burnt the best, Cassandra, as Mr Chapman himself conjectures, may not have been an inspiring correspondent, and nearly all the letters are addressed to Cassandra. One can qualify the unfavourable verdict this way and that but the verdict remains. Are not most of these two volumes catalogues of trivialities which do not come alive? They were alive at the time, but they have not the magic that outlasts ink: they are the letters of Miss Austen, not of Jane Austen: and Miss Austen would think us silly to read them, for she knows that we have not and cannot have their key. When the breath left her body it was lost, though a ghost of it lingered for a time in the hands of those who had loved her. Cassandra understood, her niece Fanny Knight understood, the Austen Leighs and Lord Brabourne had some conception – but we students of today, unrelated to her by blood, what part have we in this family talk, and whose triviality do we expose but our own?

It would be incorrect to say that the letters do not suggest the novels. They suggest them constantly: the quiet houses, the miry lanes, the conundrums, the absence of the very rich and the very poor, the snobbery which flourishes where distinctions of incomes are slight – all are present, and some of the characters are also present in solution. But never the finer characters. These never seem to get uppermost when Miss Austen writes a letter. They belong to another part of her mind. Neither Emma Woodhouse nor Anne Elliot nor even Frank Churchill or Mary Crawford dominates her pen. The controls are rather Lydia Bennet, Mrs Jennings, and Sir Thomas Bertram, a bizarre and inauspicious combine. In the earlier letters Lydia Bennet is all-pervading; balls, officers, giggling, dresses, officers, balls, fill sheet after sheet until everyone except Kitty grows weary. Nothing came of it. Nothing could have come of it except a husband. It has none of the disinterested rapture which fills Catherine Morland in the pump room at Bath, or Natasha Rostov in the far-distant universe of *War and Peace*, dancing the polonaise, dancing, dancing, because she is young. The young girl dances here and her eyes sparkle duly, but they are observant and hard; officers, dresses, officers, giggling, balls, and it is no wonder that a hostile critic (Miss Mitford) should compare her at once to a poker and to a butterfly. And when Lydia Bennet retires we may catch the tread of Mrs Jennings, and that eighteenth-century frankness of hers which has somehow strayed into too small a room and become unacceptable. In the novels, how well advised was the authoress of *Sense and Sensibility* to become a prude, and to curtail in its second edition the reference to a natural daughter! In the letters, how Miss Austen's occasional comments on expectant motherhood do jar! She faces the facts, but they are not her facts, and her lapses of taste over carnality can be deplorable, no doubt because they arise from lack of feeling. She can write, for instance, and write it as a jolly joke, that 'Mrs Hall of Sherborne was brought to bed yesterday of a dead child, some weeks before she expected, owing to a fright. I suppose she happened unawares to look at her husband.' Did Cassandra laugh? Probably, but all that we catch at this distance is the whinnying of harpies.

And then we come to the serious moments. Mrs Jennings follows Lydia Bennet and Sir Thomas Bertram takes the stage, unapproachable, uncontrovertible. Listen how his spirit, though not his style, sums up the merits and demerits of Sir John Moore:

I am sorry to find that Sir J. Moore has a mother living, but tho' a very Heroick son, he might not be a very necessary one to her happiness. – Deacon Morrell may be more to Mrs Morrell. – I wish Sir John had united something of the Christian with the Hero in his death.

And when an intimate sorrow comes (the death of her own father) she yields to formalism and writes: 'Your mind will already forestall the sort of event which I have to communicate. – Our dear Father has closed his virtuous & happy life, in a death almost as free from suffering as his Children could have wished.' It is adequate. Sir Thomas Bertram is always that: but it gives no freedom to the heart, it has none of the outpour which we found in that letter quoted above from Cassandra.

Triviality, varied by touches of ill breeding and of sententiousness, characterizes these letters as a whole, particularly the earlier letters; and certain critics of weight, Mr Chapman among them, find the triviality delightful, and rightly point out that there is a charm in little things. Yes, when it is the charm of Cowper. But the little things must hold out their little hands to one another; and here there is a scrappiness which prevents even tartness from telling. This brings us to the heart of the matter, to Miss Austen's fundamental weakness as a letter-writer. She has not enough subject matter on which to exercise her powers. Her character and sex as well as her environment removed her from public affairs, and she was too sincere and spontaneous to affect any interest which she did not feel. She takes no account of politics or religion, and none of the war except when it brings prize-money to her brothers. Her comments on literature are provincial and perfunctory – with one exception, and a significant one, which we shall cite in a moment. When she writes a letter she has nothing in her mind except the wish to tell her sister everything; and so she flits from the cows to the currant bushes, from the currant bushes to Mrs Hall of Sherborne, gives Mrs Hall a tap, and flits back again. She suffers from a poverty of material which did no injury to the novels, and indeed contributes to their triumph. Miss Bates may flit and Mrs Norris tap as much as they like, because they do so inside a frame which has been provided by a great artist, and Meryton may reproduce the atmosphere of Steventon because it imports something else – some alignment not to be found on any map. The letters lack direction. What an improvement when she is startled, an elm falls, they have to go to the dentist! Then her powers of description find fuller play, and to the affection which she always feels for her correspondents she adds concentration, and an interest in the subject-matter.

The improvement becomes more noticeable in the second volume, that is to say after 1811. She had received a series of pleasant surprises. Her novels, which had always found favour in private readings, began to get published and gain wider audiences. Warren Hastings admired them, and *Emma* was dedicated to the Prince Regent shortly after his victory at Waterloo. She went to London oftener, perhaps saw Mr Crabbe in the distance, and had a note from Mrs Hannah More. While rating these joys at their proper worth, she could not but gain the notion of a more amusing and varied world; and perhaps she is one of the few country writers whom wider experience and consort with the literary would not have ruined.

Meanwhile her success reacted on her family. Her seven brothers (with the exception of a mysterious George who is never mentioned), her sister, her sisters-in-law, her nephews and, most of all, her nieces were deeply impressed. One of the nieces, Anna, took to scribbling on her own, and sent Aunt Jane from time to time instalments of a novel to read aloud to Aunt Cassandra. Miss Austen's replies are admirable. She is stimulated because the writer is a relation, and she pours out helpful criticisms, all put in a kindly, easy way. Most of them are connected with 'getting things right' – always a preoccupation with English novelists, from Defoe to Arnold Bennett. Times, places, and probabilities must be considered, but Anna must beware of copying life slavishly, for life sometimes gets things wrong:

I have scratched out Sir Thos: from walking with the other Men to the Stables &ct the very day after breaking his arm – for though I find your Papa *did* walk out immediately after his arm was set, I think it can be so little usual as to *appear* unnatural in a book – & it does not seem to be material that Sir Thos: should go with them. – Lyme will not do. Lyme is towards 40 miles distant from Dawlish & would not be talked of there. – I have put Starcross instead. If you prefer *Exeter*, that must be always safe.

Thursday. We finished it last night, after our return from drinking tea at the Gt House. – The last chapter does not please us so well, we do not thoroughly like the *Play*: perhaps from having had too much of Plays in that way lately. And we think you had better not leave England. Let the Portmans go to Ireland, but as you know nothing of the Manners there you had better not go with them. You will be in danger of giving false representations. Stick to Bath and the Foresters. There you will be quite at home. – Your Aunt C. does not like desultory novels and is rather fearful yours will be too much so, that there will be too frequently a change from one set of people to another, & that circumstances will be sometimes introduced of apparent consequence, which will lead to nothing. – It will not be so great an objection to *me*, if it does. I allow much more Latitude than she does – & think Nature and Spirit cover many sins of a wandering story.

Here, again, the English school of fiction speaks, and puts its case amiably and privately, as it should. Manifestoes belong to abroad. Aunt Cassandra likes a book to be neat and tidy: Aunt Jane does not much mind. And Anna, receiving these letters, in which detailed comment is mixed with sound generalizations, must have been delighted; she must have found her novel much better than she thought and yet been stimulated to correct in it what was wrong. We share the enthusiasm. It sounds a lovely novel, and we turn to the terminal notes to see what more Mr Chapman has to tell us about it. Alas; he can tell us too much:

The story to which most of these letters of Aunt Jane's refer was never finished. It was laid aside because my mother's hands were so full . . . The story was laid by for years, and then one day in a fit of despondency burnt. I remember sitting on the rug and watching its destruction, amused with the flames and the sparks which kept breaking out in the blackened paper.

Thus writes Anna's daughter; and Anna's novel, with the Portmans and Foresters, who seemed so fascinating, has gone up the chimney for ever. But the tiny flicker of light which it casts backwards is valuable. We see Miss Austen and Jane Austen for a moment as one person. The letter-writer and the novelist have fused, because a letter is being written to a niece about a novel. Family feeling has done the trick; and, after all, whatever opinion we hold about her, we must agree that the supreme thing in life to her was the family. She knew no other allegiance; if there was an early love affair in the west of England, and if her lover died, as did her sister Cassandra's, she never clung to his memory, unless she utilizes it in *Persuasion*. Intimacy out of the unknown never overwhelmed her. No single person ever claimed her. She was part of a family, and her dearest Cassandra only the dearest in that family. The family was the unit within which her heart had liberty of choice; friends, neighbours, plays and fame were all objects to be picked up in the course of a flight outside and brought back to the nest for examination. They often laughed over the alien trophies, for they were a hard humorous family. And these letters, however we judge them on their own count, are invaluable as a document. They show, more clearly than ever, that Miss Austen was part of the Austens, the Knights, the Leighs, the Lefroys. The accidents of birth and relationship were more sacred to her than anything else in the world, and she introduced this faith as the groundwork of her six great novels.

[1932]

PART III

THE PAST

THE CONSOLATIONS OF HISTORY

IT is pleasant to be transferred from an office where one is afraid of a sergeant-major into an office where one can intimidate generals, and perhaps this is why History is so attractive to the more timid amongst us. We can recover self-confidence by snubbing the dead. The captains and the kings depart at our slightest censure, while as for the 'hosts of minor officials' who cumber court and camp, we heed them not, although in actual life they entirely block our social horizon. We cannot visit either the great or the rich when they are our contemporaries, but by a fortunate arrangement the palaces of Ujjain and the warehouses of Ormus are open for ever, and we can even behave outrageously in them without being expelled. The King of Ujjain, we announce, is extravagant, the merchants of Ormus unspeakably licentious . . . and sure enough Ormus is a desert now and Ujjain a jungle. Difficult to realize that the past was once the present, and that, transferred to it, one would be just the same little worm as today, unimportant, parasitic, nervous, occupied with trifles, unable to go anywhere or alter anything, friendly only with the obscure, and only at ease with the dead; while up on the heights the figures and forces who make History would contend in their habitual fashion, with incomprehensible noises or in ominous quiet. 'There is money in my house . . . there is no money . . . no house.' That is all that our sort can ever know about doom. The extravagant king, the licentious merchants – they escape, knowing the ropes.

If only the sense of actuality can be lulled – and it sleeps for ever in most historians – there is no passion that cannot be gratified in the past. The past is devoid of all dangers, social and moral, and one can meet with perfect ease not only kings, but people who are even rarer on one's visiting list. We are alluding to courtesans. It is seemly and decent to meditate upon dead courtesans. Some, like Aspasia, are in themselves a liberal education, and turning from these as almost too awful one can still converse unblamed with their sisters. There is no objection, for instance, against recalling the arrangements of the sixteenth-century Hindu kingdom of Vijayanagar. The courtesans of Vijayanagar were beautiful and rich – one of them left over £32,000. They were highly esteemed, which also seems right; some were housemaids, others cooks, and five hundred were attached on a peace basis to the army, 'all great musicians, dancers, and acrobats, and very quick and nimble at their performances.' In war the number was increased; indeed, the king sent the entire of the personable population into the field, judging that its presence would enhearten the troops. So many ladies hampered his strategy, it is true, but the opposing army was equally hampered, and when its soldiers ran away, its ladies sat still, and accrued to the victors. With existence as it threatens today – a draggled mass of elderly people and barbed wire – it is agreeable to glance back at those enchanted carnages, and to croon over conditions that we now subscribe to exterminate. Tight little faces from Oxford, fish-shaped faces from Cambridge – we cannot help having our dreams. Was life then warm and tremendous? Did the Vijayanagar Government really succeed in adjusting the balance between society and sex? – a task that has baffled even Mrs Humphry Ward. We cannot tell; we can only be certain that it acted with circumspection and pomposity, and that most of its subjects did not know what it was up to. The myriads of nonentities who thronged its courts and camps, and were allotted inferior courtesans or none at all – alas! it is with these alone that readers of my pages can claim kinship.

Yet sweet though it is to dally with the past, one returns to the finer pleasures of morality in the end. The schoolmaster in each of us awakes, examines the facts of History, and marks them on the result of the examination. Not all the marks need be bad. Some incidents, like the Risorgimento, get excellent as a matter of course, while others, such as the character of Queen Elizabeth, get excellent in the long run. Nor must events be marked at their face value. Why was it right of Drake to play bowls when he heard the Armada was approaching, but wrong of Charles II to catch moths when he heard that the Dutch Fleet had entered the Medway? The answer is 'Because Drake won.' Why was it right of Alexander the Great to throw away water when his army was perishing, but wrong of Marie Antoinette to say 'Let them eat cake'? The answer is 'Because Marie Antoinette was executed.' Why was George Washington right because he would not tell a lie, and Jael right because she told nothing else? Answers on similar lines. We must take a larger view of the past than of the present, because when examining the present we can never be sure what is going to pay. As a general rule, anything that ends abruptly must be given bad marks; for instance, the fourth century B.C. at Athens, the year 1492 in Italy, and the summer of 1914 everywhere. A civilization that passes quickly must be decadent, therefore let us censure those epochs that thought themselves so bright, let us show that their joys were hectic and their pleasures vile, and clouded by the premonition of doom. On the other hand, a civilization that does not pass, like the Chinese, must be stagnant, and is to be censured on that account. Nor can one approve anarchy. What then survives? Oh, a greater purpose, the slow evolution of Good through the centuries – an evolution less slow than it seems, because a thousand years are as yesterday, and consequently Christianity was only, so to speak, established on Wednesday last. And if this argument should seem flimsy (it is the Bishop of London's, not our own – he put it into his Christmas sermon) one can at all events return to an indubitable triumph of evolution – oneself, sitting untouched and untouchable in the professorial chair, and giving marks to men.

Sweet then is dalliance, censure sweeter. Yet sweetest of all is pity, because it subtly combines the pleasures of the other two. To pity the dead because they are dead is to experience an exquisite pleasure, identical with the agreeable heat that comes to the eyes in a churchyard. The heat has nothing to do with sorrow, it has no connexion with anything that one has personally known and held dear. It is half a sensuous delight, half gratified vanity, and Shakespeare knew what he was about when he ascribed such a sensation to the fantastical Armado. They had been laughing at Hector, and Armado, with every appearance of generosity, exclaims: 'The sweet war-man is dead and rotten; sweet chucks, beat not the bones of the buried; when he breathed he was a man.' It was his happiest moment; he had never felt more certain either that he was alive himself, or that he was Hector. And it is a happiness that we can all experience until the sense of actuality breaks in. Pity wraps the student of the past in an ambrosial cloud, and washes his limbs with eternal youth. 'Dear dead women with such hair too,' but not 'I feel chilly and grown old.' That comes with the awakening.

[1920]

MACOLNIA SHOPS

ROME is crowded in the early months of the year, but few people go to the Kirchner Museum. It consists chiefly of prehistoric remains, idols from Peru, and weapons from Abyssinia; and there are only three objects of which Baedeker condescends to give a special account. One is that famous graffito of the Crucifixion, lately discovered on the Palatine. Another is known as the 'Treasure of Praeneste' – a curious collection of Egyptian valuables that belonged to a ruler of Palestrina during the sixth century B.C.

The third object was also found at Praeneste. It would seem that Dindia Macolnia, a wealthy lady of the town, went down one day to the sovereign city of Rome to buy a present for her daughter. A record of her visit would be interesting. Marius was in Rome at the time, or, if not Marius, Sulla, or, if Sulla was dead, Cicero was speaking, or, if Cicero was silent, Macolnia might have looked with well-bred curiosity on the face of Augustus Imperator. But Dindia Macolnia was there to shop.

She found a beautiful bronze toilet case, cylindrical in form, nicely engraved with figures, both at the top and round the sides. It was an old-fashioned thing, and the decorations were out of date – no Cupids, no garlands, no charming banquet-scene of tipsy ladies and gentlemen which should fill her daughter with tender reminiscences of home. Nevertheless, with the addition of three legs and a handle, it would do splendidly, especially for a relation. These additions were made by Novius Plautius – no heaven-born artist – who commemorated the two facts on the handle: 'Novius Plautius made me at Rome', 'Dindia Macolnia gave me to her daughter'. Of course everyone would take 'me' to be the entire toilet case; and thus, by a harmless quibble, the whole thing became as good as new. It is only the prying criticism of the twentieth century that has decided that the toilet case and the legs were not made by the same hand.

In due time the daughter of Dindia Macolnia died and was buried, and, more important still, her toilet case was buried with her, and was dug up during the eighteenth century A.D., and called the Cista Ficoroniana, and buried again in the Kirchner Museum.

It is a Greek work, and it tells the story of the punishment of Amycus by Pollux. The Argonauts had landed in Amycus's country, and asked for water; and he, from sheer barbarian churlishness – one might say from sheer nervousness – would not let them drink. So Pollux the boxer has vanquished him and bound him naked to a tree, and round them are a group of admiring onlookers, divine and human – Zeus, Athene, and the winged Boreas; Jason and Heracles; while Victory flies through the air to place the wreath on Pollux's head. Rather a conventional group, it must be confessed, Athene, the only female figure in the whole design, being particularly unattractive. Yet here, as everywhere, are that unerring beauty and that economy of line which make noble and refined the slightest detail of thrown-off clothes or twisted rope.

But it is only when we turn to the other figures that the encircling motive of the composition becomes plain – or motives, one should say, for there are two, the outer motive, that is plainly and easily followed, and the inner motive, whose expression is more constrained and delicate.

The plain motive is the Praise of Water. Pollux, the boxer, has unsealed the spring, and from the Argo, anchored in the salt sea, the heroes step ashore to drink. It is a good thing to satisfy the body: some are hurrying forward to fill their jars: one is drinking water from a wine-cup as he leans on his spear beside the splashing spring: others have drunk and are sitting in perfect physical bliss, having reached the goal of their desire, and found its happiness not illusory. But one, cast in a severer and more modern mould, is already up and practising boxing on a blown-out skin, in order that he too, when occasion offers, may have this water-compelling power. And, close below him, a little Pan is very properly mocking his actions: Work is at all times unseemly, and why this pother over water when the one thing needful is wine?

Dindia Macolnia and her daughter, if Etruscan antiquities

reflect truly, agreed with the little Pan. They did not understand water, and it is not likely that they understood Friendship either, which is the second motive that their toilet case reveals to us today. It declares that when the body is feeble the soul is feeble: cherish the body and you will cherish the soul. That was the belief of the Greeks; the belief in wearing away the body by penance, in order that the quivering soul may be exposed, had not yet entered into the world.

As the heroes are refreshed, their faculties awake in their fullness, and strong and vivid is the love they bear and have borne for each other. That love has never died, but it has shared the eclipse and weakness of the body. Two – the most beautiful figures of the whole composition – are standing together, leaning on their spears, with the knowledge that they have passed through one more labour in company. Another has hastened back to the Argo, and is pouring water down the throat of a sick friend. But he has drunk himself first. That man is as many centuries from self-denial as he is from self-consciousness. In spirit he is further still from the magnanimous Alexander, who empties water on the sand in the midst of a dying army.

Thus the motives go: the Praise of Water and the Praise of Friendship. The second is greater than the first; but it must needs come after it in place.

'Praise of Water! Praise of Friendship!' cries the angry shade of Dindia Macolnia, rising on its elbow out of the quaint Etruscan Hell. 'I bought the thing because it was pretty, and stood nicely on the chest of drawers.'

It may be that the Greek artist, sitting solitary and content amidst Elysian asphodels, now values that praise more than ours.

[1903]

CNIDUS

CNIDUS is not yet a seaside resort, nor am I afraid of making it one by describing my visit to it. There are some places that are safe from popularity – for example, the peninsula in Southern Asia Minor, townless, roadless, three miles across and fifty miles long, at the end of which lies Cnidus.

Greek captains never will use a chart. They sometimes have one, but it is always locked up in a drawer; for, as they truly say, it is nothing but paper and lines, which are not the least like the sea, and it is far better to trust to yourself, especially in parts where you have never been before. But, as they combine instinct with caution, progress is sometimes slow; and, instead of having a long afternoon at Cnidus, we did not anchor till five o'clock, and it was pouring with rain.

Desire for information tempted some of us ashore; the name of Asia others. By some mischance, we were landed on the broken edge of the town wall, and had to stumble upwards over vast blocks of dislodged stone, amid the rapture of competent observers, who had discovered that the iron clamps were those used in classical times, and that we were straining our ankles over masonry of the best period. Within the walls were darkness and much mud, such as there is within the Hades of Aristophanes, and heavy dropping drain, such as befouls the Limbo of Dante, and at first the great silence that befits a city dead a thousand years.

So I have never seen Cnidus, for the land was only an outline, and the sea ran into the sky. And who would expect visions from a dripping silhouette, when, time after time, the imagination has dwelt in vain desire amidst sun and blue sky and perfect colonnades, and found in them nothing but colonnades and sky and sun? But, that evening, under those weeping clouds, the imagination became creative, taking wings because there was nothing to bid it rise, flying impertinently against all archaeology and sense, uttering bird-like cries of 'Greek! Greek!' as it flew, declaring that it heard voices because all was so silent, and saw faces because it was too dark to see. I am ashamed of its outbreak, and will confine myself to facts, such as they are.

Cnidus, then, is only an outline. The high mountains of the peninsula are on the right, and on the left is the great Triopian promontory, joined to the mountains by a flat and narrow strip of sand. Thus the city is shaped like a dumb-bell – athletic similes are pardonable when the theme is Greek – having a throne on the mountains, a throne on Triopia, and a smooth causeway whereby she may pass between them. I do not know whether Greek art has ever embodied Cnidus as a maiden dominating the Aegean from a double seat of empire. It might very well be; for has not Eutychides personified Antioch bending over the side of a hill, to dip her feet in the waters of Orontes? Such conceptions, I ought to add, do not date from the best period of art, and therefore give no pleasure to those whose taste is really pure.

There are two harbours. Our steamer was in one, and the other was the Trireme harbour beyond the causeway, and our destination. We went to one or two temples, I think, and an agora; and I know we went to the theatre, for I fell off the stage into the orchestra, to the confusion of the competent observers, who, in the uncertain light, had mistaken the stage for the base of the harbour pier. The orchestra is planted with Jerusalem artichokes, and the mud in it is more glutinous than the mud outside.

Somewhere or other there must have been the temple of Apollo, and the temple of Poseidon, and the shrine of the nymphs, in whose honour all the men of the Dorian Hexapolis came yearly to race; and somewhere else there must have been the ruined house of the Cnidian Aphrodite. But I did see the home of the Goddess who has made Cnidus famous to us, for, up on the right, the mountain had been scarped and a platform levelled, and someone pointed it out and said: 'That is the precinct of the Infernal Deities, where they got the Demeter' – that Demeter of Cnidus, whom we hold in the British Museum now. She was there at that moment, warm and comfortable in that little recess of hers between the Ephesian Room and the Archaic Room, with the electric light fizzling above her, and casting blue shadows over her chin. She is dusted twice a week, and there is a railing in front, with 'No Admittance', so that she cannot be touched. And if human industry can find that lost arm of hers, and that broken nose, and human ingenuity can put them on, she shall be made as good as new.

I am not going to turn sentimental, and pity the exiled Demeter, and declare that her sorrowful eyes are straining for the scarped rock, and the twin harbours, and Triopia, and the sea. She is doing nothing of the sort. If her eyes see anything, it must be the Choiseul Apollo who is in the niche opposite; and she might easily do worse. And if, as I believe, she is alive, she must know that she has come among people who love her, for all they are so weak-chested and anaemic and feeble-kneed, and who pay her such prosaic homage as they can. Demeter alone among gods has true immortality. The others continue, perchance, their existence, but are forgotten, because the time came when they could not be loved. But to her, all over the world, rise prayers of idolatry from suffering men as well as suffering women, for she has transcended sex. And Poets too, generation after generation, have sung in passionate incompetence of the hundred-flowered Narcissus and the rape of Persephone, and the wanderings of the Goddess, and her gift to us of corn and tears; so that generations of critics, obeying also their need, have censured the poets for reviving the effete mythology of Greece, and urged them to themes of living interest which shall touch the heart of today.

There have been other finds in that mountain precinct – some fascinating terracotta pigs, for example, broad of back and steady poise, and a number of those interesting Katadesmoi, leaded tablets stamped with curses, which have thrown such a flood of light on the subject of classical vituperation. But we had no time to go up there, and plunged along, over a real ploughed field, to reach the Trireme harbour while there was yet a vestige of light.

The rain hammered down on our umbrellas, and filled our ears with fictitious uproar. It was only when we put the umbrellas down to speak or listen to each other that we heard what was really happening. There were sounds then from the black and the illimitable grey – the bark of a dog, a sheep coughing in the wet, and the most certainly the sound of human voices. We put up our umbrellas again and hurried on; for human voices are alarming when they cease to be imaginary. It is not pleasant to meet new people in the dark.

The long ploughed field ended in a stone wall and a sharp slope of cliff. Looking down, I saw the Trireme harbour at last – a perfect curve of grey that bit into the black. It must face west; for it still shone, though not with colour, being to the eye without substance or perspective – a vast well that went through the middle of the earth into nothing. Some great building had fallen into the shallows; and pillars, capitals, and cornices were isolated mysteriously, as if in air. Only by the delicate smell and the delicate whisper of ripples on the sand, was it revealed to us that it was a harbour, and filled with the sea.

We had to turn at once and hurry back over the fields to our own harbour; for the rain was wetting us through, and it was quite dark now, and late, and voices were calling all about the hills. There was light of a kind by the boats, the light of phosphorescence, that was born when the ripples clashed and died when they subsided. And a small Japanese lantern, grotesquely incongruous, assisted us to embark.

Heads were counted, to see that no one was missing. There were ten already in the boats, and seven pressing to get in, stumbling about amid sea urchins and wet rocks ere they did so. And five more were coming up behind, all blurred out of the night. We were twenty-two in all; but that was hardly satisfactory, for we had started out twenty-one. Someone had joined us.

It is well known (is it not?) who that extra person always is. This time he came hurrying down to the beach at the last moment, and tried to peer into our faces. I could hardly see his; but it was young, and it did not look unkind. He made no answer to our tremulous greetings, but raised his hand to his head and then laid it across his breast, meaning I understand, that his brain and his heart were ours. Everyone made clumsy imitations of his gesture to keep him in a good temper. His manners were perfect. I am not sure that he did not offer to lift people into the boats. But there was a general tendency to avoid his attentions, and we put off in an incredibly short space of time. He melted away in the darkness after a couple of strokes, and we before long were back on the steamer, amid light, and the smell of hot meat, and the pity and self-gratulations of those who had been wise enough to stop on board.

It was indeed an absurd expedition. We returned soaked and shivering, without a photograph, without a sketch, without so much as an imprecatory tablet to link the place with reality and the world of facts. It lies a defenceless prey to the sentimental imagination and, as I am absolutely certain never to go there again, I do not see how it is to be rescued. I never cease to dry up its puddles, and brush away its clouds, and span it over with blue sky in which is hanging a mid-day sun that never moves. Even over that extra person the brain will not keep steady.

[1904]

GEMISTUS PLETHO

I

THE traveller who has gone into the Peloponnese for the purpose of visiting ancient Sparta will find his attention diverted from classical scenes to a place whose name is probably unfamiliar to him, and whose appearance is certainly unexpected. From the base of Mount Taygetus a small but steep hill projects into the plain, bearing the ruins of a castle on its summit, and the ruins of churches, palaces, and monasteries on its sides. The castle is surprisingly big, and, though the churches are surprisingly tiny, each has, or has had, its little dome and battered marble pillars, its mosaic pavement under foot, its perishing frescoes of mysterious saints upon the walls. Fifteen people live here now, and act as guides. But the place was once closely – perhaps too closely – populated, and has witnessed an elaborate if defective civilization. Such a place has no business in Greece. Yet the traveller may possibly neglect the Sparta museum, where he had intended to spend so much time over the archaic reliefs, and wander instead through the remnants of this unfamiliar world, nearer in its date than the world of Lycurgus, yet in its spirit even more remote.

The great castle looks up a gorge into the white ridges of Taygetus behind, and in front it looks over the broad blue valley of the Eurotas: over New Sparta with its large pink cathedral and dreary boulevards; over the spacious site of Old Sparta, whose simple buildings have crumbled into the plain and are buried underneath the corn. But, when we inquire into the history of a place which is so wonderful in itself and in its situation, we meet with disappointment. We read that the Franks built it in the thirteenth century and called it Misithras or Mistrà; that it became the chief fortress in the Peloponnese during an uninteresting period; that it was taken from the Franks by the Byzantines, and from the Byzantines by the Turks; that it was governed by a long succession of tyrants whose lives were short and brutal.

Yet one man did live here whose name is worthy of remembrance; and the place is curiously symbolical of him. For his ways were huddled and medieval; and his cramped limbs were never freed from the barbarism and the stupid pomp and the dirt. But his eyes were fixed outside the narrow enclosure of his century, on the serene plains of antiquity, on temples that stood among gardens, on cities that had no walls, on the spacious country where man had once been beautiful and noble and happy, and whither he hoped men might yet return. We, who also stand looking at that country, owe him gratitude as well as sympathy. For if we stand nearer to it than he did, it is in some measure owing to him.

Georgious Gemistus, afterwards surnamed 'Pletho', was born at Constantinople in 1355. He came to Mistrà when he was quite young, and, with one brief but important interval, remained there until he died. The town was then ruled by younger members of the Palaeologus family, nominally in the interests of the Byzantine Emperor. With them, and with the Emperors also, Gemistus kept on friendly terms. He had some high judicial post at Mistrà, and seems to have given political advice to the Governors, who were generally in sore need of it. He advised them to fortify the Isthmus of Corinth against the Turks; and his advice was taken. He advised them to undertake a complete revolution – social, agrarian, and economic – in the Peloponnese; and his advice was fortunately neglected. He wrote congratulatory orations when they ceased quarrelling; he wrote funeral orations when they died; and when they wrote an oration, he wrote an oration in praise of it.

It is as philosopher, not as politician, that he becomes important, or at all events interesting. The European world then knew of three religions – the Christian, the Mohammedan, and the Jewish; and to one of them, or to one of their modifications, every man subscribed himself. Gemistus, from an early age, adopted an attitude that was new. He severed himself from his own church, but he did not join any of her rivals. Truth, he believed, might be in the past rather than the present. Where his intellectual sympathies lay, he placed his spiritual hopes also. He looked for his religion among the half-forgotten rites of ancient Greece.

The story of the extraordinary scheme which he evolved belongs to a later period of his life. It is a matter for surprise that he was ever permitted to evolve it. His pagan tendencies were early suspected, yet he came to a natural end at the age of ninety-five. Orthodoxy has indeed often distinguished between paganism and heresy, treating the former with a leniency which she will not show to the latter. Such may have been the attitude of the Greek Church towards Gemistus. At all events, he suffered no practical discomfort; and his long life is creditable to his contemporaries as well as to himself.

His reputation as a philosopher was not confined to Mistrà and Constantinople. Italy, entering on her Renaissance, soon learnt that there lived in the heart of Greece a Greek, marvellously learned, marvellously wise, who had studied Zoroaster and Pythagoras, Plato and Plotinus, Menes and Euhemerus; who was discovering the inner significance of the ancient religions. Many a student, puzzling out the meaning of Plato with little philosophy and less Greek, longed for Gemistus to come over and interpret. Meanwhile, some scholars went to

Mistrà, of whom the most important was Bessarion, first a bishop in the Greek Church, and afterwards a cardinal in the Roman. Gemistus had no inclination to alter his quiet but not ignoble life. He studied, and thought, and wrote, and gave advice; and it was not till he was eighty that an event occurred which introduced him in person to the world.

For many years negotiations had been going on between the Pope and the Byzantine Emperor, with the object of uniting the Roman and Greek Churches. The Pope suggested that a Council should be held, at which the theological differences, which were bitter rather than important, could be discussed, and a reconciliation, which was desirable politically, might be effected. The Emperor consulted Gemistus, who warned him to make no advances to the Pope unless the Pope would first promise a substantial army for the defence of Constantinople against the Turk. The advice was good, and characteristic of the man. But the Emperor was in such straits that he was willing to make religious concessions for even a small subsidy. He was also persuaded by Joseph, the aged Patriarch of Constantinople, whose vanity hoped to effect the conversion of the Latin Church without any concessions at all.

Gemistus, seeing that the Council was inevitable, took the most important step in his life. He determined to attend it personally, and defend the cause of Greek Christianity. It is difficult to account for his behaviour. Patriotism may have had much to do with it, vanity something. And it is well to recollect that, in the fifteenth century, men were more open in their inconsistencies than they dare to be today. The orthodox party seem to have been more flattered than puzzled by his support; but at all events, in the autumn of 1437, he, the Emperor, the Patriarch, and many bishops, set sail for Italy at the Pope's expense. With them sailed the orthodox theologian Gennadius, who was afterwards to play so important a part in Gemistus' fortunes. 'It was once believed,' says Gibbon, 'that there were two men of this name. But recent investigations have restored the identity of his person and the duplicity of his character.' As far as Gemistus is concerned, the epigram is unfair. Gennadius was certainly consistent in his hostility. Nor was he, on the whole, an unattractive man. He has testified to the genius of his rival, and to the nobility of his character. Only against his opinions did he wage a cunning and not unreasonable war.

Trouble began at Venice, where the Emperor and the Patriarch Joseph quarrelled. The Emperor hurried on to meet the Pope at Ferrara; the Patriarch would not be parted from his luggage. The emperor sent him word that he must greet the Pope by kissing his foot. He replied: 'If the Pope is older than I am, I will treat him as a father; if of the same age, as a brother; if younger, as a son.' The Pope, of course, was younger. At last the matter was adjusted. The Pope promised that the Patriarch should kiss him on the cheek, provided that not more than six bishops were looking on at the time. Then a new difficulty arose. The Pope, and the Emperor, and the Patriarch, all claimed the most honourable seat at the Council; and a triangular struggle took place, which resulted in the erection of four seats, one for the Pope, one for the Emperor of the West, which remained empty, one for the Byzantine Emperor, and, behind him, one for the exasperated Patriarch. The Pope's chair had trimming to it. The Patriarch put trimming on his chair, but was obliged to take it off.

It would be a mistake to suppose that Gemistus watched these proceedings with any great cynicism. Such incidents are only ludicrous to posterity; and he probably regarded them as seriously as we regard similar incidents at the Durbar today. Moreover, though he was indifferent to the Greek Church, he was jealous for the Greek honour. Patriotism, as well as orthodoxy, demanded that the Patriarch should have trimming to his chair.

At the beginning of 1439, the plague broke out at Ferrara;

and the Council fled over the Apennines to Florence. Here Cosimo de' Medici had recently established himself, and was impressing the peculiar stamp of his dynasty upon the city. The medieval Florence of Dante had passed; the Florence that had blindly worshipped the Antique was passing. The new Florence was bound to no one period, to the imitation of no one model. She loved things that are incompatible with each other; and so far only was she eclectic. Illogical, not because she was weak but because she was strong, she could welcome all doctrines and all ideals, even as her merchant despots, a little later, could sing to peasants and make themselves agreeable to princes.

In such a city a scholar from Greece was always welcome, though he now represented only one influence out of many. And Greeks hitherto had been so rude and so dirty that it was an extra pleasure to receive Gemistus, who was at all events polite. His beautiful voice, his venerable beard and dignified manners, accorded well with his eloquence and learning. Painstaking theologians were unimportant beside a man who would give a new, if not a final, interpretation of the classical world. He explained Plato with great success, discoursing for hours upon the Beautiful to men who were then filling the world with beauty, and who listened to him with a patience which we can hardly comprehend. At the instance of Cosimo de' Medici, he wrote a tract *Concerning the difference between Plato and Aristotle*. Hitherto it had not been known that there was any difference; and as the Church's philosophy was based on Aristotle, while Gemistus preferred Plato, a conflict began which divided the learned world for some fifty years.

For the defence of Plato, Gemistus helped Cosimo to found the Neo-Platonic Academy at Florence, and indicated Marsilio Ficino as its first president. Ficino was enthusiastic rather than able; he celebrated Plato's birthday with a banquet, and burnt lamps before his bust, but did not translate him into Latin with striking success. However, he was well suited for the post. Unlike Gemistus, he remained through all his speculations an orthodox member of his Church; while he sought for an element of truth, not in one religion, but in all. To him Plato was a reconciler rather than a new apostle, and had risen from his grave to bring peace, not war, upon the earth. Later on there was an attempt to canonize Plato as a saint. But the Pope was unable to give the movement any official encouragement. The opinions of Ficino were echoed throughout Italy by wise and thoughtful men, until a new attitude towards spiritual questions was instituted by Savonarola.

People who understand Plato say that the Florentines misunderstood him, and that their philosophy is most unsound. A nation of artists is perhaps seldom sound in its philosophy, and is apt to produce masterpieces which have no metaphysical justification. But in one respect at all events they used him rightly. Through him they recaptured for the world one of the secrets of ancient Greece – the secret of civilized conversation. The Middle Ages had separated serious discussion from daily life, confining it to the study and the lecture room and the hall of disputation. Florence, like Athens, summoned it into the open air, and bade it take its chance against birds and trees, evolve, if it could, from a dinner or a game of fives, yield, if it must, to a dance or to a song. The result might be desultory, but it was certainly spontaneous. The influence of the Florentine Academy was anything but academic; and the sincerity, if not the wisdom of the Cephissus, emerged beside the Arno.

It is by this work in Florence that Gemistus is best remembered. It is true that the work would have been done by others. The ground was already prepared for him; and perhaps the seed did not germinate quite as he expected, for his Platonism and the Platonism of the Academy were to develop on very different lines. But his impulse was decisive;

and it is now that he assumes, or permits himself to be given, the surname of 'Pletho'. Plato means 'broad shouldered'. Gemistus, perhaps thinking broad shoulders unsuitable for a philosopher, interpreted it to mean 'full', 'replete with wisdom', and adopted 'Pletho', as a purer form. In time his disciples asserted that he had inherited not only Plato's name but also his soul.

Meanwhile, he did not neglect his duties at the Council, where he was invaluable. As he had missed the spirit of Christianity, there was no reason why he should not keep to the letter. Men like Gennadius, who were sincere in their faith, might make concessions, but nothing could move the orthodoxy of Gemistus. His arguments were sometimes startling, but always effective; and if his patrons failed, it was not owing to him.

The Council of Florence broke up in July 1439. Shortly before its conclusion, the Patriarch Joseph died, and his tomb is to be seen in the church of Santa Maria Novella.

> Happy I lived, and happy I expire,
> Lord of myself, and of my heart's desire.

But the epitaph lies horribly, for the Patriarch lost his labours quite as much as he had lost his temper. He had intended to unite the Latin Church to the Greek, instead of which the Greek Church had become united to the Latin. In the hope of a political alliance with Western Christianity, the Byzantine Emperor had sacrificed his national ritual. Religious riots greeted him on his return to Constantinople; and, for all his efforts, he did not save the city from the Turk.

Gemistus had never approved of the Council, and it had been even more disastrous than he expected. However, his experiences had been pleasant. He was scarcely capable of appreciating the wonders of Italy for a Greek still found barbarism in anything west of the Adriatic. But, old as he was, his visit stimulated him. The ideas which had long been floating in his brain now took clear, if fantastic, shape. 'Before long,' he told the Florentines, 'the world will see a new religion, which will be neither of Christ nor of Mahomet, but will differ not greatly from the religion of the ancient Greeks.' He was understood to be contemplating a work on this new religion, and, when the Council closed, he returned to Mistrà to compose it.

He was constantly interrupted. His enemy Gennadius led him into a weary controversy on the merits of Plato and Aristotle, and delayed his great work – possibly with intention. And he wasted his own time by composing orthodox pamphlets, in which he seems to have found a kind of intellectual pleasure. One of them – *Concerning the Procession of the Holy Ghost* – drew a clever letter from Gennadius, who still kept on civil terms.

My dear friend, why did you not tell me about this admirable pamphlet? How reticent you are! It almost looks as if you were annoyed with me. I am delighted to think that your splendid talents are so well employed, and are in no way tainted by any pagan sympathies. In these enlightened days, any attempt to recall the darkness of the Antique would be an unpardonable crime. Just imagine! There are philosophers who are seeking for a new Olympus, a new ritual, a 'simplified religion' which is to remodel society according to the notions of Plato! If such blasphemies ever find publication in a book, I look forward to confuting that book. Truth and reason would be my weapons; I should not throw it into the fire. *That* I should reserve for the author.

Gemistus did not reply; but the publication of his life's work was still further delayed. There is a great difference between letting out startling opinions in the course of conversation, and presenting them formally in a book. Hitherto he had been sure of the Emperor's favour. But Gennadius was high in favour also. Two Turkish invasions further distracted his old age, and that revival of ancient Greece which he so ardently desired became even more impossible. He did not see that the revival had really taken place in Italy; that Greece is a spirit which can appear, not only at any time, but also in any land. He died in 1450, three years before the fall of Constantinople, nine years before the fall of Mistrà. He was given Christian burial, and passed away without offering his new pagan religion to the world.

2

The Princess Asanina, wife of the last Imperial Governor of Mistrà, had no reason to love Gemistus. The old man had once called her a nasty little thing, and other things besides – '*expression bien irrévérencieuse*,' remarks the French editor, '*ne ût-elle même pas appliquée à une princesse.*' It was into her hand that the manuscript of the new religion fell; and, when she was carried by the Turks to Constantinople, she carried it with her. Instead of destroying it, she sent it to Gennadius, remarking that it was a shocking book. Gennadius returned it, saying it was indeed shocking, and that the fact of its being so interesting only made it all the worse. He advised the Princess to burn it at once; the Church would applaud her. Both parties were strikingly deficient in zeal; they seem to have been positively unwilling to destroy a book which they took to be a work of genius. Gennadius, though now Patriarch of Constantinople, received his salary from the Turkish government; and the Princess Asanina was now one of the Sultan's mothers-in-law. In such circumstances, their orthodoxy may well have relaxed. No one would mind if they let the matter pass. The Princess again sent the manuscript to Gennadius; she wished to have no more responsibility. Gennadius, after some hesitation, burnt it – with the exception of some extracts left to show how bad it was. The result is that quite enough of it survives; and there is no difficulty in listening to the message of Gemistus, should we chose to do so.

The work, which bears the Platonic title of *The Laws*, opens with a promise of sanity that is not fulfilled. With grave pity Gemistus reviews the diverse opinions by which men are distracted in their pursuit of happiness. Some believe in knowledge or in virtue; others despise them; some put their trust in religious ceremonial; others reject it; none agree about it; some think an anchorite holy; others that a husband or a father is still holier. Even about the gods men are uncertain whether there are any, what they are, or in what relation they stand to men. How can we hope to attain happiness while such bewilderment remains? Let us attempt first to dispel it; and by so doing we may discover the perfect law which alone can guide us to the happy life.

Such thoughts were not original, and perhaps never have been. But any man who repeats them with sincerity is entitled to a hearing, and everything proves that Gemistus was sincere. It is disappointing to think that this sober introduction introduces nothing. With the shameless inconsistency of his century, Gemistus passes without apology to dogmatism of the wildest and most uninspiring kind, and stands forth as the high priest of a creed which cannot even be called ingenious.

The new religion which he is presenting as a cure for humanity's ills is nothing else but the religion of ancient Greece, 'adapted to the needs of philosophy, and freed from the idle additions of the poets'. Accordingly he begins with Zeus, who has little connexion with the Zeus who once swam upon the Eurotas to Leda, two miles away. The Zeus of Mistrà is a Neo-Platonic abstraction, without parents or wife, the father of all. He dwells on Olympus, together with those gods who are his legitimate children – Poseidon his first-born, Hera, the wife of Poseidon, Apollo, Artemis, and Hephaestus, and about a dozen more. The illegitimate children of Zeus – and why they are thus branded is never explained – live by themselves in Tartarus, presided over by Cronos and his wife, Aphrodite. A third class of deities falls into two divisions, the first consisting of the Sun, Moon, and Stars, legitimate children of Poseidon, the second of Demons, who are numerous but kindly. The fourth class, though of divine parentage, is not divine. In it are men, animals, and plants.

Thus did Gemistus awake the ancient gods of his country, and thrust new emblems into their bewildered hands. Apollo found himself presiding over 'identity', and his sister over 'diversity'. Dionysus saw to spontaneous movements, while all transmitted movements were owing to Pallas Athene. Zeus, through Poseidon, with the concurrence of Hera and the assistance of Pluto and Persephone, created the human soul. The gods had lost Homeric fierceness during their long sleep. Orderly and decorous, they performed their allotted tasks, never interfering with each other or losing their tempers. They, who have, in the idle additions of the poets, an immortality which Gemistus did not suspect, could endure the philosophy of that day, just as they will endure the archaeology of this.

The gods were served by an elaborate ritual. Every morning, before breakfast, they were addressed in an allocution, which informed them at great length of their nature, parentage, and limitations. There were three more allocutions in the afternoon, and another in the evening. The style of Gemistus, never very clear, now becomes hopelessly involved; nor is he more successful in the 'Hymns' – chilly little things in hexameters, to be sung by the assembled people. 'O Artemis, thou dost preside over diversity; thou hast received the universe united and thou dost divide it as far as thou canst. Permit us to escape what is bad, O venerable goddess, and rule our lives.' On festal days these hymns were to be accompanied by music. There are also directions for annual sacrifices. But the part dealing with the duties of the priesthood was too bad, or not bad enough, to be preserved; and Gennadius has burnt it.

'This theology is the foundation of everything; only those who believe it can attain to happiness.' Perhaps there has never been a scheme so equally unattractive to the heart and to the head. The mere intellectual effort of remembering who is who among the gods is very trying, and it is difficult to believe that the most eccentric of souls could here find any consolation. Yet much of the ritual had probably been actually performed by the little band of disciples who gathered round Gemistus in his closing years. And he directs that 'any sophist who speaks against it shall be burnt alive'. This was the traditional language of enthusiasm; after his death his disciples found him a place in the heaven he had constructed so carefully and defended so bravely.

Only occasionally are there moments of sobriety which recall the introduction, and moments of insight which justify it. 'It is not enough to be happy, fools can be that. We must know what happiness is, and how it comes.' 'A great name may be defiled by bad usage; yet once used rightly, it again becomes pure.' Speaking of religious inquiry, Gemistus says: 'There is no defect in heavenly things, nor any petty jealousy, that could make the gods ashamed to reveal themselves to us.' And his choice of ancient Greece as an ideal was not always arbitrary. He saw in it a rule of temperate life, a possible escape from the asceticism which medievalism had professed, and from the sensuality which it had practised. 'Neither is pleasing to the gods. The animals in this respect are better than we, for their instinct guides them infallibly; whereas we have only our reason, which is still uncertain and weak. Let us pray the gods to strengthen it, and to preserve us from either extreme.'

It is easy to say that the book is wearisome and absurd. Gemistus tried to recall antiquity by catchwords – by the names of the Greek gods. These names had for him a mysterious virtue: he attached them like labels to his uninspiring scheme, while he rejected all that makes the gods immortal – their radiant visible beauty, their wonderful adventures, their capacity for happiness and laughter. That was as much as his dim, troubled surroundings allowed to him. If he is absurd, it is in a very touching way; his dream of antiquity is grotesque and incongruous, but it has a dream's intensity, and something of a dream's imperishable value.

During his lifetime, by paths he had not suspected, the gods had found their way to Italy, sometimes openly, sometimes in more questionable shape, bearing the emblems of saints and the crowns of martyrs; and there they remain, beautiful in fresco and marble, to this very day. He was, after all, to take up his abode among them. In 1465, Sismondo Malatesta of Rimini captured Mistrà from the Turks, and, out of the great love he had for Gemistus, exhumed his body and translated it to Italy. At Mistrà the medieval world surveys the empty site of Sparta; in the church of San Francesco at Rimini the Gothic brickwork has disappeared behind the marble arcades of Alberti. Gemistus lived in the one, and is buried in the other. The Renaissance can point to many a career which is greater, but to none which is so strangely symbolical.

[1905]

CARDAN

The name of Girolamo Cardano, who was born at Pavia in 1501 and died at Rome in 1576, would be familiar to a student of the history of medicine or of mathematics. But the ordinary person, who alone confers immortality, will hesitate to accept him on such trivial grounds, rightly considering that his science has long been superseded, and that his contributions to algebra are now no more deserving of special celebrity than are the waters of a river when they are once mingled in the sea.

If Cardan escapes the oblivion he so much dreaded, it will be neither as doctor nor as mathematician, but because at the end of his life he wrote a little book about himself, and wrote it in the right way. He had always been interested in the subject, and fragments of autobiography occur in most of his works. Now he gives it undivided attention, and endeavours through fifty-four chapters to describe his character, constitution, and fortunes. He might have been to us merely a person of some importance in his time, a funny old man who pottered about, four centuries ago, beside the springs of science. Hitherto his egotism has rescued him. He is so supremely interesting to himself that he cannot but interest others; and his little book ranks among the great autobiographies of the world.

The first statement in it is in some ways the most remarkable, and indicates the spirit in which he will review his life. 'Before my birth, my mother endeavoured to procure abortion, and failed.' Another writer, if he had the courage to make such a statement, would certainly turn it to some literary use. He would become sentimental over the poor infant, entering the world so unwillingly, so ungraciously received. He would try to arouse pity or indignation. He would probably say that it was better for him if he had never been born. Cardan does nothing of the sort. Here is a fact, and a fact of some importance, to be related without lamentation, and without apology. If people are shocked at it, they are silly; if they pity him for it they are sillier still. He proceeds to calculate his horoscope.

It is this absence of sentimentality that gives Cardan his value – one might say his charm. Strictly speaking, there is nothing very attractive about him; there is certainly nothing poetic. But he has the ability, as well as the wish to be sincere, and his writing affects us with the power of a spoken work, making us blush sometimes for him, and more frequently for ourselves. Truthfulness is one of the few virtues to which he lays claim, and for this reason his biographers have accused him of untruthfulness. 'A man,' they argue, 'who makes such a claim, must be a liar: we should never think of making it ourselves.' It is a difficult point; however, it is worth while remembering that evidence against Cardan's truthfulness is both scarce and doubtful. 'It has never been my habit,' he says, 'to tell lies.' His autobiography may be assumed to be a fairly trustworthy, as well as a readable book; and on it the following account of him is based.

Fazio Cardano, his father, was a Milanese lawyer, a man of good birth and some ability, who had hoped to go down to posterity as the commentator of a book called *Peckham's Perspectives*. He was very ugly, like his son, having white eyes, no teeth, a stammer, and a round back, and he did not carry off his ugliness by any charm of disposition. He was never married to Cardan's mother, which may partly account for the boy's ill-regulated childhood, and for the persecution he encountered from respectable people in later years. 'My mother,' says Cardan, 'had a bad temper and a good memory. She was short, fat, and pious. Indeed, both my parents had bad tempers, and they did not love their son for long at a time. However, they spoilt me; my father insisted on me laying in bed every morning till eight o'clock, and I think it did me a great deal of good. If I may say so my father was on the whole kinder and nicer than my mother.' The household was completed by 'my Aunt Margaret, a woman from whose composition all venom seemed to have been omitted'.

The child, in spite of a tolerable horoscope, was unlucky from the first. At the age of one month he caught the plague, and his face was covered with carbuncles. Up to the age of seven years, his family whipped him, and he had to tug his father's heavy bag through the streets of Milan. After seven, when whipping would have done him some good, he was left in peace. At eight, he ate a bunch of unripe grapes, and nearly died. He could remember being lifted up, in his convalescence, to see the French troops returning in triumph from the battles of 1509. Then he went to call on a friend, and a small smooth-haired dog bit him in the stomach. He climbed up a ladder, and the ladder fell. Sitting on a doorstep, safe for once, he thought, a tile slipped off a neighbouring roof, and stretched him senseless. Fazio thought it time to move; and 'we changed our house, but not our fortune'. There was no money, the country was harassed by perpetual wars, and the question of a profession had to be decided. Fazio wished the law; Cardan, in a notable passage, explains why he rejected it. From boyhood he had realized the dignity of life, and he desired to understand men in all ages and in all places. Law differed country by country, and altered year by year: he must have a profession which dealt with all humanity. Such an attitude might have made him a philosopher: Fazio hoped that it might. It made him a doctor instead. It made him a mathematician also. His father, with very elementary knowledge, had produced a tolerable commentary on *Peckham's Perspectives*; he would do better. So he did; and at the present day, if anyone remembers that — 3 can be the root of 9, it is owing to him.

This squalid childhood, so full of disasters and disagreements, made a great impression on Cardan. 'A family,' he says, pathetically, 'is kept together neither by fear nor love, but by a certain reverence.' Both fear and love were present in his; but the reverence was lacking.

It is not necessary to quote the detailed catalogue of his physical defects, which he relates with the interest of a physician rather than with the horrid zest of an invalid. Nowadays, a man so miserably constituted would be regarded as an oddity, and treated with consideration; in the sixteenth century he was allowed to take his chance of becoming great. He himself is conscious of nothing disgraceful; for at times the mender of flesh can attain to the serenity of the maker. Occasionally he wished for death, but the wish did not last long, nor was it violent while it lasted. 'I think,' he adds, 'that others have wished for it also, though they have never had the courage to say so in a book.'

He is equally sincere over the defects of his character, though here the moralist may object that sincerity is not enough, and that a little shame would be very desirable. Cardan is so interested in self-analysis that he often forgets to deplore the results he has arrived at. He relates, in quick succession, his bad temper, his stupidity, his licentiousness, his inordinate love of revenge, without pausing to take breath and repent. Several times he had ruined himself by gambling: he sold all his wife's jewels, and the furniture, to pay his debts. But he can look back with pleasure on the days when he had luck and adds: 'Never play unless you play for money; nothing else can excuse the waste of time.' When his vices are inconvenient to himself, we have a more decorous state of things. 'I wish I had a stronger character; I ought to give the servants notice, and I can't. And I have allowed people to give me presents of goats, lambs, storks, hares, and conies, till the house smells like a farmyard.' But sometimes, when we should most desire it, he is truly penitent: he cannot forgive himself for his habit of deliberately saying things that will vex his hearers: he has done it all his life: it is so strange, this sudden impulse to be rude and to inflict pain. Evidently Cardan had the desire to shock others which is so often found in unconventional people, and which is so often taken as a mark of unconventionality. But he had the head to know that it was wrong, and the heart to be sorry for it.

Such instances of tenderness are comparatively rare. To Cardan, the greatest things in life were work, self-examination, and the hope of immortality. Human intercourse was unimportant beside these. The only time he is stirred to great emotion is at the death of his son, and even here it is the feeling that his name will not survive on earth that pains him most. He regarded friends as useful aids to existence: he took care that Cardinals should be among them, and Senators, and the Imperial Viceroys of Milan. 'When you are choosing a friend, see first whether he gets on with others' – admirable advice, but not the best. He is conscious of the risk of great affection: 'only the gods know how to love and how to be wise.' It may be conceded that, in this respect, Cardan is less interesting than his contemporaries, whether we take Michelangelo on the one hand, or Benvenuto Cellini on the other. Only once is he at all impressive – when he describes how he meets his future wife. And, even here, he grows strangely frigid towards the close. The passage opens with rather a beautiful account of a dream.

I was practising at Sacco, and things were going rather well with me, when one night I dreamt I was in a garden. It was delightful: there were flowers and fruit and gentle wind: no poet or painter could have imagined anything so charming. The garden gate was open, and outside it stood a girl dressed in white. I ran out to embrace her, and immediately the gardener shut the gate, and would not let me return. I burst into tears, and, clinging to the girl, was excluded from the garden for ever.

A few days later, Altobello Bandarini, a retired officer of the Venetian militia, moved into the house next door, and his daughter, both in face and clothing, was exactly like the lady of my dream.

I said to myself: 'What am I to do with this girl? I am poor and she is poor, and stifled by a crowd of brothers and sisters. How can I marry her? and if I attempt seduction her father lives close by, and is a military man besides. Whatever am I to do?' The end of it was, that I married her, and her parents were quite pressing about it, and offered every facility. She lived with me fifteen years, and was the cause of every misfortune that happened to me throughout my life.

But he had the grace to add that Lucia Bandarini made a good wife. It is only as the mother of his sons that she can be said to be the cause of his misfortune.

It is characteristic of Cardan that the approach of his marriage should be thus indicated by a dream. Never was a man so anxious to establish a connexion between the spiritual world and our own. He believed in dreams, omens, familiar spirits, ghosts, astrology, necromancy, cheiromancy, and metoposcopy. The supernatural powers were assiduous in their comments on his life, but they were singularly ill informed, and rarely told him the truth. They never prophesied what happened, and they prophesied what never happened. He is to die at the age of forty-one, and frames his life accordingly. He lives till seventy-six, thus finding himself with thirty-five unexpected years. He goes for a walk, and a crow seizes on to his clothes and tears a hole in them. Nothing happens. He dreams of a large red hen. He fears it will speak to him. It does speak to him. He cannot remember what it says and nothing happens. His little dog, generally so well behaved, jumps on to the shelf in his absence and chews up all his manuscripts, with the exception of a dialogue on Fate, though it was the easiest to chew. This time something does happen: before the year is out he gives up his practice in Milan.

Such were the connexions that Cardan tried to establish with the other world. He thinks he is impartial, but, obviously, here is a matter of faith: he never would have tolerated such incapacity in a human adviser. Here he is characteristic of his age. He lived at a period when the Catholic religion seemed to be breaking down, and each man was trying to make a religion for himself. The result was not attractive. A little later, and the Jesuits put an end to private enterprise in superstition, and reorganized it in the interests of the Church.

It is instructive to follow the career of a man so curiously equipped. But, as we are concerned with Cardan's character, rather than with his achievements, it is sufficient to note three events of his life – his visit to Scotland, his quarrel with Julius Caesar Scaliger, and the tragedy of his sons.

The visit to Scotland, which took place in 1552, marks the highest point to which Cardan's worldly fortunes attained. For forty years he had struggled against poverty, which his marriage had increased. The College of Physicians at Milan would not admit him, because he was of illegitimate birth. He was the victim of snobbishness, which, if it is not coeval with human nature, may be dated from the Counter-Reformation. But his extraordinary ability as a doctor compelled people to notice him. He records over 180 successful cures, and of patients whom he has definitely killed he can only remember three. Since he believed he could cure consumption, it was natural that he should be invited to attend on the Archbishop of St Andrews, John Hamilton, who believed that he was suffering from it.

Fortunately for both parties, the Archbishop's complaint turned out to be not consumption but asthma. Cardan owed his success mainly to his common sense. If he saw the patient was growing worse, he changed the treatment. He was less scientific than his contemporaries, but, as their science was wrong, this was to his advantage. In the present case, he profited by the failure of others, and in a month the Archbishop, if not restored to health, was at all events saved from death. He was to live regularly, with proper allowance for sleep, and he was not to sleep on a feather bed. Every morning he was to take a shower bath. He was to have plenty of turtle soup, and was not to overwork. Such advice, then, if not now, was more valuable than drugs, and Cardan is not to be considered a quack because his reputation rested on it. Before he left, he calculated Hamilton's horoscope, but did not discover that his patient would be hanged in 1571.

On his way back through London, Cardan had an audience of Edward VI, who was recovering from an attack of measles. He was greatly struck by the ability of the king, who asked him some intelligent questions about the Milky Way. At the request of the courtiers, he calculated the king's horoscope, and found that he would live till he was fifty-five at least. Next year the king died, and Cardan wrote a dissertation called *What I thought afterwards about the subject*. He frankly confesses his failure. He is to blame, but not the stars. The horoscope, indeed, was a perfunctory piece of work. Cardan wanted to get away from London. He was frightened at the overwhelming power and ambition of Northumberland, and he foresaw, by common sense, though not by astrology, that horrible tragedies were at hand.

His general impression of Great Britain was favourable.

It is worth consideration that the English care little for death. With kisses and salutations parents and children part: the dying say that they depart into immortal life, that they shall there await those left behind, and each exhorts the other to retain him in his memory. They dress like the Italians, for they are very fond of us. All the northern nations love us more than they love each other. Perhaps they don't know how wicked we are. They are faithful, liberal, and brave. But bravest of all are the Highlanders, who take pipes with them when they are led to execution, and go dancing up to their death.

It is interesting to contrast this with the lurid account of Italy given by the Englishman Roger Ascham. But whether the contrast is to the credit of the English, or of the Italians, is another question.

Three years later, in 1555, Cardan was attacked by the scholar and physician Julius Caesar Scaliger. Scaliger was a great, healthy bully, who had begun life as a soldier. He was born in Italy, but so hated Italians, that he became a French subject and settled at Agen, where he reared his devoted family. 'My father was a terrible man,' says his son. 'All the gentry respected him. He had a face like any king's, yes, like an emperor's. There is no king or emperor who has so grand a way as he had. Look at me; I am exactly like him. As for my sister, she is a poor creature, a beast.' Scaliger, for the sake of notoriety, had already quarrelled with Erasmus. Now he attacked Cardan, whom he could not bear, thinking him a puny, affected, diseased Italian, who had no right to exist in a world which was meant for the strong. Cardan's work, *Concerning Subtlety* – the greatest of his works – furnished an excuse. Scaliger wrote fifteen books of *Esoteric Exercitations* to confute it, loading his adversary with every kind of insult.

Cardan received a copy of this work, but, having other occupations, did not immediately reply to it. Scaliger and his family waited, month after month, in the greatest anxiety. At last the silence was explained. News arrived that Cardan was dead. The *Esoteric Exercitations* had killed him.

Then the strong man was seized with remorse. He im-mediately composed a funeral oration on his victim, which begins as follows:

Since fate has been so unkind to me as to combine my private achievement with a public misfortune, and to connect my efforts, so noteworthy and so necessary, with a calamity so disproportionately dire, I think it only fair to inform posterity that I did not vex Cardan more by my trifling corrections than he has vexed me by his death.

He continues in the same strain of complacent magnan-imity and gentlemanly regret, and loudly calls to heaven to witness that he had meant no harm. He had done no harm either. Cardan survived the oration by twenty-one years, and the orator by seventeen. Unfortunately, the oration was never published, and the greatest joke of the sixteenth century could only have been enjoyed by a few.

The younger Scaliger notes it as an odd thing that, when Cardan did reply to his father, he never mentioned him by name. He only called him a 'certain accuser'. This restraint is typical of the man. Though he might be violent with his tongue, he tried to govern his pen. The printing press, then only a century old, had been mistaken for an engine of immortality, and men hastened to commit to it their deeds and passions for the benefit of future ages. Cardan, though he shared the illusion, had a higher conception of the responsibility. Though he was pitiless to himself, he desired that the follies and incompetencies of others should often remain anonymous. For this reason, Scaliger is only 'a certain accuser' in the reply.

The end of Cardan's life was embittered by the tragedy of his sons. His own father and mother were long since dead, and his wife had died also. He was left to educate three children, Gianbattista, Aldo, and a daughter Chiara. Chiara was a good girl, and never cost her father more than a dowry. Aldo was wicked and worthless from the first. Cardan, after much unhappiness, was obliged to disinherit him. All the love of which he was capable went to his elder son, Gianbattista. It is all probably for Gianbattista that he composed the *Precepts* which are printed at the end of his autobiography, and which are a pleasant contrast to the dusty piety, and still more dusty cynicism, with which great men have so often regaled their offspring. Gianbattista, who had some ability, studied medicine in Milan. There was an earthquake in the night; and, next morning, Cardan heard that his son had married a disreputable woman who had neither character, connexions, nor dowry. He refused to receive them; and the quarrel lasted nearly a year. Then he forgave his son, and tried to make the best of the catastrophe.

But greater misfortunes were at hand. Gianbattista's wife had not become respectable by marriage, and their life was one continual squabble, in which she was supported by her father, mother, and three brothers. At last the young man could no longer bear the consequences of his folly. He bought some arsenic and put it into a cake, which he offered to the household. His father-in-law and mother-in-law were violently ill, but recovered. His wife, who had recently given birth to a child, died in great agony. The cause of her death was obvious. The next day Gianbattista was taken to prison.

As usual, Cardan was warned by portents and dreams. He noticed a fiery mark on his hand, which took the shape of a sword. He left Pavia, where he was living, and tried to save the life of his son. There was just a chance that death might be commuted for exile. To this end Cardan used all the curious scholastic arguments which still found favour in the courts. He proved that poison was a nobler weapon than a dagger. He proved that it was sometimes used as medicine, and might therefore be considered beneficial. But the Milanese had never liked him. His affection moved them as little as his arguments. On the 7th of April, 1560, Gianbattista, then twenty-six years old, was executed in the prison.

Cardan was ruined. Not only had he spent large sums over the trial, but his reputation as a doctor was destroyed. The father of a murderer could not inspire patients with the necessary confidence. Then, as now, ability without respect-ability was useless. Fifty years earlier, in the prime of the Renaissance, when a man was judged by himself, not by his relatives, he might have recovered quickly from the blow. But the Counter-Reformation had begun. The Council of Trent was sitting, the Index had been started, the Inquisition was being developed. Cardan lived too late, a fate even more tragic than living too early. He was a martyr without being an apostle. He moved to Bologna; and, for a time, his fortunes improved. Then, without warning, he was accused of impiety, and imprisoned.

Hitherto, the Church had shown little opposition to science. In Italy, at all events, men were permitted to say, 'I hold this as a philosopher; as a Christian, I hold the reverse.' And Cardan had always been strictly orthodox: he had even refused to go to Denmark as a royal physician because the Lutheran heresy had been established in that country. But now the Church was determined to combat inconsistency as well as dissent. This, in Cardan's 237 volumes, was not difficult to find. The most serious charge was that he had calculated the horoscope of Christ. He was accused of atheism, and, since there were then grades in atheism, he was placed in the first division of the second class.

The life that had been so tragic ended like a farce. Cardan was released from prison by Cardinal Morone, and by Cardinal, afterwards Saint, Carlo Borromeo. He was taken to Rome, and he died there in the receipt of a pension from the Pope. It seems that his accusers had no desire to persecute him. He was an old man, and it was improbable that he would give them such trouble in future. All they required was a decent submission to the new order that they were establishing, and, having obtained that, they left him to die off in peace. His great learning, and his past achievements, conferred a certain distinction on anyone who would protect him. He was kept carefully, the product of a talented but misguided age, just as the marble gods and goddesses were kept carefully locked up in the galleries of the Vatican.

He entered Rome in 1571. There he had time in which to consider his eventful life, and, for all its misery, he finds that it has been good.

It has been my peculiar fortune to live in the century which discovered the whole world – America, Brazil, Patagonia, Peru, Quito, Florida, New France, New Spain, countries to the North and East and South. And what is more marvellous than the human thunder-bolt, which in its power far exceeds the heavenly? Nor will I be silent about thee, magnificent Magnet, who dost guide us through vast oceans, and night and storms, into countries we have never known. Then there is our printing press, conceived by man's genius, fashioned by his hands, yet a miracle equal to the divine.

It is true that, to compensate these things, great tribulations are probably at hand: heresy has grown, the arts of life will be despised, certainties will be relinquished for uncertainty. But that time has not yet come. We can still rejoice in the flowering meadow of spring.

I cannot say that I regret my lot. I am the happier for having known so many things which are important and certain and rare. And I know that I have the immortal element within me, and that I shall not wholly die.

Besides hoping for immortality beyond the grave, for which there is some justification, Cardan hoped for immortality this side of it, for which there is no justification at all. The Italians of the Renaissance found their life so wonderful, that they believed that men would remember for ever that they had lived, and that intensity of their emotions could not be dissipated by time. Cardan, who is the last of that Renaissance, is less ambitious in his demands. 'I do not mind whether it is known what kind of a man I was, but I should like it to be known that I existed.' Sir Thomas Browne, who lived still later, and who is prepared for total oblivion, sees the futility of such a compromise. 'To be content that times to come should only know there was such a man, not caring whether they knew more of him, was a frigid ambition in Cardan, disparaging his horoscopal inclination and judgement of himself.'

To raise up a skeleton, and make it dance, brings indeed little credit either to the skeleton or to us. But those ghosts who are still clothed with passion or thought are profitable companions. If we are to remember Cardan today let us not remember him as an oddity.

[1905]

VOLTAIRE'S LABORATORY

1. *How They Weighed Fire*

DURING the spring of 1737 the iron foundries in a remote district of Lorraine were often visited by a thin, middle-aged man with a notebook. He would weigh out two pounds of iron, have them heated till they were red-hot, and then weigh them again. He repeated the experiment, increasing the amount until he had weighed up to a thousand pounds. Three cauldrons were next prepared under his directions, they were placed on scales, so that their weight could be estimated, and then molten metal was poured into them from the furnace, a hundred pounds into the first cauldron, thirty-five pounds into the second, twenty-five into the third, and when the cauldrons were cold the mass was weighed again. As the title of this article suggests, the thin, middle-aged man is Voltaire, but what on earth is he doing in an iron foundry? Wait a minute. Here comes a still more remarkable figure.

The newcomer is a lady of about thirty, with a long thin face, a commanding nose, and greenish eyes. Her appearance is masculine but not mannish; in spite of her earnest mien she is gay and charming, she dresses well, and is very kind-hearted. It will be easy to make fun of her. For she, too, holds a notebook in her hand, in which she enters the weights of the hot and cold iron. She is quite as keen as Voltaire, and even more serious. She has taken up science, not because it is fashionable and brings her into contact with celebrities, but because she hopes to discover the nature of the universe. Facts, facts! A theory may come later – if there is one. She gives up acting, dancing, games, in order to do experiments. Voltaire calls her 'divine Emilie'. She is his mistress, Madame du Châtelet, and she owns Cirey, the great house where he is stopping.

On returning to Cirey, the investigators separate, and Voltaire goes to his own suite, which contains half a dozen ground-floor rooms, beautifully furnished; passing through a tiny ante-chamber, and a bedroom of crimson velvet, he comes to the long gallery, and sits down there. The long gallery is lacquered in yellow, with panels of Indian paper; it is ornamented with statues, one of which, a statue of Love, conceals the stove; there are cupboards full of books and scientific instruments; there are windows opening into the garden or on to the chapel – so that without disturbing himself too much he can hear Mass. At the end is a camera obscura and another room, not yet in order. Voltaire drinks a cup of coffee. Establishing himself at a superb writing-desk, he takes up his pen in despair. For he is going in for a prize competition on the subject of the Nature and Propagation of Fire, and he has been unable to find out whether fire weighs anything. Since fire is an element, one expects it to weigh something, yet the hot iron at the foundry was only occasionally heavier than the cold: sometimes it was the same weight and sometimes actually lighter. Nor is this all: other problems connected with fire are equally obscure. If he shuts up burning coals in a metal box, sometimes they continue to burn, at other times they go out. If he prepares sections of little trees and places them on a red-hot surface, the time in which they are reduced to ashes varies considerably, although they are of exactly the same thickness and size, and even come from the same plantation. 'I then repeated this experiment with vegetables'; but the vegetables burned unevenly too. An experiment with objects painted different colours had been more satisfactory: black objects got hot quicker than green ones, yellow than white; but even here there were exceptions, and all he can do is to add to the Laws of Fire a supplementary law to the effect that they do not always work.

'My dear Abbé, we are surrounded by uncertainties,' he writes to his agent in Paris. 'To discover the least scrap of truth entails endless labour,' and he implores the Abbé to inquire of people who are likely to know whether fire really does weigh anything; also whether a burning glass has a normal effect on objects in a vacuum; also, is it true that Persian naphtha of the best quality flames under water; also he wants writing-paper of various sizes, sealing-wax, an astrolabe, two globes on stands, thermometers, barometers, earthenware pans, retorts, crucibles; also a complete sportsman's outfit – gun, costume; also face-powder, hair-powder, scent, nail-scissors, sponges, two very large pots of orange-flower pomatum; also a young priest who will officiate in the chapel, and knows a little chemistry besides; and a young mathematician who knows astronomy; also he does *not* want the publications of the French Academy, but the publications of the Academy of Sciences: the good Abbé has confused the two institutions, and sent the wrong volumes, so that Voltaire feels like the man who ordered eighteen swans for his ornamental water, and received eighteen monkeys by mistake; also – also – the list of wants rolls on; what, meantime, is Madame du Châtelet doing at her end of the house?

She, too, is entering for the prize competition on the Nature and Propagation of Fire, but she has not told her lover this. It is to be a surprise. An indefatigable inquirer, she has visited foundries and scorched vegetables until she is left with very little time for the actual writing, and she has to dip her hand constantly in cold water, it aches so. Her suite is even more gorgeous than his: everything matches in blue and yellow, down to the little dog's basket, the bed is covered with blue satin, Veroneses and Watteaus adorn the walls, her writing table, inlaid with amber, was the gift of Prince Frederick of

Prussia, her bathroom is tiled, and paved with marble, the chandeliers are exquisite, a looking-glass door leads from the bedroom into the library. Far into the night she writes; so does Voltaire; and between them slumbers the dilapidated central portion of the house, possibly occupied by her husband.

Life at Cirey was certainly comic, but before we have our good laugh at it we had better remind ourselves that Voltaire and Madame du Châtelet were abreast of their age, and their science relatively no more absurd than our own – indeed, it may well prove to be less absurd, for they were highly intelligent. We find them funny because we know more, but if we patronize them for not knowing more it is we who become funny. For example, their difficulties over fire were shared by all their contemporaries. Chemistry now informs us that fire is not an element, but a state through which bodies are passing, and which is likely to be accompanied by certain reactions: under some conditions, when they are heated, they give out gas, and so get lighter; under other conditions they generate solid oxide, and so get heavier. In a hundred years' time chemistry will inform us of something else. The eighteenth century had not discovered even what we know, so the experiments at the foundry seemed to give contradictory results. Moreover, the apparatus was hopelessly inaccurate; however good a pendulum clock the Abbé sent from Paris, and however carefully he packed it, it still could not record the exact times two cauliflowers took to burn. 'My dear Abbé, we are surrounded by uncertainties.' The uncertainties thrilled him, he dashed hither and thither to put them right and took genuine pleasure in the complexity of the universe.

It has been well said that Voltaire is not a journalist but a newspaper. Every sort of activity gets mentioned in his columns. The literary side is strongest, but science jottings constantly appear, and first become prominent during his exile in England. He picked up in England many scraps that

moved his respect or mirth: inoculation; a woman who bore
rabbits; an Irishman who saw worms through a miscroscope
in mutton broth. But it was not until he returned to France
and fell under Madame du Châtelet's influence that his interests concentrated. She inclined him to the subjects she herself
had studied – that is to say to physics and to astronomy – and
his chief scientific work, an exposition of Newton's theory, was
composed under her protection. He presented the theory
accurately, criticized it intelligently, and has the undivided
credit of introducing Newton to the French public. Orthodoxy was alarmed; it had invested in the whirlwinds of Des-
cartes as a suitable basis for the physical universe, and resented
the possibility of gravitation. On account of gravitation, and
on account of other laxities, which included an improper
poem on Joan of Arc, Voltaire kept away from Paris. He was
not yet the very great Voltaire who quarrelled with Frederick
the Great and avenged Calas. But he was a considerable figure,
tragedian, poet, wit, philosopher, and now science was to
place her metallic wreath a little crookedly upon his brows.

He and his hostess had arrived at Cirey earlier in that same
year, 1737. They had driven by night and through the snow,
and the wheel had come off the carriage on Voltaire's side, so
that Madame du Châtelet, her maid, and a quantity of luggage fell on him. At the same moment all the menservants fell
off the box. It was long before the luggage, the maid, the mistress, and the great man could be progressively extracted, and
he uttered a series of short, sharp shrieks. As so often happened, he was enjoying himself. Cushions were spread in the
frozen road, and he and Madame du Châtelet sat on them and
pointed out to one another the glories of the night sky. 'The
stars shone brilliantly,' one of the servants writes. 'Not a tree,
not a house disturbed the expanse of the horizon. M. de Voltaire and Madame du Châtelet were in ecstasies: wrapped in
furs, they discussed the nature and the orbits of the stars and

their destination in space while their teeth chattered. If only they had had a telescope, their joy would have been complete.' There they sat, half laughing and wholly serious, until the carriage could be repaired and take them on to their home.

When they got there, they evolved a routine which both impressed and annoyed their visitors. They took themselves seriously, in which they were fully justified, and they were obliged to organize their work, or it would not have got done. Eleven in the morning and nine at night were the only hours in the twenty-four when they were certain to be visible. At eleven there was coffee in Voltaire's gallery; in the evening came the great event – supper – occasionally marred by a quarrel. After supper, if all had gone well, Voltaire showed the magic lantern, or directed a telescope at the moon, or played tricks with prisms, being screamingly funny all the time, or read Joan of Arc aloud in the marble bathroom, or had plays performed in a barn. Science was much discussed, also religion; at no time of his life was he either an atheist or an agnostic, he believed firmly in God, provided God is given nothing to do, and he always insisted that physics must rest upon metaphysics, and that metaphysics are divine. When the party broke up, they retired to their work, and somewhere or other in the house, well looked after but seldom seen, slept her little boy. The variety, the vigour of Cirey, is most impressive; the imagination flits from room to room until it wearies, and fails even to reach the huge woods which shut in the domain, and the peasants whose labour supported it. What stands out in the end is the laboratory work. That the experiments were primitive, ill-directed, and unsuccessful, did not trouble the investigators, and need not trouble us if we understand what they felt: they saw a new world opening in every direction and asking to be interpreted.

Madame du Châtelet was certainly a most remarkable creature – tiresome, but not too tiresome, and therefore an ideal mate for a very tiresome man. 'Venus-Newton', Frederick of Prussia calls her, while Madame du Deffand insinuates that she was only Newton because she could not be Venus, and also accuses her of spending more on her dresses than on her underthings – gravest of charges that one woman of quality can bring against another. Voltaire adored her. She irritated him, but he also irritated her, which he enjoyed doing, and they were too affectionate and gay to subside into sourness. The relationship between them is very odd: it included emotion, and lasted twelve years, yet it cannot be classed among famous love-affairs. He was not a lover – he had all the ingredients that make up love, such as tenderness, pity, lust, selfishness, unselfishness, but they never combined: he was a chemical experiment, which, if love be the desired result, may be said to have failed. Madame du Châtelet was more normal, and it was she in the end who tired of the liaison, or rather tried for an additional one which ended in a ghastly catastrophe. With their tragedy I am not concerned here: at the moment I visualize them they were wholly in accord, and in accord with her husband and now that the eighteenth century is no longer here to sneer or the nineteenth century to lecture, they are perhaps coming into their own. What kept them together was their interest in outside things – science, the drama, philosophy, art. They can never have said – at least I cannot imagine them ever saying – 'What is this? What has brought us so close? We had better not inquire, lest it vanish away.' They were held by their common interests, and so the nerve-storms that occasionally swept over them left no wreckage behind.

Neither he nor she obtained the prize for the Nature and Propagation of Fire. The judges complimented him on being a poet and her on being a lady, but appear to have been slightly shocked by the number of facts they mentioned, and divided the prize between three other competitors, who confined themselves to theory. In the opinion of modern authorities, the award ought to have been made to Madame du Châtelet: her essay is much the best.

2. *Troublesome Molluscs*

Thirty years have passed, and Voltaire, now at the height of his fame, holds a pair of scissors in one hand and a slug in the other. Let me repeat: in the one hand he holds a large brown slug, and in the other a pair of scissors. The slug is of Swiss extraction, and comes off one of his estates, where it has been eating the lettuces. *Ecrasez l'infame*? But no: he reserves it for another purpose. Looking into its face, he surveys the gloomy unresponsive snout which is all a slug offers, he compares it with the face of a snail, so much more piquant, and both with the face of a man. All three are different, but all are faces, and he does not know whether he trembles at the edge of a great discovery or of a joke. Beneath him are the blue waters of the Lake Leman, beyond them the walls of Mont Blanc, he stands with one foot in Genevan territory to escape the French, and the other in France, to be safe from the Swiss. He stands triumphant, all his possessions are around him, thousands of his trees grow, his contented peasantry work, his invalid cousin dozes, the bells of the church he built chime – and he cuts off the slug's head.

His niece, Madame Denis, keeps house for him now – or rather houses, for he possesses three. Awkward and torpid, Madame Denis holds at bay the ambassadors, savants, mountebanks, princesses, who have come from all over Europe to see her uncle. He is researching, he must not be disturbed. The scissors approach again, and a second slug is decapitated, and a third, until there are twelve. Nor does this conclude the gruesome tale: in a box hard by seethes a clot of headless snails. Voltaire surveys his victims with affability. He does not like the slugs much, but has great sympathy with the snails, he finds their courtships gallant if curious, their contours intelligent, and their taste delightful. Nevertheless, he continues to snip off their heads. It is Science. He is trying to find out whether heads grow again.

Once more, the results are conflicting. As in the case of fire, it is as if all nature combines to conceal the truth. Slugs behave differently to snails, which might be expected, but they also behave differently among themselves. All molluscs lack earnestness of purpose, so to speak – sometimes they die when their heads are removed, sometimes they grow fresh heads and live, sometimes they live without heads. Voltaire is delighted, but puzzled. On the whole, slugs grow new heads, snails don't; though snails when mutilated merely between the horns repair the damage more frequently than do slugs whose heads have been removed entirely. What may we deduce from this? Well – not much, and at the end of one of his solemn works (his *Questions on the Encyclopaedia*) he suddenly exclaims 'Retraction! I retract the scissors with which I cut off the snails' heads.' For they had grown in 1772 but not in 1773, and what can one build on such creatures? He can only say that Nature is always admirable, and that what we call 'Nature' is really an art that we have not yet understood. 'All is art, from the Zodiac down to my snails.'

To retract and to relinquish are, however, different things, and Voltaire had the happy idea of turning his failures into a joke, and fathering them on the unfortunate clergy. He invents a charming monk, Père l'Escarbotier, who is also a cook, and causes him to pour out his difficulties to Père Elie, who is a Doctor in Theology in another convent. The correspondence between the two is superb. 'People used only to talk about Jesuits, but now they are completely occupied with snails,' begins Père l'Escarbotier with modest pride, and he goes on to describe his own inconclusive experiments in the kitchen; he has often mentioned them in his sermons: 'I could compare certain of my snails only to Saint Denis, who, after his head had been cut off, carried it tenderly for six miles in his arms.' Père Elie receives this miracle in silence. In a second letter the reverend cook asks what, when the heads are cut off, happens to the souls. He replies to this readily enough: the question is simple, though it requires a different answer in the case of snails and of slugs, for the souls of snails are in their heads, but slugs have their souls anywhere. But a third letter, raising the question of a 'vital germ', from which all species have developed, elicits a sharp rebuke; Père Elie reminds Père l'Escarbotier that 'corruption is the mother of all things' and warns him against heretical speculations which lead to no good. '*Adieu!*' he concludes, on a kinder note. 'May the snails who are set beneath you and the insects who accompany you ever bless your reverence.' And there is a further conclusion as from the pen of Voltaire himself: 'we must marvel and be silent.' Gaily and charmingly he has turned his foolish scientific experiments into a humorous pamphlet: he has begun as a goose and ended as a mocking bird.

Since Madame du Châtelet's death he had taken science less seriously. He had never married, and his niece urged him towards the drama, if anywhere, for she enjoyed acting. Now and then the old ardour would break out: he would wonder whether Hannibal had really dissolved the Alps with hot vinegar, as the historian Livy reports, so he heated some vinegar and poured it on a piece of Mont Blanc. As soon as Mont Blanc adequately cracked, his mind was at rest, and he went on to other matters. The fact is that his seriousness was taking another direction: all his wit and wisdom were being marshalled for his struggle against the Church. He believed in God, he even built a church: but he loathed the Church, and the depth of his hatred appears in the extraordinary difficulties into which he got over sea-shells.

Sea-shells do not, to the outsider, seem more troublesome than other molluscs, but Voltaire regarded them from a very special point of view: they were traitors, who attempted to demonstrate the truth of revealed religion instead of advancing the cause of Liberty, as natural objects should. Had they remained in the sea, all would have been well, but straying from their proper element they appeared in large heaps in the middle of Touraine and elsewhere, or in fossil forms, or on the tops of mountains. Why, you may ask, did this disconcert Voltaire? Why, because it suggested that they had been left when the waters of the Flood subsided, so that Genesis was true. He could not allow this, and he set out with his usual energy and ingenuity to put shells in their places. He had not been trained by the Jesuits for nothing, and the arguments he brought forward are rather too conclusive to be convincing.

In the first place, he argued that the shells in question are not from the sea at all, but are either the shells of fresh-water oysters or the property of his old friends the snails. 'In a rainy year, there are more snails in a space of thirty miles than there are men in the whole earth,' and this being so, the deposits in Touraine and elsewhere can be easily accounted for. Then he argues that the shells were engendered spontaneously in the earth, 'and grew just as stones do'. A correspondent of his, a gentleman who had property near Chinon, had actually watched empty shells growing; twice in eighty years a heavy crop had been produced, they were microscopic at first, and gradually swelled, and stuck against one another until they formed a soft stone, suitable for building; there were five or six species of these empty shells, and since the tenants and neighbours of the gentleman had seen them too, doubt was impossible. Indeed, we can all of us watch the process for ourselves, for the reason that the so-called Ammonite fossils vary in size: the curves of their spirals must obviously increase the longer they lie in the earth. And, finally, let us grant, for the sake of argument, that all the above arguments are false, and that the shells which have given such support to superstition really did originate in the sea. No matter – all is not lost: they can still be accounted for in three ways. Firstly, since so many of them are cockles, they may have dropped from the hats of Palmers who were going to the shrine of St James at Compostella in the Middle Ages. Secondly, since so many are edible, they may be the debris of picnic parties. And thirdly, since so many of them are different, they may have come from the collections of dead conchologists. To this last argument – which leaves us almost more breathless than its companions – Voltaire returns more than once. He was vexed by the bones of a reindeer and of a hippopotamus which were found near Etampes. 'Are we to conclude from this,' he asks, 'that the Nile and Lapland once shared the Orleans–Paris road?' Surely, it is simpler to suppose that the bones once adorned the cabinet of a connoisseur!

His anxiety over shells led him even further than we should expect. He feared that if once a flood was admitted Noah's Ark would come sailing in, and consequently had to ridicule all theories of the universe that emphasized water. There was the fish Oannes, who came out of the Euphrates to preach to the Babylonians. There was Thales, who thought that the stars lived on mist. There was Buffon, who ascribes mountains to the action of waves. There was Maillet, who deduced from a heap of shells at Cairo that Egypt had once been under the sea and the Egyptians fish. Voltaire mocks them all indiscriminately. 'In spite of the present passion for genealogies, there are not many people who would claim descent from a turbot or a cod.' Then the coral insects strike his eye, and seeing that they may give trouble he makes short work of their claims. They must not be allowed to build coral reefs, or the land will appear once to have been under the sea. 'Certainly, one does find little insects in coral, but where does one not

find little insects? Old walls are full of them, but no one sup-
poses that they build the old walls. So is old cheese – but no
one argues that the cheese has been made by the mites.' One
way and another, the sea is prevented from encroaching on
human destiny; not even in the name of science may it cover
the earth, lest when the waters decrease Mount Ararat should
appear and our race again enter into bondage. Voltaire's
attitude here is, in a cruder form, the attitude of certain unorthodox people today, who are disquieted by the work of
Eddington and Jeans, because of the support for Christianity
that may be extracted from it. He hated religion, having witnessed the misery it caused, and he was not detached enough to
admit that because a thing is baneful it is not necessarily untrue. Indeed, he was not detached at all, and if we think he was
we misread both him and his age; he loved freedom, not
truth, so that when the coral insects appeared to be helping the
Jesuits he used casuistry to discredit them. Never, never, if he
could help it, should Noah's Ark sail over the world again.
And if he had lived today, and been told that in the opinion of
many biologists all life, including human life, had a marine or
intertidal origin, he would once more bring up his armoury
and produce arguments which, alas! we should no longer
find devastating. For Voltaire, today, would seem a much
smaller figure than he was in the eighteenth century; we
should admire his personality, fear his tongue, and adore his
short stories, but dismiss his 'serious' utterances as journalism.

Probably he could have been an eminent scientist if he
liked – he was intelligent enough for anything, and while he
was under Madame du Châtelet's influence he showed
powers of application: his treatise on Newton proves this. But
after her death he became desultory and a tease; his mistrust
of theories led him to the theory that other people's conclusions must be wrong. He was hampered by his need of fun;
both scientists and their pursuits can be irresistibly amusing,

and Voltaire was not the man to check his own mirth. He came, he saw, he laughed, and the slugs and snails that might have led a serious anatomist towards the discovery of the pharyngeal ring suggested instead a correspondence between two comic monks.

Nevertheless, he did science one good turn: he impressed the general public with her importance. This is all that a literary man can do for science, and perhaps only a literary man can do it. The expert scientist is too conscious of the difficulties of his subject; he knows that he can only communicate his discoveries to us by simplifying and therefore falsifying them, and that even when he can state a fact correctly we receive it incorrectly, because we cannot relate it to the thousands of other facts relevant. The literary man has no such misgivings. His imagination is touched by the infinite variety of the natural world; he reads books about it, skipping the statistics, he forgets most of what he does read, and perhaps he performs a few experiments in order to grasp the meaning of research. Then, in the course of his other activities, he writes about science, with a spurious lucidity that makes the expert smile. Spurious, but stimulating; the public does realize, from the remarks of such men as Lucretius, Voltaire, Charles Kingsley, Samuel Butler, Mr Aldous Huxley, Mr Gerald Heard, that something is happening. It does get a misty idea of the expanding empire of mankind.

'Certainly, one must admit that Nature is varied,' said the traveller.
'Yes, Nature is like a bed of flowers, where——'
'Oh, never mind the bed of flowers!'
'She is,' the secretary continued, 'like an assemblage of blondes and of brunettes, whose tresses——'
'Oh, bother the blondes and brunettes!'
'Well, she is like a picture gallery, where the features——'
'No, no; Nature is like Nature; why introduce similes?'

'To amuse you!' the secretary replied.

'I don't want to be amused,' said the traveller; 'I want to learn!'

In this passage – it comes from his charming fantasy *Micromegas* – Voltaire neatly contrasts the literary man and the scientist. The literary man loves images, and as soon as he has found a vivid one, his interest in the truth it is supposed to illustrate is apt to cease. But the scientist knows that Nature is Nature. Voltaire himself was literary, yet he had enough sense of science to perceive his own limitations, and though he amuses us and is amused by hot iron and slugs, he has realized – perhaps through Madame du Châtelet – that the universe has not been created for our stylistic exercises. For what, then, has it been created? He cannot say: '*cultiver son jardin*' is a reaction, not a reply. But he could ask the question, he could cause others to ask it, and if 'popular interest in science' has any importance (for my own part, I think it has immense importance), he must be honoured as an early popularizer.

[1931]

CAPTAIN EDWARD GIBBON

I

THE garden where I am writing slopes down to a field, the field to a road, and along that road exactly a hundred and seventy years ago passed a young officer with a rather large head. If he had turned the head to the right, he would have seen not me, not the garden, but he would have seen the elms that still border the garden – they were already recognizable trees. And on his left, outrunning him as it had outlived him, ran a little stream called the Tillingbourne. The gorse and the may were just over when he passed, the dog-roses coming out, the bracken rising, but although he was unusually observant he has left no record of these events. 'June was absolutely lost' is his only comment; June, which he might have spent reading Strabo, he was condemned to spend marching across Kent, Surrey, and Hants.

He does, however, mention that the previous night he slept at Dorking, and visited there 'a whimsical pretty place in the style of Vauxhall'. I am glad he should have had that relaxation. The pretty place was Denbighs, on the slope of the downs. It was not merely in the style of the Vauxhall gardens. It actually belonged to the proprietor, an ingenious gentleman who contrived at every turn some 'singularity', something that amused and amazed, and the last turn was the most marvellous of all, for it was none other than the Valley of the Shadow of Death itself. A guide book of the period thus describes the scene:

The view on a descent into this gloomy vale was awful. There was a large alcove, divided into two compartments, in one of which the Unbeliever was represented dying in great agony. Near him were his books which encouraged him in his libertine course, such as Hobbes, Tindal, etc. In the other was the good Christian, calm and serene, taking a solemn leave of the World, and anticipating the joys of immortality.

The young officer must have regarded the alcove with an easy and an equal smile. He was rather conceited and he may have foreseen that before long, in the Libertine's library, a work of his own would be lying, a work more suggestive than even Tindal and Hobbes, and entitled *The Decline and Fall of the Roman Empire*.

Yes; it is Edward Gibbon who passes at the bottom of this garden on June 8th, 1761. He strikes me as a little dissatisfied. He is fresh from a wretched love-affair; he wanted to marry a Swiss girl, and his father objected. 'I sighed as a lover, I obeyed as a son,' he will write in after years, but the episode is not yet an epigram. He is vaguely unhappy, and his father has married again – depressing. Then there is money – he needs it for books and dissipation, and has consented to cutting off an entail in return for £300 a year – a bad bargain. Then there is religion – it is all very well to smile at the alcove, but one must belong somewhere, and he has already changed from Protestantism to Catholicism and back again; the Swiss girl was a protestant, and then – overshadowing everything – is a vexatious war. England is at war with France. Our ally, Prussia, is beating France, yet we are afraid of a French invasion, and a militia Bill has been passed authorizing the raising of troops for home defence. It seemed an excellent measure, and he and his father were both enthusiastic. Alas! Their services have been accepted, and here they are, a captain and a major in the South Hampshire Militia, and they are making constant route marches, drilling, recruiting, guarding dirty prisoners, entertaining people whom they do not want to meet, quarrelling with people whom they have never seen, and engaged in a war otherwise unknown to history – the war between the South Hampshire Militia and the North. The major is bored – still, he wastes his life wherever he is, and we need not pity him. The captain wants to read, study, think, but this aggravating little trap has caught him. Nor is he feeling physically well – the grotesque disease which will finally carry him off has already declared itself. However, this he mentions to no one, any more than he mentions the love-affair, and his outward deportment is frigid and bland. Westward he goes, and, looked at through all those years and those myriads of fallen leaves, he seems romantic to me – the greatest historian England has ever produced, trying his paces on the English roads. But he found no romance in them himself, not anywhere until he heard vespers in the church of Ara Coeli. His head – moving away from mine by now – is not yet concentrated on the decline and fall. Other schemes contend inside it, such as the life of Sir Walter Raleigh, or a history of that noble people, the Swiss, or a monograph of the talented Medici at Florence. And his little book about literature has just come out written in French, and he will present a copy to the Duke of York if opportunity offers. Nursing his secrets, he disappears in the direction of Guildford and I lose him as a neighbour. It is surprising he ever came so near.

Now, when Gibbon wrote his famous Autobiography (or to be more accurate, when he wrote the various memoirs – which were afterwards combined into an autobiography by his executor), he has become a great man with a fixed attitude towards life and an assured style, and such a man can never interpret his own youth. He has ripened but he has hardened. Gibbon did not harden into a prig, he never concealed immaturities through hypocrisy. But he often omitted them because they no longer interested him, and were unlikely to interest his public, and if he did refer to them it was jestingly and in general terms, as befitted an eminent and sarcastic historian. 'By degrees a mimic Bellona unveiled her naked deformity, and before our final dissolution I had longed, sighed for my release.' That was how the South Hampshire Militia appeared in retrospect, but how did it appear to the militiaman? Did he 'sigh' for release, any more than he 'sighed' as a lover? We can answer these questions, thanks to the militiaman's journal, which was published not long ago. It is like anyone else's journal, the author never intended us to see it and that is its value, because if Gibbon has a literary fault it is the fault of presenting himself to us too commandingly. His mastery of style entails a mastery of his audience which becomes monotonous. Even when he is personally appealing – as in the passage that describes the inception of the *Decline and Fall* at Rome or in the still more touching passage that describes its conclusions in the summer-house at Lausanne – we are conscious of reacting precisely as he intended, we have no chance of bringing a free-will offering to that august shrine, all has been pre-arranged. He insists on our hearing what he says to us until we long for a chance of hearing what he says to himself, and thanks to the Journal that chance is now ours. We find not a new Gibbon but a more vulnerable one, and the mere fact that he does not finish all his sentences endears him to me. When he was worried and when he was young, he did not always know what he wanted to say. Nor did he always know where things led to. For instance, on Sunday, December 22nd, 1762, we get the entry: 'Captain Perkins dined with us today, and led us into an intemperance we have not known for some time past,' followed on Monday by: 'I could do nothing this morning but spew. I scarce wonder at the Confessor who enjoined getting drunk as a pennance.'

But I must keep to more serious matters. I have already mentioned a war between England and France. It occasioned little inconvenience, but the war between Sir Thomas and the Duke was a very different affair, and some account of it is necessary if we are to understand Gibbon's military career.

2

Charles Paulet, fifth Duke of Bolton, and Lord Lieutenant of the County of Hampshire, was admittedly Colonel of the North Hampshire Militia. But he wanted to be Colonel of the South Hampshires as well, to which Sir Thomas Worsley objected. Sir Thomas had already been instituted as colonel by another authority, and nothing would induce him to resign. In vain did the Duke argue that the two battalions really constituted a single regiment, so that he commanded both. Sir Thomas retorted from his cups that, by Act of Parliament, no regiment could exceed a certain size, and that if the two battalions were added together that size would be exceeded; consequently the South Hampshires were an individual unit, which he commanded. The Duke was a Whig, Sir Thomas a Tory. Both of them had influential friends in London, to whom they wrote, and since Sir Thomas was not good at letters, his were drafted for him by Captain Gibbon. Both colonels complained to their general, who affected not to understand them, and finally Pitt was asked to lay the dispute before the King. Pitt declined to do this – perhaps the rival contest between England and France distracted him – and the struggle had to go on as best it might. We can read the details in Gibbon's journal. The Duke had begun the campaign with a notable success; he split the enemy ranks by imposing on the South Hampshires as adjutant an officer of his own, McCombe by name, and instructing him to make all the official returns to himself, and not to Sir Thomas. But he had reckoned without honest Sergeant Firth. Firth, on hearing that McCombe was coming, 'said publicly he had been a prizefighter and an alehouse keeper, and that when they had been together in another regiment McCombe was broke for having cheated as Paymaster.' This came to McCombe's ears. He demanded a court-martial on Firth. Sir Thomas countered by demanding a court-martial on McCombe because he insisted on sending his official returns to the Duke; all Hampshire society was rent in twain, and before the court-martial could be held King George II died and a truce had to be called while the belligerents went into mourning. Gibbon was actually coming back from the King's funeral at the moment I visualize him – the funniest funeral that Westminster Abbey has ever seen, if Horace Walpole is correct, the funeral where the Duke of Newcastle stood on the Duke of Cumberland's train for fear of catching a chill from the marble. The courts-martial were finally held at Southampton; both Firth and McCombe were reprimanded and Gibbon was made a burgess of the city, and entertained the Corporation to dinner in the Old Assembly room: 'six dishes of turtle, eight of Game with jellies, Syllabubs, tarts, puddings, pineapples, in all three and twenty things besides a large piece of roast of beef on the side table. The whole made a pretty appearance and (reckoning port, white wine and punch) cost me only thirteen pounds odd.' McCombe was invited, the Duke began to weary and the war died out by common consent.

While the gentlemen of England thus rallied in her hour of need, the common people showed no enthusiasm. Recent events were fresh in their mind, and they knew that though they had been called up for home service they might be drafted overseas. Recruits were difficult to get. Each parish had to provide its quota, they were chosen by lot, and each man chosen had either to serve or to provide a substitute or pay £10. Men with three children born in wedlock were exempt, and it was extraordinary how prolific and how moral the population proved; nearly all the weavers of Alton got off. Finally a reluctant crowd of three hundred yokels were collected, in place of the scheduled five hundred, and were marched about their native soil, and sometimes given uniforms. 'I am afraid,' writes an anonymous satirist of the period, 'if you should take your firearms with you, that John in the Rear will be firing his Piece into the Back-side of his friend Tom in the Front; or which would be still worse, blow out the brains of his noble Captain.' No such disaster occurred to Captain Gibbon. He did no good, but came to no harm, and when, after three wasted years, the militia was disbanded, he could return with a good conscience to his studies, and to his beloved Europe.

He had studied, as best he could, in the midst of his duties, and the list of the books he read and the extracts he compiled are formidable. As yet, he scarcely knew what he was reading for, but he had grasped his vocation, and, if historians did nothing but read, he might well have complained that the militia nearly stultified him with its pettiness, its scrappiness, and 'more than all, the disagreeable society I was obliged to live in. No manners, no conversation, they were only a set of fellows all whose behaviour was low, and most of whose characters were despicable. Luckily I was their superior in every sense, and through Sir Thomas (whose prime Minister I was) in fact I commanded the Battallion.'

A severe, unattractive young man! But a just one. He goes on to summarize the advantages. His health seems better, he has had amusement and change of scene, he has become conscious of 'a new field, that military affairs which, both in my studies and travels, will give me eyes for a new world of things. . . . But what I value most, is the knowledge it has given me of mankind in general, and of my own country in particular. So that the sum of all is, that I am glad the militia has been, and glad it is no more.'

This is the summary not so much of a philosopher as of a historian who realizes that it is impossible, through reading alone, to interpret the past. Nor is emotion enough. The historian must have a third quality as well: some conception of how men who are not historians behave. Otherwise he will move in a world of the dead. He can only gain that conception through personal experience, and he can only use his personal experiences when he is a genius. In Gibbon, as in no other English historian, this tenuous circle was complete. He was a genius who read, dreamed, and also knew – knew by direct contact – a fragment of the rough stuff of society, and extended his knowledge through the ages. Thus the lane that passes under this garden reminds me at moments of the enormous stretches of road he was later to traverse – the roads that led all over Europe and back through the centuries into Rome, then all over Europe again until they frayed out in the forests of Germany and the sands of Syria. As he jogged away through Surrey and Hampshire, he had already in his mind premonitions of a larger route, though its direction remained obscure, and when Sergeant Firth accused McCombe or Sir Thomas dictated another letter about the Duke, his mind was preparing for brawls where the disputants were Caesars and the prize the civilized world.

[1931]

TROOPER SILAS TOMKYN COMBERBACKE

THE workhouse at Henley-on-Thames has, or rather had, a garden attached to it, in the midst of which stood a solitary hut, reserved for inmates who were suffering from infectious diseases. At the moment our eyes rest upon this hut – that is to say at a moment during the February of 1794 – it was occupied by two troopers of the King's Light Dragoons. One of them was sick of the confluent smallpox; he raved in delirium, and the other, who held him down, was covered with ominous spots. The unfortunate men had been left behind by their regiment to look after themselves as best they could, and their situation was appalling, for the weather was bitter, the hut possessed four windows and little else, and though the paupers in the main building were sympathetic they approached with circumspection. We do not know the name of the trooper who had the smallpox, but the one covered with spots was called Comberbacke.

Comberbacke was a clumsy young man, with a drooping lower lip and aspiring eyes, and somewhat of a puzzle to his mates. They saw easily enough that he was a 'natural', but he was a talking natural, a rare and rather agreeable species; he could speak and even write upon a variety of topics with a fluency they felt bound to admire. Although he could neither mount his horse nor groom it he was grand when he came to the wars of the past, and he was always willing to describe them in an interminable and interesting way. There was an expedition entailing the Hellespont – probably the mouth of the Thames being a broad space of water – leading to Thermopple [*sic*] a place up north, and General Alexander – no doubt from Truro, where it is a well-known name. He talked and laughed, didn't mind being teased, changed from subject to subject; he was superb; nothing could stop him when once he had started, and if asked to write a letter for you it was the same: the ink poured out in a torrent, so that by the time she had got to the fourth page the girl couldn't do otherwise than give in. Thus he gained a curious reputation, where even his imbecilities were admired. For instance, 'Whose rusty gun is this?' the inspecting officer would ask. 'Is it *very* rusty?' replied Comberbacke, 'because if it is I think it must be mine.' What a reply! But how successful! For the inspecting officer was dumbfounded. And again, Comberbacke's idea that a horse ought to 'rub himself down and so shine in all his native beauty' – well, it was the idea of a zany, still when the letter was written and the girl on the way there or back there was no reason you shouldn't brighten his horse up for him; it didn't take long, and you knew which end kicked and which bit, more than he did. At last he proved so incompetent that his horse was withdrawn from beneath him permanently, and he was employed upon matters relating to sanitation: that was why he was in the garden-hut now. When his comrade's delirium lessened, he procured pen and ink and wrote the following letter:

My assumed name is Silas Tomkyn Comberbacke, 15th or King's Regiment of Light Dragoons, G. Troop. My number I do not know. It is of no import. The bounty I received was six guineas and a half: but a light horse man's bounty is a mere lure: it is expended for him in things which he must have had without a bounty – gaiters, a pair of leather breeches, stable jacket, and shell; horse-cloth, surcingle, watering bridle, brushes and the long etc. of military accoutrement. I enlisted the 2nd of December 1793, was attested and sworn the 4th.

I am at present nurse to a sick man, and shall, I believe, stay at Henley another week. There will be a large draught from our regiment to complete our troops abroad. The men were picked out today. I suppose I am not one, being a very indocile equestrian. Farewell.

Love, extravagance, and a too reckless support of Unitarianism had combined to put him in this plight. A clergyman's son, he had been sent by his brothers up to Cambridge, where he had successfully composed a Latin declaration on Posthumous Fame, and a poem entitled *To a Young Ass*, and seemed to be settling down. Then he ran away and enlisted. He was always like that. He would start suddenly and collapse suddenly, and he was about to collapse now. The hut, his mate's illness, his own eruptive spots, were going to be too much for him, and to induce in him his favourite reaction – a sense of guilt. For the moment he played the man, and a beautiful girl even ventured into the garden and flirted with him from a distance. Though he mourned for a lost girl of his own, he was touched, and in after years he thought of writing a poem called *The Soother in Absence* to commemorate the visitor, but like so much else that he planned this was never accomplished. He seldom did what he or what others hoped, and posterity has marked him as her prey in consequence. She has never ceased to hold up her plump finger to him, and shake it and say that he has disappointed her. And he has acquiesced because he is a darling. But if one turns on posterity and says, 'Well! what else do you want him to do? Would you rather have Comberbacke as he is or not at all?' she is apt to be silent or to change the conversation.

His Cambridge career included typical irregularities. 'We have veal, sir, tottering on the verge of beef,' he had shouted out in Hall upon one occasion; and on another, when the Master of his college met him and said, 'When will you get rid of that shameful gown?' he had retorted, 'Why, sir, I think I have got rid of the best part of it already.' More serious was the unholy row in the Senate House on the occasion of the expulsion of a Mr Frend for his Unitarian principles. The undergraduates sympathized with Mr Frend, because they associated him with revolutionary ideas and they attended in great numbers to applaud his defence. Comberbacke clapped with the rest, and when the Proctor approached him he deftly exchanged places with a man who had scarcely any arms. 'Sir, you were applauding,' said the Proctor; the man retorted 'Would that I could,' showing his stumps. And there were drinking parties. Nothing very much, but on to it all fell a love-disappointment: his affection for the sister of an old schoolfellow was not returned. So one night he crossed the court from his rooms to the entrance gate, passed down the long paved passage called 'the chimney', gained the street, and entered the world. It was not his first escapade. At the age of seven he had nearly killed his brother Frank in a quarrel over some toasted cheese; then, stricken with remorse, he had rushed into the twilight and had watched the river and some calves on the farther side of it, and so poignant had been the misery that in later years a chance sound would invoke the whole scene: 'There would come on my mind that night I slept out at Ottery and the calf across the river whose lowing so deeply impressed me. Chill and child and calf and lowing.' And he was to have other escapades in the future: there was another journey – alas! someone interrupted it – along the course of an underground river, and there was a voyage – perhaps the most marvellous any navigator has ever undertaken – into the Antarctic seas.

He went by coach from Cambridge to London, got off at Holborn, bought a ticket for the Irish Lottery (not yet illegal), composed a poem on it beginning –

> Promptress of unnumber'd sighs,
> O snatch that circling bandage from thine eyes.

– sent the poem to the *Morning Chronicle*, went to the King's mews, and enlisted.

An old schoolfellow was the first to find out what had happened; then it got round to the family; and as soon as his brothers started writing to him he fell to pieces. He rushed at once from heroics to morbidity ('Mine is a sensibility gangrened with inward corruption'), to mawkishness ('Alas, my poor mother!' – whom he did not like), to self-abasement ('Oh, my wayward soul! I have been a fool even to madness!'), to solemn fudge ('In a mind which vice has not utterly divested of sensibility, few occurrences can inflict a more acute pang than the receiving proofs of tenderness and love where only resentment and reproach were expected and deserved'), and finally to a deprecating and uneasy gaiety. But his troubles were not at an end. He had to be got out of the Dragoons, and it proved to be less easy than getting in; and he had to be got back into Cambridge, if Cambridge would receive him.

His brothers, one of whom held a commission, got in touch with the War Office, and, so far as we know, it is through this channel that he was released. But he never was very truthful, and in after years he used to tell dramatic tales. They centre round one of his own officers, a Captain Ogle. According to one of these tales, he was standing sentry outside a ballroom, when Captain Ogle, who was passing in with another officer, quoted two lines in Greek, and ascribed them to Euripides. 'I hope your honour will excuse me,' said Trooper Comberbacke, 'but the lines you have repeated are not quite accurately cited; moreover, instead of being in Euripides they will be found in the second antistrophe of the *Œdipus* of Sophocles.' In another version, it is through Latin that he attracts the Captain's attention; he wrote up some pathetic lines in the stable where he had failed to groom his horse. At this point Miss Mitford, authoress of *Our Village*, takes up the thread. Captain Ogle's father and Miss Mitford's father were friends. They were at dinner at Reading and Captain Ogle was with them. To amuse them he told them of the scholar-trooper, and his yearnings for release, but, says Miss Mitford, 'kind and clever as Captain Ogle was, he was so indolent a man that without a flapper the matter might have slept in his hands till the Greek Kalends.' The company exerted themselves. The difficulty was to find a substitute, for troopers were scarce. One of the servants who was waiting at the table was called, and agreed to serve for a suitable honorarium. The matter was fixed up there and then, and so grateful was Comberbacke that in after years he looked through two of Miss Mitford's works, entitled *Christina* and *Blanch*, and gave her good advice, which was, however, of no use to her, she feared.

As release approached, he became more and more school-boyish and hysterical. He was afraid of annoying his brothers further, particularly George the clergyman, and now asks advice on every detail. Should he, or should he not, order new clothes?

They are gone irrevocably. My shirts, which I have with me, are, all but one, worn to rags, mere rags; their texture was ill adapted to the labour of the stables. . . . I have ordered therefore a pair of breeches, which will be nineteen shillings, a waistcoat at twelve shillings, a pair of shoes at seven shillings and four pence. Besides these I must have a hat. Have I done wrong in ordering these things? I have so seldom acted right that in every step I take of my own accord I tremble lest I should be wrong. I forgot in the above account to mention a flannel waistcoat; it will be six shillings. The military dress is almost oppressively warm, and so very ill as I am at present I think it imprudent to Hazard cold.

Besides the clothes, there is a terrible confession about some books; he sold books that were worth forty shillings for four-teen; he will do all he can to buy them back. Moreover, should he write a contrite letter to Dr Pearce, the master of his College, imploring to be taken back, or would it show truer humility if he remained dumb? His brothers seem to have behaved decently – it cost them at least forty guineas to buy his discharge; and the college authorities were sympathetic and made no difficulties in receiving him. Some censure had to be administered, and, consequently, the Register of Jesus, Cambridge, contains the famous entry: '1794 Apr: *Coleridge admonitus est per magistrum in praesentia sociorum.*' And now you know who Comberbacke is if you did not know it before.

As soon as Comberbacke felt himself Coleridge again, he began to perk up. He had really been treated most leniently, but 'Dr Pearce behaved with great asperity,' he complains, and has confined him to college for a month and ordered him to translate the works of Demetrius Phalereus. 'All the fellows tried to persuade the Master to leniency, but in vain.' Then he turns cheeky: 'Without the least affectation, I applaud his conduct and think nothing of it. The confinement is nothing. I have the field and grove of the College to walk in, and what can I wish more? What do I wish more? Nothing. The Demetrius is dry.' He gets up at 5.0 a.m.; he has dropped all his old acquaintances; he is finishing a Greek Ode; really, his brother need not worry about him any more.

The rooms he occupied at Jesus' are still to be seen. They are in the front court, on the ground floor – charming rooms – and Malthus, if one seeks for a contrast, once occupied the rooms opposite. It is natural to assume that after his military career he would settle quietly down. But it is dangerous to assume anything about Coleridge. If life is a lesson, he never learnt it. He did not settle down to his Demetrius, he did not proceed to his degree, and in the autumn of that same year the College register contains a second Latin entry, to the effect that Coleridge went away and did not return.

He had disgraced himself irretrievably, and three years later he wrote *The Ancient Mariner*.

[1931]

MR AND MRS ABBEY'S DIFFICULTIES

THE death of Mrs Rawlings, followed four years afterwards by that of Mrs Jennings, her respectable parent, involved Mr and Mrs Abbey in appreciable difficulties finally. They did not at first realize the possible consequences of becoming guardian to the four children – John, George, Tom, and Fanny – the offspring of Mrs Rawlings by a previous union; indeed, Mr Abbey acted with unusual precipitancy, and, without troubling Mr Sandall, his co-executor under Mrs Jennings's will, undertook sole charge even in the grandmother's lifetime. The sum of £8,000 – and £8,000 was a substantial sum a hundred years ago – passed into his control, and he proceeded to administer it for the benefit of the young people as only a business man can.

The connexion of the two deceased ladies had been with the livery trade. They had kept the stables attached to the Swan and Hoop, Finsbury Pavement, and the first husband of Mrs Rawlings had actually been killed by falling off one of his own horses on a dark night not far from Southgate. Mr Abbey's own position was more secure. A broker in tea, and in coffee also, although scarcely in coffee to an equal extent, he had added to his office in Pancras Lane a residence at Walthamstow, and to the latter a conservatory, and to everything that he undertook the conviction of some ultimate issue. It was at Walthamstow that he made provision for the child Fanny, who was aged but seven years only when she came under his charge. He arranged that she should live with Mrs and Miss Abbey, she should attend a young ladies' school where she might acquire such education as her sex necessitated. The education of her brother John was already complete, for

251

he had attained his sixteenth year, and Mr Abbey was prompt
to remove him from his studies and to apprentice him to a
surgeon. George (aged thirteen) and Tom (eleven) were received as clerks into his own office. Thus suitable provision
for all concerned was rapidly and adequately made.

Unfortunately the children were restless – a defect inherited
from their father, who had been of rustic origin. John would
not stick to his gallipots, nor George and Tom to their stools;
and Fanny wished to learn the flageolet. They were always
asking for money to satisfy their whims, and since Mr Abbey
had in view their ultimate good alone and had reinvested the
£8,000 to that end, he negatived all such demands. What they
wasted on letter-paper alone was deplorable, for, as the three
boys grew up, they were in constant correspondence with one
another and with their sister. Mr and Mrs Abbey valued a
united family highly, none higher; but saw no advantage in
Tom communicating with George that it was raining in
Devonshire, or in John informing Fanny that he had counted
the buns and tarts in a pastry-cook's window, and 'was just
beginning with the jellies'. Mrs Abbey, in particular, felt that
family affection was used as a cloak for something else: that
they communicated, as she expressed it, 'behind my back' and
were not so much devoted to each other, which is all very
proper and well, as interested in what each other thought. An
unfortunate discovery gave her some pain. Fanny left her letters lying about, as young girls will, and Mrs Abbey's eye was
caught by the strange appearance of one of them. It was
written in short lines, certainly just nonsense, yet she did not
relish it, the more so since it was in John's handwriting, and he
a notorious makegame.

> Two or three Posies
> With two or three simples –
> Two or three Noses
> With two or three pimples –

Two or three sandies
And two or three tabbies –
Two or three dandies
And two Mrs — mum!

Who might 'Mrs — mum!' be? Mrs Abbey reread the paragraph and then saw that it was a crambo or forfeit, the last line of which concealed her own name. She was affronted, the more so since the name must be in the plural gender. 'Two Mrs Abbeys,' she repeated to herself. 'And why two?' She inquired of her husband next time he came down from Pancras Lane, of Miss Caley, the headmistress of Fanny's school, of Miss Tucker, the headmistress of the school to which she was subsequently transferred. They all agreed that an unkindness was intended. She kept a look-out for John's letters in the future, and discovered in another that she was to be sent up to the London office 'to count coffee-berries', while the grass plot was used for dancing. Elsewhere Fanny was to 'pay no attention to Mrs Abbey's unfeeling and ignorant gabble. You can't stop an old woman's crying any more than you can a child's. The old woman is the greatest nuisance, because she is too old for the rod. Many people live opposite a blacksmith's till they cannot hear the hammer.' Here all was too plain, except, indeed, the blacksmith, whose forge was at the farther extremity of the village; and Mrs Abbey was obliged to take up a different line with Fanny. She would not allow the girl to go up to see her brother in town, and she discouraged his visiting Walthamstow.

How necessary her strictness was, the following anecdote will evince. While the children were deficient in character and breeding on the one side, they had inherited from their mother, Mrs Rawlings, on the other, a tendency to consumption, and Tom was the first to sicken. Fanny professed to be heartbroken, and permission for a visit to his bedside could not well be withheld. She went up to Hampstead, and saw him, thus paying lip service to truth, but afterwards proceeded to act the fine lady, and made a round of calls with her brother John. She returned to Walthamstow in an unseemly state, could give Mrs Abbey no interesting details as to the progress of Tom's malady, nothing but chatter about Mr So-and-so and Miss T'other, what they said and ate and wore and contributed to the newspapers, and might she buy a magazine once a month, even if it meant giving up her spaniel, and she did not think Miss Tucker would object, for newspapers opened the world as Mr Dilke had remarked, and Mrs Dilke was at Brighton. She was easily silenced, but the Abbeys realized how susceptible she was to bad influences, and how sternly they must guard her against them. Letters like the following could not be indefinitely allowed to arrive:

My Dear Fanny

I called on Mr Abbey in the beginning of last week, when he seemed averse to letting you come again from having heard that you had been to other places besides Well Walk. I do not mean to say you did wrongly in speaking of it, for there should rightly be no objection to such things: but you know with what People we are obliged in the course of Childhood to associate, whose conduct forces us into duplicity and falsehood to them. . . . Perhaps I am talking too deeply for you: if you do not know, you will understand what I mean in the course of a few years. I think poor Tom is a little Better, he sends his love to you. I shall call on Mr Abbey tomorrow: when I hope to settle when to see you again. Mrs Dilke is expected home in a day or two. She will be pleased, I am sure, with your present. I will try for permission for you to remain all Night should Mrs D. return in time.

> Your affectionate brother
> John.

Permission was refused. The Dilkes and their set were no companions for a growing girl of fourteen, and Fanny remained under discipline at the time of Tom's death. The discipline had even to be increased, as the following letter, dated four months later, indicates; it had proved impossible to keep her in a healthy and modest frame of mind without almost entirely forbidding any intercourse between her and the rest of her family; it had also proved desirable to remove her from Miss Tucker's, owing to the expense:

My Dear Fanny

Your letter to me at Bedhampton hurt me very much. What objection can there be to your receiving a letter from me? At Bedhampton I was unwell and did not go out of the Garden Gate but twice or thrice during the fortnight I was there – Since I came back I have been taking care of myself – I have been obliged to do so, and am now in hopes that by this care I shall get rid of a sore throat which has haunted me at intervals nearly a twelvemonth. I always had a presentiment of not being able to succeed in persuading Mr Abbey to let you remain longer at School – I am very sorry that he will not consent. I recommend you to keep up all that you know and to learn more by yourself, however little. The time will come when you will be more pleased with Life – look forward to that time, and though it may be a trifle be careful not to let the idle and retired Life you lead fix any awkward habit or behaviour on you – whether you sit or walk endeavour to let it be in a seemly and, if possible, a graceful manner. We have been very little together: but you have not the less been with me in thought. You have no one in the world besides me who would sacrifice anything for you—I feel myself the only Protector you have. In all your little troubles think of me with the thought that there is at least one person in England who, if he could, would help you out of them – I live in hopes of being able to make you happy – I should not perhaps write in this manner if it were not for the fear of not being able to see you often or long together. I am in hopes that Mr Abbey will not object any more to your receiving a letter now and then from me. How unreasonable!

Your affectionate brother
John.

Though less coarse in tone than its predecessors, this letter was even more calculated to undermine authority. O mark the impudence of calling life at Walthamstow 'idle' – he who had never done a stroke of real work for years, had weakened his constitution by dissipation and drift, falling in love with his landlady's daughter, and had vainly tried, when it was too late, to continue his medical career and obtain a post as surgeon upon an East Indiaman! The 'sore throat' of which he complained was the precursor of the usual hereditary trouble, its later developments proving fatal. Kindly Mr and Mrs Abbey were distressed, and, Fanny herself falling ill, called in the family practitioner to attend her. Yet they could not but feel that sickness had all along been used to claim illicit privileges and to undermine their authority as guardians, and that just as in the case of Tom so in the case of John there had been duplicity. In view of his departure abroad, John was permitted to write his sister as often as he wished, and almost his last letter to her contained the venomous sentence, 'In case my strength returns, I will do all in my power to extricate you from the Abbies.' He could not even spell.

Blessed with excellent health himself Mr Abbey left illness to doctors. But in money matters he left himself on firmer ground, and, a man of business through and through, brooked no interference in his own domain. When the three boys had abandoned the professions assigned to them, he could not prevent them, but he could cut off their supplies whenever fit without giving a reason. There was so much that boys could not understand. In the first place, the reinvestment of the £8,000 had, he owned frankly to himself, not been a success. In the second place, old Mr Jennings, the original stableman, had left a confused will. He had died worth £13,160 19s. 5d., £9,343 2s. of which had gone to his widow and thence in more compact form to the grandchildren as £8,000; but he had also left his grandchildren £1,000 direct and £50 a year besides in reversion after their mother's death.

Mr Abbey was aware of these additional legacies, but they were not often in his mind, for, like all city men, he had much to think about, and he deemed it fitter to leave them alone;

they would do no harm, the interest would accumulate in Chancery, and when documents came about them it was his habit to clear his throat, and drop everything together into a safe. And as years went on and the children failed to mention the legacies to him, he ceased mentioning them to himself. He had so much to think about. After the first excitement of guardianship, he had done what nine men out of ten of substance would do in his place: nothing; so he said nothing. When John and George called with troubled faces at Pancras Lane and asked exactly how poor they were, he rightly replied, 'This is no ordinary question,' and silenced them by some reference to their own inexperience. Or, 'Ask your Aunt Midgely,' he would say. They knew not what he meant, nor did he, for Mrs Midgely Jennings was unlikely to afford information, since she was herself dissatisfied with her income, and periodically threatened to bring suits, against whom or for what Mr Abbey was not quite cognizant.

He was not clear either about the great Chancery suit, Rawlings v. Jennings, which the mother and grandmother had initiated by mutual consent in their lifetimes in order to clear up in an amicable spirit the obscurities of Mr Jennings's will. Not one to interfere with another man's job, Mr Abbey left law to the lawyers, and thanks to his attitude the Chancery suit lasted twenty years. Ah, he did not know much, but he always knew a little more than his wards; he performed that duty, and Tom and John remained ignorant until the day of their death, while Fanny believed for many years that she was a pauper and owed Mrs Abbey for her board and lodging. Much extravagance was averted by this timely reticence, many loans to undesirable friends, and tours both in England and on the Continent, which could have led to no useful purposes. 'Ever let the fancy roam, pleasure never is at home,' wrote John to George openly in one of his letters; atrocious advice as coming from an elder brother to a younger, and alluding to the fact that George had decamped with the daughter of a sea-captain to America. All this Mr Abbey realized, deprecated, and strove to check, and it was not his fault when Fanny terminated her connexion with Walthamstow in the arms of a Spaniard.

The last years of the stewardship were very painful. Being small and sickly, and two of her brothers dead and the third abroad, Fanny seemed inclined to settle down. She spoke little, she dressed plainly, and never tossed her head when Mrs Abbey repeated that she resembled her father, who had fallen off the horse, and that naught but idleness had ever been found on that side of the family. But, unfortunately, George came from America on a visit. Fanny was upset again, and all the careful accumulations of so many years came tumbling down. George was more robust than his brothers, had married, and had acquired a hard effrontery which passed for business ability among the Yankees, though it was not so estimated by Mr Abbey. Retrenchment and deliberation were to Mr Abbey the twin pillars of commercial achievement, he never hurried others and he did not expect to be hurried. He greeted the prodigal in measured tones, and received in reply a point-blank demand that the trust should be wound up. 'Ask your Aunt Midgely,' he said; but retorting that he knew whom to ask, George prepared to take the case into court. He insisted on the safe being opened, he discovered that the two additional legacies, ever Mr Abbey's weak point, had been invested twenty years previously in Consols by order of the court, £1,550 7s. 10d. of Consols in the one case and £1,666 13s. 4d. in the other, and that the interest had been accumulating ever since his mother's death. He dragged every detail, including what had been paid as lawyer's fees, to the light, and before Mr Abbey could collect himself had returned to America with £1,147 5s. 1d. in his pocket.

Worse was to follow; when Fanny came of age, which she

did two years after George's visit, she claimed her share also. Mr Abbey might have ceded it without protest, had she not claimed in addition the shares of her two dead brothers. Such rapacity was childish, and Mr Abbey was quick to reply that the arrangement would be unfair to George. Fanny retorted 'No, George's own wish!' and she applied to Mr Dilke, who produced the necessary documents. Fanny annexed the balance, no less than £3,375 5s. 7d. and quitted Walthamstow. Her Spanish adventurer married her soon afterwards, but Mr and Mrs Abbey could never feel it retribution sufficient. Although the money was not theirs to spend, they had come to feel that it was theirs to keep, and they would have liked it to accumulate at compound interest for ever. Bitter words had passed, Fanny insolently hinting that, if Tom and John had been given their proper dues, the additional procurable comfort might have prolonged their lives.

Of course it would not have, and in any case what is the use of such people, Mr Abbey could not help thinking as he sat at Walthamstow in the evening of his own life. Now that the worrying and badgering was over and the trust that he had so faithfully administered was filched from him, now that Rawlings *v.* Jennings was wound up, and idle verses about his wife no longer fell through the letter-box, he could not feel that his four wards had ever existed in the sense in which he, in which Mrs Abbey, in which Miss Abbey and the conservatory existed. Already were they forgotten – George in America, Fanny in Spain, Tom in the graveyard of St Stephen's, Coleman Street, John at Rome. On the tomb of the last-mentioned had been placed a text which rather pleased the old gentleman, despite its fanciful wording. He found it appropriate to the whole family. 'Here lies one whose name was writ in water,' it said. He had written in water himself once with the point of a wet umbrella, and he remembered that almost before the servant arrived to open the door, his signature had evaporated. He himself has expressed the same truth in sounder English in the one letter of his that has been preserved, a business letter addressed to Messrs Taylor and Hessey, publishers, Waterloo Place; he has summed up once for all the world's judgment upon inefficiency:

> Pancras Lane,
> Cheapside.
> April 18, 1821

Sir

I beg pardon for not replying to your favour of the 30th ult. respecting the late Mr Jno. Keats.

I am obliged by your note, but he having withdrawn himself from my controul, and acted contrary to my advice, I cannot interfere with his affairs.

> I am, Sir,
> Yr. mo. Hble. St.
> Richard Abbey

> [1925]

MRS HANNAH MORE

HANNAH MORE was the godmother of my great-aunt. Her picture is before me as I write. I sit upon one of her chairs, the sloping grass outside is said to be imitated from her garden, and once I had a red mitten she knitted, but gave it away. The name of the picture is 'Mrs Hannah More and favourite squirrel'. They too are seated – the old lady at a Chippendale table, the squirrel upon it. They face one another, they bend their necks with identical gesture, and the calm light of a hundred years ago flows in through square panes of glass upon the letter and the nut that they are opening. It must be Barley Wood, for she is very old – Barley Wood where she hoped to die, but her servants mishandled and betrayed her. 'I am driven, like Eve, out of Paradise,' she said, 'but, unlike Eve, not by angels.' It was Zachary Macaulay who rescued her, having discovered licentiousness in the kitchen, in which even Louisa was involved. Who was Louisa? A trusted orphan. Who on earth was Zachary Macaulay? Mr R. C. Trevelyan's great-grandfather. Yes, here is the Hannah More of our tradition, fragile and philanthropic. The earlier Hannah, who quipped it with Garrick and scribbled it with Walpole – she is less to our taste.

Yet earlier and later were connected. Had it not been for *Percy*, a five-act tragedy in blank verse, I do not think she could have sat on that chair so calmly. She had received a certain amount of money from a gentleman who failed to marry her, but it was on the broader and more substantial basis of *Percy* that her fortunes really rested. It held the stage for years. Poetry assisted it; when Mrs Montague read *The Bleeding Rock* she exclaimed: 'Your "Rock" will stand unimpaired by ages,' nor was she wholly wrong. And when secular royalties decreased, Hannah turned to other themes, cautiously descending the social ladder in the process, but never losing touch with the booksellers. The success of *Parley the Porter* and other tracts was enormous. *Charles the Footman* was translated into Russian; *Moses in the Bulrushes* into Cingalese; two Persian noblemen called at Barley Wood and carried away a volume of *Practical Piety* for the use of the Shah; *The Newcastle Collier* solved all difficulties with Labour in the North; while of her full-length novel, *Coelebs in Search of a Wife*, thirty thousand copies were sold in America alone. Her income was assured, and she and her sisters, having begun as Bristol governesses, were able to move into the country and practise philanthropy upon a commanding scale.

There were five of them – Mrs Mary, Mrs Betty, Mrs Sally, Mrs Hannah, Mrs Patty – and though I have often encountered them in old letters and read long praises of their gaiety and goodness, they have never seemed the least alive. Three sisters one can visualize, but who can get any conception of five – of old-maidism triumphant and militant, raised from the domestic to the conventual? (Had Selina Mills kept faith, there would have been six.) Five, all attaining the age of seventy, all lively, hospitable, and jabbering, all suppressing the Slave Trade and elevating the poor. Mrs Hannah, thanks to her London flutters, was the best known, but shrewd observers thought Mrs Patty the more formidable, and a letter of hers, presently to be quoted, confirms them. But oh, the schools and the hostile farmers! Oh, the hostile curates and the appeals to the Bishop of Bath and Wells! Lachrymose epistles, stilted diaries ('Lord, look upon Cheddar, suffer not the work begun there to fail,' etc.). Abundance of strawberries and cream in the house. What can it have been like? It only becomes real to me in this little squirrel picture, painted when the sands were running out. Something faint and delicate emerges, the books rise to the ceiling, but the trees stir in the garden. The lovely provincialism of England takes shape, detaches itself from our suburbanism, smiles, says, 'I like my books, I like my garden, I like elevating the lower orders,' and manages not to be absurd. Presently the old mistress will ring a bell, Louisa will fail to answer it, there will be horror, disillusionment, flight, the Industrial Revolution, Tolstoy, Walt Whitman, Mr and Mrs Sidney Webb. But the glass is unshattered for the moment, and though all it mirrors is temporary, yet there exist in its depths gleams independent of fashion or creed.

Surely she had charm, and her sisters some share in it also. Otherwise how explain the power they exercised from the depths of Somersetshire? And perhaps there is some truth in our family tradition which declares that Hannah's letters were altered by her editor, William Roberts, after her death, and that posterity will consequently never know the nature of her attraction.

She calls Sir Thomas Acland in one of her notes to me (writes her god-daughter) 'the recreant Knight of Devonshire', which Roberts, thinking uncivil, I suppose, has altered into 'the excellent and estimable Sir T. Acland', two words that playful woman never used in her life. Somewhere else she began to me, 'When I think of you I am gladerer and gladerer and gladerer,' which he, thinking bad English, has done into 'I am very glad.' Now if such an oaf as that will write a book, at least he should be honest.

It is on the labours of the oaf that subsequent editors depend.

Her piety, unlike her charm, can be documented. It centred round Sunday. The Protestant time-complex (so much more teasing than the Catholic complex of place) had her in its grip. Recurring as it does once in every seven days, Sunday ended by making an enormous impression on her, and drove her into some very strange corners, for she was fond of pleasure and fun.

Going to the opera, like getting drunk, is a sin that carries its own punishment with it, and that a very severe one (she writes in her youth). Thank my dear Doctor Stonehouse for his kind and seasonable admonition on my last Sunday's engagement at Mrs Montagu's. Conscience had done its office before; nay, was busy at the time; and if it did not dash the cup of pleasure to the ground, infused at least a tincture of wormwood into it. I *did* think of the alarming call: 'What doest thou here, Elijah?' and I thought of it tonight at the opera.

Sunday night

Perhaps you will say I ought to have thought of it again today, when I tell you I have dined abroad; but it is a day I reflect on without those uneasy sensations one has when one is conscious it has been spent in trifling company. I have been at Mrs Boscawen's.

In her later life she wished to dine out less, became intimate with the Clapham Sect, and ended by thinking nearly everything sinful: 'The word Trinity, you know, means three. I once lived in a street called Trinity Street. I do think it very wrong to give such sacred names to common things.' And 'He who is taught arithmetic on a Sunday when a boy, will, when a man, open his shop on a Sunday.' For my own part I prefer her like this. She gained nothing by being broadminded; what is the point of just being able to tolerate Gibbon? She is more herself in the country, shocked and busy, and surrounded by her sisters.

As to her work, it was good, if education is good. She taught the poor to read and wash, observe Sunday, and honour the King, and before her day no one had taught them anything. They had taught themselves. Her desire to meddle in their affairs was mixed with genuine pity and affection, and in some ways she came nearer to them than do those who approach them with respect. Unless her pupils were farmers' sons she did not allow them to write, and she was horrified at the suggestion they should acquire history or science, while the suggestion that she had anything to learn from them would have evoked the French Revolution in her mind. Nevertheless, 'If I know a little of anything in this world it is about the poor.' She shared their sentimentality, and that love of anniversaries and funerals which supplies the absence of Art, and though she checked the vice which was their chief solace, she was not wild or stupid about it; she could even accept help from 'a woman of loose morals but good natural sense, who became our friend sooner than some of the decent and the formal'. If the destruction of instinct and the creation of an interest in the outside world are good things, then her work must be praised, for she effected the beginnings of both. Around her house for a radius of many miles the faint glimmer of education spread – samplers and alphabets, the sparks of our present conflagration. The farmers, wiser than she, foresaw that in time it would be impossible to find a 'boy to plough or a wench to dress a shoulder of mutton', and that the evil old days might come back when the monks had preached Christianity from the top of Glastonbury Tor.

The funeral of Mrs Baber, not in itself a historical landmark, may help us to realize the sisters' outlook. Mrs Baber died in August, 1795. She was one of the teachers whom they engaged to help them in their schools. Mrs Baber did her duty for many years, then she died, and rather fortunately Hannah was away at the time. Patty takes up the pen, and produces one of the great masterpieces of macabre literature. The lid has been removed and she lets herself boil over. 'I took my letter yesterday to finish it at Cheddar, but alas! heavy grief and agitation render it almost impossible for me to write another word.' It is a promising beginning: no short letter ever started with such a phrase. Images pour from her at once – the black dresses, the little handkerchiefs through which the tears drip on to the earth.

When the procession moved off, Mr Boak, who was so good as to come to the very house, preceded the corpse, with his hatband and gown on, which, as being unusual, added somewhat to the scene; then the body; then her sister and myself as chief mourners: a presumptuous title amidst such a weeping multitude; then the gentry, two and two; next her children, near two hundred: then all the parish in the same order: and, though the stones were rugged, you did not hear one single footstep.

When we came to the outer gate of the churchyard, where all the people used to pay their duty to her by bows and courtesies, we were obliged to wait for Mr Boak to go in and get his surplice on, to receive the corpse with the usual texts. This was almost too much for every creature, and Mr Boak's voice was nearly lost; when he came to 'I know that my Redeemer liveth,' he could scarcely utter it; but to feel it was a better thing. On our entrance into the church, the little remaining sight we had left discovered to us that it was almost full. How we were to be disposed of I could not tell. I took my old seat with the children, and close to her place. Mr Boak gave us a discourse of thirty-five minutes, entirely upon the subject. They feared at one time Mr Gilling must have been taken out. If you could for a moment doubt my account, I would add that the undertaker from Bristol wept like a child, and confessed that, without emolument, it was worth going a hundred miles to see such a sight.

Patty goes on from height to height:

I forgot to mention, the children sobbed a suitable hymn over the grave. I said a great deal to them afterwards, and wrung their little hearts; for I knew but too well that the world and young blood would make an excellent sponge to wipe out, full soon, the awful lessons of that day; as we have not that exalted opinion of the dignity of human nature that some gentlemen and ladies have. I promised to go next Sunday to open the school if I am able. I think I shall go on horseback.

Then back again to her prey. She had longed to cry out and speak, 'but I recollected that I had heard somewhere a woman must not speak in the church. Oh had she been interred in the churchyard, a messenger from Mr Pitt should not have restrained me.' And then silence. We hear no more of Mrs Baber, and not much of the emotions that must for years have racked and sustained the sisterhood. No wonder they were suspected of 'enthusiasm'. The line that divided them from Joanna Southcott or Elspeth Buchan was not too clearly drawn.

Let us take one more peep at them, then lower for ever those venetian blinds. They are all together now, and with them is a younger virgin, Miss Selina Mills. Zachary Macaulay arrives to say good-bye: he is off to free some slaves in Sierra Leone. He wants to see the five Miss Mores, but he does want to see Miss Mills also. Hannah thinks this last wish undesirable, for Patty is passionately devoted to Miss Mills, and the harmony and usefulness of the house must not be disturbed. She makes excuses for the girl's absence, and when he inquires if his affection is returned, she says 'No,' telling a lie. But as he went downstairs he heard sobs from a secluded room, dashed in, and his Selina fell into his arms. There was a terrible scene, in the course of which the young man expressed his surprise 'that those women who possessed the greatest share of intrinsic worth did not seem to possess that degree of estimation in the eyes of men which they merited.' He could have 'bitten out his tongue with vexation' for making such a remark, still he managed to make it, and it was long before he and his bride were forgiven. In after years the offspring of their union, little Tom Macaulay, visited Barley Wood and recited *all* "Palestine" while we breakfasted'. Thus did time make amends, thus do the generations touch, and old Hannah, now sisterless and very gentle, observed that — But enough, enough. Release the squirrel, for he is also one of God's creatures. Cover up the chairs.

[1928]

BATTERSEA RISE

BATTERSEA RISE! What a thrill the name gives me in the publisher's list! Is it just a fancy title, or can it really be the house which once belonged to my family? It really is the house, and Miss Pym, the writer of the book before me, is the great-grandchild, as I am, of Henry Thornton the elder. And did I ever go to the house in the early eighties, led by some cousin in my peacock-blue velvet suit? I seem dimly to remember an enormous and heavily varnished globe. However, Miss Pym, who knows the furniture so well, mentions maps on rollers, not a globe, so perhaps I was never taken there. Anyhow here is the house, evoked unexpectedly, and with sympathy, and perhaps for the last time. Battersea Rise? The name can mean nothing to the post-war generation, and may even sound faintly funny.

It was originally a small Queen Anne building, standing at the edge of that very wild tract, Clapham Common. In 1792 our great-grandfather Henry Thornton bought and enlarged it and its great feature was a library designed by his friend William Pitt. In this library the evangelicals and philanthropists of the Clapham Sect would meet – William Wilberforce, James Stephen, Zachary Macaulay, Thomas Babington, Charles Grant, etc., joined on occasion by Mrs Hannah More from Somerset. Thornton was of Yorkshire stock, but his family had lived in the district for two generations. They were business people; his grandfather and brother had been governors of the Bank of England, his father a merchant in the Russia trade, and he himself was a partner in the bank now known as Williams Deacon. He was for over thirty years M.P. for Southwark, and no doubt he found the house convenient, because he could easily drive up to Westminster. This early period of its history is the best known. Riches, evangelical piety, genuine goodness, narrowness, complacency, integrity, censoriousness, clannishness, and a noble public spirit managed to flourish together in its ample bosom without mutual discomfort. No dancing and no cards; but heaps of food. Constant self-examination; but it was constant rather than painful. Lord Crewe, who writes a foreword to Miss Pym's book, rightly compares the Thornton set to the Quakers, but they were less attractive than the Quakers in that they never deviate into mysticism. Solidly religious, they give one the impression of having no sense whatever of the unseen. That they had no sense of art goes without saying, nor were they interested in literature unless it was of an intellectual or formative character. Miss Pym, like myself, is out of touch with them, though she goes further than I can when she quizzes them for suppressing the slave trade. Surely that was a great work, and a source for family pride so long as we are a family. Her view of them is perhaps coloured by non-Thornton influences, and when she generalizes about them it is in the following strain:

Their manners were perfect, so that they would often appear to give in, but to those people who knew them well it was evident that the acquiescence was only seeming and a concession to good manners which they rightly held in high esteem.

Not so however when their loyalty was really aroused and when they thought that matters had gone too far. Then their caustic tongue would give vent, lashed by the fact that something had been hurt or neglected, and in ominously quiet tones they would ask the why and wherefore of the question, until their pitiless logic would split into pieces whatever excuses the unfortunate offender had to offer and reduce him to the frame of mind which they considered should be his. . . . Nothing escaped their lightning intelligence, and be it some individual who was trying to make himself out grander than he was; some sycophant whose intentions were too marked; some would-be Christian whose tenets did not fit in with his actions – they were down on such frailty like a knife, and in one caustic and witty sentence would lay bare the truth which such pains had been taken to hide, and destroy for ever the aspirations which had started out so grandly.

No, it could not have been an easy family to marry into. There are stories of one poor little bride bursting into tears and of another saying thoughtfully, 'If there was a spot upon the glorious Sun himself, the Thorntons would notice it.'

Henry Thornton, after a few years of bachelor occupation with Wilberforce, married a Yorkshire girl and quickly filled Battersea Rise with children, and then, in the second decade of the nineteenth century, and within a year of one another, he and his wife both died. There follows a gracious interlude, of which Miss Pym does not speak. The young guardian of the children, Sir Robert Inglis, Tory member for Oxford, comes into residence with his wife, and rules over the six girls and the three boys with urbanity and charm. Battersea Rise becomes youthful, though not frivolous. Most of the tales I have heard of it date from this Inglis regency, rather than from more recent years, and one gets an increasing sense of the garden, a garden as big as a park, and containing a tulip tree which, the children believed, would have been cut down by Napoleon had he succeeded in invading England. The interlude ends in 1833, when Henry Thornton the younger (Miss Pym's grandfather) marries in his turn. The Inglises retired to their own estate in Bedfordshire, the brothers and sisters gradually dispersed, though they kept the Clapham connexion, and one of the sisters, Marianne, only moved to the other side of the Common, 'where I can hear the sound of the Battersea Rise dinner bell.' In those big easy houses of the past, with their abundance of servants, and their governesses who had to use the back staircase, there was not the fight for privacy in which we now are all involved. Relatives could live together without running into each other, and perhaps there never was a moment in the hundred years of Battersea Rise when every aunt and sister definitely cleared out.

The younger Henry Thornton inherited his father's banking capacity. The money continued to come down from London, London itself crept nearer, and he drove up every day to the City in a spider-like gig, wearing a stove-pipe hat. I should like at this point to quote not from Miss Pym's book but from some manuscript recollections of my own aunt's, the late Miss L. M. Forster. No doubt I am partial, but my aunt's words seem to me to have much beauty, and to call up a lovely picture of that lost house and garden – lost, if the vision of a child had not preserved it.

I doubt if I was three years old, for we walked about the house at a very early age, and what I remember is being carried into the library at Battersea Rise one cold morning, and being put down by the glass door to watch the men rolling great balls of snow on the lawn and leaving green paths behind them as they went. It was a most fascinating sight and I stood entranced, balancing myself with outspread hands on the glass, and I remember a feeling of acute disappointment, and of being baulked, when someone came behind me and gently took my hands from the window, saying I should get them too cold if I kept them there. I obeyed, but felt the men and the great snowballs were no longer so close to me as before. I have no doubt that my parents were in the group of people breakfasting at the round table in the Library, and I remember the pleasant smell of coffee and toast when I was carried to the window, but I do not know in whose arms I was borne, nor which aunt made me take my hands off the window panes, but I feel sure it was not my mother. I believe I should have said 'need I?' to her, and that her sympathy would have set me free to stand as I liked. The wide lawn and snow-covered trees glittering in the sun with the men plodding steadily on, rolling the great snowballs before them, is the very first of many beautiful landscapes that hang like pictures in my memory.

The date to which this passage refers is about 1842. My aunt goes on to give a pleasant and fantastic account of her uncle Henry, her host: 'He said that when he was little he had been told he must never play with fire or he should get burnt, but now he was a man he knew better, and would show us he could play with fire nicely, and not get burnt at all. He lit a good sized piece of newspaper at the fire, put it all blazing on his leather chair, and sat down on it, to our delight and horror.' On such scenes, at times, could the Hoppner portrait of the first Henry and the architecture of William Pitt look down.

The second Henry died in 1881, but his widow continued to live at Battersea Rise after his death. One of their daughters had married Miss Pym's father, the other had married a cousin, Percy Thornton. Percy was for many years conservative member for Clapham, and the opponent of John Burns, so modern do we now become; he was also an eminent cricketer. The house continued its tradition of sobriety and solidity, though the zeal of its early years did not revive. London came nearer and nearer. Clapham, once infested by

highwaymen, turned first into a pleasant and then into an unpleasant suburb. The house faced the road and the coming on-
slaught, but its garden behind retained the illusion of untouched
country. The tulip tree grew higher, the Japanese Anemones
and St John's Wort increased, the rabbits and other pets multiplied, the books stood unaltered and unopened in the library,
the maids still whitened the white squares and avoided the
black squares of the tesselated pavement in the hall. This is the
house through which Miss Pym strays, half-sentimental, half-
amused, wholly affectionate. She lingers with the servants of
the moment, begins to catalogue the furniture, breaks off to
walk through the greenhouses or to have a hit at Hannah
More. And as she reminisces, the last act opens, the old generation passes, and in 1907 Battersea Rise completely disappears.
There was an attempt to preserve it – I remember sending a
small contribution, which was honourably returned – but not
enough people cared, and indeed it has neither played a leading part in national life, nor has it produced any outstanding
individual. It was just the abode of an unusually upright and
intelligent middle-class family. The whole organism seems to
have functioned to the very end – the greenhouses, the special
cows, the maps on rollers, the Nankeen Rooms, the gloxinias,
the large vase into which they were stuck, the sofa under
whose weight two footmen staggered on to the lawn. London
knocked and everything vanished – vanished absolutely, and
has left no ghost behind, for the Thorntons do not approve of
ghosts.

[1934]

PART IV

THE EAST

SALUTE TO THE ORIENT!

I

SALUTE to the Orient! Given at Port Said presumably, where the statue of M. de Lesseps points to the Suez Canal with one hand and waves in the other a heavy bunch of large stone sausages. '*Me voici!*' he gesticulates, adding '*Le voilà*' as an afterthought. Voilà Egypt and Africa to the right, Syria and Asia to the left, while in front of M. de Lesseps is the sausages' outcome, the narrow trough that he has contrived across the sands to the Red Sea. It leads rather too far, that trough, to the mouths of the Indus and the Ganges, unmanageable streams. Nearer Port Said lie trouble and interest enough, skies that are not quite tropic, religions that are just comprehensible, people who grade into the unknown steeply, yet who sometimes recall European friends.

Prayers to be offered up after saluting the Orient. Numerous prayers.

May I never resemble M. de Lesseps in the first place; may no achievement upon an imposing scale be mine, no statistics, philanthropy, coordination, or uplift. Good deeds, but scattered deeds, that shall be remembered for a few years only, like a wayward tomb. Oh, deliver my soul from efficiency! When obstacles cease to occur in my plans, when I always get the utmost out of Orientals, it will be the surest proof that I have lost the East. – A prayer against impropriety may follow – against hashish, almées, odalisques, the cancan; coupled with a prayer against propriety, which is more difficult to frame. Beware of impeccable introduction. Seek not that which is best in native society, for it leads to mutual log-rolling,

275

not to the best. 'Sons of the Desert, I too am a gentleman. All hail!' This will not do at all. – Then there is the prayer against cynicism which if a man forget he shall be damned, shall not even notice the sunlight in time, or that the sea is dark blue and the sky light blue, or that there are kites in Cairo and none in Alexandria. So when the old residents say to me, as they will, 'There is no such country as the Orient, there is only Dagoland': I must reply to them: 'You may be right, but I must gain my own disillusionment, not adopt yours; you know much, I nothing, yet I cannot learn from you.' Oh, reject the bitter tradition of mistrust that is served to the new-comer with his first cocktail, reject the little hints that the Club provides, so helpful in detail, so harmful in bulk! In India the tradition has lasted too long, the bitterness is irremediable, the hints have usurped the whole of speech. But in this nearer East there is still hope. Cynicism has not yet won, and I may help to defeat it. There's a nobler literature anyhow; Kinglake, Morier, Doughty, Blunt, Lucie Duff-Gordon discovered more than Dagoland: they found gravity and mirth here, also health, friendship, peace. . . . Prayers against timidity.

The above prayers are all negative, dangers to avoid, fears to overcome. They are clinched by a prayer which is positive and which seems their contradiction: a prayer for dignity and impressiveness. The perfect traveller whom we are building up is a charming creature, with every advantage of heart and head, but he is diffident, and diffidence will not succeed in the East. Unless I have a touch of the regal about me, a glint of outward armour, my exquisite qualities will be wasted, my tact and insight ignored. The East is a bit of a snob, in fact. It does require its sympathizers to seem great as well as to be good, and I must do my best to oblige it in this little matter; so may I be mistaken for a king!

Moreover, it is desirable to be young. But this, alas! cannot be phrased as a prayer. 'God,' says a cruel Egyptian proverb, 'has given earrings to those who have no ears,' and few elderly travellers have escaped this irony of Allah's. They have letters of introduction and facilities, but not ears in any useful sense, and the jewels that they bring back are 'I am much struck with the alterations in Bethlehem – not to say improvements, since my previous visit in 1885,' or 'representative institutions should be introduced into the Oasis of Siwa', or 'after an interesting conversation with the Mufti, in which Henry acted as interpreter, Lucy and I proceeded to inspect the so-called tomb of Potiphar's wife.' Elderly travellers don't write *Eothen*. It is hard to be generous and direct after thirty, even when the desire to be so remains, and even in England. And it is harder in the East. Prejudices or ideals (they amount to the same under a vertical sun) will arise in the mind and distort the horizon and slop pieces of sky into the sand. Only in youth or through memories of youth, only in the joyous light of the morning, can the lines of the Oriental landscape be seen, and the salutation accomplished.

2

We had better start properly in a dahabiyeh – that 'trip in a dahabiyeh as far as Biskra' which Mr Max Beerbohm so commends to lady novelists, and which has so often been taken by Mr Robert Hichens. You know what it is like: how the song of the Nubian boatmen mingles with the cry of the muezzin on his passing minaret and the aromatic wind that blows from the Sahara where horsemen in their white burnouses are silently riding towards the Nile to intercept the dahabiyeh with the connivance of Lady Concannon, who, the picture of aristocratic beauty, but with dark rings under her eyes that betray that sinister vigil in the Temple of Pasht, is now all animation to the doting Sir Ambrose, and is pointing out to him a flight of scarlet flamingoes, whom the song of the muezzin has disturbed so that they circle higher and higher into the evening sky until their glory is one with the glory of the Moab hills. It is a superb trip as far as style goes, but, oh, the expense! We cannot stir in such an East without a *maître d'hôtel*. We must attempt something on cheaper lines, even if it means parting with Lady Concannon.

So here is another journey and sunset, both deplorably cheap; we are only in a third-class carriage now in the Egyptian delta, squashed between country folk and joining in their talk.

To avoid their gaze, which troubled him, he looked out of the window, and saw the suburbs of the town slip by and the cultivated plain appear, stretching away to a line of low hills, the colour of a lion's back, the desert frontier. Sakeihs and clumps of palm-trees, with here and there a cake of mud-built hovels, stood forth like islands. The fields were full of life: men and women ploughing or reaping green clover; children herding grey, unwieldy buffaloes, brown sheep, or munching camels. Along the dyke moved a scarce inter-mitted procession of country people, of camels, oxen, mules, but chiefly asses, in clouds of dust made warm by the declining sun. Shocked by the inelegance of the rustic scene, Mabruk Effendi tried to read.

'Camels, oxen, mules, but chiefly asses.' This is neither great writing nor a great landscape, but – *Le voilà*! We can greet it, for it is true, and so is the psychology of Mabruk Effendi. If we place such a passage against any products of the dahabiyeh school we shall learn the difference between the real East, however quiet its tone, and the faked East, which is often sumptuous and skilful, but which exists to be the background of some European adultery. The faking began long ago. Cleo-patra was the original excuse, and the Emperor Augustus (wanting to keep the Egyptian corn-trade in his own hands) pretended that the country would corrupt his pure-hearted Romans, and forbade them to land without a permit. It is a long cry from Virgil to Mr Hichens, but the germs of the exotic fallacy may be found in the eighth book of the *Aeneid*. Adultery in the East is no more universal than the mummies with which writers of the dahabiyeh school entwine it. Cancel it off against sin in England, and pass on.

The above quotation is from *The Children of the Nile*, by Marmaduke Pickthall, a writer of much merit who has not yet come into his own. He is the only contemporary English novelist who understands the nearer East, nor is he challenged outside England except by the isolated masterpiece of MM. Adès and Josipovici. He has written novels about England also, and their badness is instructive: he appears to be one of those rare writers who only feel at home when they are abroad. As a pose such an attitude is common, but can easily be detected by the scorn with which the poser always treats tourists, Oriental Christians, and Levantines generally; they are on his nerves, because they remind him of the civilization to which he really belongs; unadulterated Islam will alone suit him, and he returns to Paris or London to say so. Pierre Loti and Claude Farrère both provide examples of such snobbery; the latter's *L'homme qui assassina* pretends to interpret Stamboul, but never ceases nagging at Pera. Whereas Mr Pickthall is much too serious to be scornful; though Islam is indeed his spiritual home, his most charming novel is about an Oriental Christian, and his most ambitious novel about a Moslem of the bad type, a cruel and treacherous swaggerer. He does not sentimentalize about the East, because he is part of it, and only incidentally does his passionate love shine out. In the preface to *Oriental Encounters* he hints at the youthful experiences that have served his art so well. He reached Port Said reputably enough, but in Palestine he delayed presenting his introductions, and fell in with 'one of the most famous jokers in all Syria' who took him in hand and taught him to eat and meet whatever came along.

I was amazed at the immense relief I found in such a life. In all my previous years I had not seen happy people. These were happy. . . . Class distinctions, as we understand them, were not. Everybody talked to everybody. With inequality they had a true fraternity. People complained that they were badly governed, which only meant that they were left to their devices save on great occasions. . . . I had a vision of the tortured peoples of the earth impelled by their own miseries to desolate the happy peoples, a vision which grew clearer in the after years. But in that easy-going Eastern life there is a power of resistance, as everybody knows who tries to change it, which may yet defeat the hosts of joyless misery.

This is the creed of Wilfred Blunt, though he has been too much of the grand seigneur to live down to it. The youthful Marmaduke did not refrain, and by the time he presented his introductions he was himself unpresentable 'in semi-native garb and with a love for Arabs which, I was made to understand, was hardly decent. My native friends were objects of suspicion. I was told that they were undesirable, and, when I stood up for them, was soon put down with the retort that I was very young.' For a time he tried to lead a double life, then broke loose entirely, and literature has gained. As soon as we open his cheerful pages, the western world vanishes without a malediction, like night at the opening of day. We sell carpets at Damascus or visit Tantah fair with no sense of strangeness; it seems our natural life, and when our compatriots do stray across the scene they seem quaint and remote, just as they must seem to an Oriental. So completely does the writer capture the reader that it is the West not the East that has to be explained. Here, for instance, come two queer afrits; let us survey them through the eyes of Said the fisherman.

One of these, whose face had somewhat the colour of a pomegranate flower, insisted on grasping Said's hand and shaking it, which is a manner of friendly greeting with the Franks. He laughed heartily with his mouth open, staring into Said's face with stupid blue eyes. His companion, who kept his face – pink and white like a painted woman's – carefully shaded by a very broad-brimmed hat, held a little aloof, but laughed heartily too. The moustache of this latter was yellow like straw.

And here is an article of mysterious purport and of high artistry, possibly the work of jinns.

Said fell to examining its framework, sitting on his heels and exclaiming 'Ma sh'Allah!' under his breath. It was almost like a table standing on six iron legs; but four of the legs reached above it as well as below, and each was crowned by a little knob like an orange, of some burnished material he took for gold. A wonderful thing! It was long ere he could tear himself away from the marvel.

Yet it is only a bed, such as we may see in the Tottenham Court Road, and the afrit with a face like a pomegranate flower was only you or I. The angle of vision remains steady, in book after book, and not until *Veiled Women* is there a hint of fatigue. The vision embraces more than trivialities: it can achieve a full-length portrait. How true, for example, is the psychology of the young Englishman in *The Valley of the Kings*, but how strange, because we see him through the eyes of Iskender, his Syrian follower! We endorse and yet we are amazed. This is the story: Iskender is a nobody, a Mission waif, who receives some politeness from the English tourist, and in return gives his heart, his fortune, and all that he can command in this world and the next with the exception of verbal accuracy. Pleased and amused with the alliance, the Englishman rejects the advice of the Old Residents, who duly warn him that no Oriental can be trusted, and he goes far into the desert with Iskender to find some gold. There is no gold. Iskender only dreamt of it, and worked the dream into a reality to pleasure his beloved master. But the Englishman does not know this, nor does Iskender, because while romancing about the gold he has come to believe that it exists. Their tour is delightful, but when they arrive at the Valley of the Kings, in whose gorge the treasure should be seen, the country is as flat as a pancake. 'Are you a liar?' inquires the Englishman in cold and terrible tones. Iskender weeps. Give him a few moments, he pleads, and the gold will come; and in a few moments a troop of Bedouin ride out of the hills and take the pair prisoner. The Englishman understands everything now . . . treachery . . . the Old Residents were right . . . and because he feels a fool he is transformed into a fiend. After much misery and muddle the captives return to civilization, the Englishman ill, Iskender distraught with grief, and worsening his position each time he tries to explain it. The West is to blame, we feel; why cannot the Englishman see what has happened? He does half see it, but he is ill and angry, he is bored, and he abandons his Salute to the Orient before it has been completed.

Oh, yes, I suppose I forgive you, and all that! Only I don't want to speak to you or see your face. You've got to be a kind of nightmare to me. I daresay I misjudged you; I don't pretend to understand you; in some ways you behaved quite well and honestly. Only I can't endure the sight of your face, the sound of your confounded voice. Get out, I tell you!

These words might serve as the epitaph of much European sentiment towards the East. Were they nearly Mr Pickthall's own epitaph? Did he not almost abandon Iskender and all that he signifies, and return to efficiency and cocktails? The Westerner is on his trial when the Oriental whom he has trusted lies to him. 'A lie is the limit,' he may think, and if he thinks it is, it is, and he had better turn back as soon as he sees the statue of M. de Lesseps at Port Said. Only he can go on who believes that there are different kinds of lies, and that those that are told in order to please a friend must be pardoned, however disastrous their consequences, and though their number be seventy times seven. *The Valley of the Kings* is written jokingly, but it is profound, and it will serve as a pocket Bible as far south as India.

3

But it will interpret only half the population. As if there were not puzzles enough, the women must needs come in, or rather fail to do so, and introduce problems that would vanish if they could be seen or talked about freely. They are present in a vague sort of way in the fields and railway stations. But what is going on inside that lump of dusty black cloth, that carriage whose shutters suggest that a commercial traveller lurks cocooned, that other part of the house? We have much information, from the Arabian Nights onward, but it arrives in so literary a condition that to me it never seems very real, and the Harem presents itself less as a mystery than an emptiness. It seems the more unreal because the tiny glimpses I have had of domestic arrangements in those parts were not the least according to recipe, and nothing that I have read has illuminated them. No doubt they were exceptional; one spends one's life among exceptions. But these other gentlemen, who write with such profusion and aplomb – what exactly were their glimpses? Those European ladies with heavy faces who enter the Harem to dispense morality and quinine – to what extent are they capable of reporting what they hear? When one visits a show interior, such as that of the House of Gamal-ud-din at Cairo, and sees the pretty little shelves, and peeps through the lattices into the street, one feels that the bird is indeed flown, and that by no possibility can its plumage or song be reconstructed. The abolition of slavery and the growth of industrialism are weakening the Harem system, so the problem may not be important practically. But the imagination abhors a void, and when the East is easiest it will suddenly reflect, 'But this is only half, and I cannot even remember that there is another half,' and will be humiliated.

Of the novels that have tried to fill the void by far the most convincing is *Le Livre de Goha le Simple*. The joint authors, Albert Adès and Albert Josipovici, are Egyptian – one of them a Cairene Jew – and they have produced a book that is certainly beautiful and possibly great. '*Je n'ai compris l'Orient, je ne l'ai vécu que le jour où j'ai lu Goha le Simple*,' writes Octave Mirbeau in his Preface, and, though some of us will suspect information that we cannot test, we can endorse the vitality. The authors plunge us into the private life of eighteenth-century Cairo without explanation or apology and we accept it as we accept the life of *Barchester Towers* or *Kipps*. It seems perfectly natural to consort with eunuchs and negresses, to attend an old Sheikh's lecture in El Azhar, to watch his young wife deceive him with their imbecile neighbour on the house-top; natural, too, that when the scandal starts it is the Sheikh not the imbecile nor the wife who is dishonoured. She is negligible as soon as she is unchaste, no one thinks of her. She is returned to her father, and he, as is natural, kills her, because her acts are a continuation of his own. And when the wanton has perished life moves forward as before, brilliant, solemn, unsentimental, and the objects that compose it present flat-coloured surfaces, and are devoid of their usual associations. It is a procession not known to the West, and proceeding to no mystic goal, yet all humanity takes part in it, so that we behold, *sub specie orientis*, acts that we have idealized or obscured at home.

The extraordinary vividness of *Goha le Simple* is mainly due to the character-drawing. We approach a remote society and clime, through individuals whom we should notice anywhere. This is true of the Sheikh and his wives, and their household, but specially true of Goha himself, whose insanity is personal and whose distortion of the universe coheres. He believes, for instance, that when a man dies he shrinks until he is the size of a baby and vanishes – a reasonable arrangement, though this planet has not adopted it. He never distinguishes the wife of the Sheikh from a granite statue of Isis that embraced him on Gezireh. His moods vary, but the errors that govern them are constant, and through them we salute an Orient which he infects, not with his madness but with his reality. The picture becomes complete in every particular. Because his state of mind is real the housetop where the lovers unite becomes indescribably beautiful, and the falling stars above the Mocattam Hills are really the blocks of fire that the angels are throwing on to the jinns lest they climb up into heaven.

A fine book; but it does not explain the women of the East. It announces them with the successful effrontery that only art can achieve. Verification is not possible, nor do we find it in two other novels, Pickthall's *Veiled Women* and *Les Désenchantées*, by Pierre Loti. They do not verify one another even, for the moral of the first is that women want to go into a Harem, and of the second that they want to come out.

The theme of *Veiled Women* is notable. Mary Smith, an English governess, is converted to Islam and marries a young Bey, a member of a distinguished Turco-Egyptian family. Gradually she is orientalized, a visit to Paris only hastening the process, and after reactions and sufferings we leave her trusted by her husband and respected by his concubines. Here are good opportunities, but the treatment is sketchy, and there are hints of propaganda. A book that recommends a Harem is bound to give an unconvincing picture. No doubt society would be simpler if the two sexes were also two distinct species, and Islam, which has favoured this doctrine in practice though never in so many words, has certainly avoided problems that distract the West. But the doctrine is nonsense biologically, and it is useless to preach it at this hour of the day when women are determined to be everything and go everywhere, even if they and civilization perish in the attempt.

This objection does not apply to *Les Désenchantées*, where the propaganda is reasonable, at all events at the first glance. But there are other objections. Pierre Loti is a sentimentalist who has voyaged hat in hand over the picturesque world. He has saluted Brittany and the Basque, India, Anam, Japan, the South Sea Islands, the whole of the North African coast from Morocco to Egypt, also the Syrian seaboard and the fringes of Asia Minor, paying particular attention to Constantinople, and from all these places he has brought back trophies. These trophies are of similar form, so far as they have any form. There is the homage of a great French artist for a misunderstood people, there are tears, there are cypresses or coco-nuts, and the genius of each country is apotheosized in an intrigue with one of its female inhabitants. *Les mariages de Loti se font partout*. The French do not tire of them, and a professor at the Sorbonne has described their author as '*le plus grand écrivain de notre génération*'. The English are less patient and grow disinclined to attend a function which is always on the same lines. *Les Désenchantées, roman des harems turcs contemporains* teaches us nothing that we did not learn from *Le Roman d'un Spahi*. Three Turkish ladies provide in this case the erotic motive. Immured in Stamboul, they are deeply versed in European philosophy and letters, and while they admire all the great writers, they naturally value '*le plus grand écrivain de notre génération*' most. Would that they could translate theory into practice, could live the life they only know in music and books, could in brief see him . . .! Moved by their appeal, he comes, and they risk death for the sake of his conversation. The story grows more refined and more diffuse on each page, until the great writer kisses the leading Turkish lady, but only once, but after death, but not on the lips. . . . *Les Désenchantées* annoys, because Loti has touched a real problem, and one wishes to see it handled decently. The psychology of a lady who lives in one civilization and is always reading and dreaming about another must be most interesting, but it will never be revealed by a professional amorist. Perhaps a woman novelist may one day tell us what does happen in the Harem, for Mr Pickthall and Loti leave us bewildered between them. But she must be a novelist, not a journalist or a missionary. Until she comes we must inflame ourselves at *Goha le Simple*, and wonder. And by the time she comes the Harem system may be only an historical curiosity.

4

For we cannot ignore the political situation – either the official influence of Europe or the unauthorized efforts of Bolshevism. We don't know yet what Bolshevism would like to do with the East, but it has reached Turkey and Persia, and it is bound to influence the social order. While all round the coast, supported by their respective fleets, are the Great Powers, solemnly competing for concessions and protectorates, as they have done for the last forty years. The situation would be comic if it did not threaten so much blood. Each Power still declares that she alone understands how to salute the Oriental, that he loves her and sees through the wiles of her rivals, and if properly supported will chase them into the sea. 'Johnny'd rather have us than anyone else' is the English version of this competition; on the lips of Pierre Loti it becomes '*La Mort de notre chère France en Orient.*' But the facts are otherwise, and brutally simple, Johnny'd like to see the death of the lot. The more an Oriental has been governed by any European nation the more does he hate that particular nation, and tend in consequence to romance over its rivals. He loveth best who knoweth least, in fact. At the moment of writing the Turks hate Germany and love France, the Syrians hate France and love England, the Egyptians hate England and love Italy and the United States, the Tripolitans hate Italy, but there is nothing stable in any of these emotions. They change rapidly, though governments pretend they will be eternal. There is no mysterious affinity, as official apologists pretend. Before long the partners, as at a country dance, will have shifted, and Tripoli may be loving Norway and hating Sweden. How it all will end politicians must decide; we who seek the truth are only concerned with politics when they deflect us from it. The individual in the East must succeed as an individual or he has failed. That is our lesson. If he relies upon the temporary popularity of his country he builds upon sand. It may clear his outlook if he remembers firstly the promises and secondly the performances of western governments in these parts. And that memory may inspire one prayer more: that the East may be delivered from Europe the known and from Russia the unknown, and may remain the East.

5

The House of Islam is written more seriously than the other novels of Mr Pickthall. In it he drops the frivolity which often disfigures him and which has hindered him from reaching certain audiences, and he dons a robe of grave beauty. The East isn't palm-trees and sunsets, or friendly rogues, or the Harem, or the cynical and discontented peoples, though it contains all these things. It is a spirit also, and though that spirit may not be the finest, we must attempt to define it, and *The House of Islam* may help.

The book opens with a prelude in Constantinople. Two Moslems, brothers, are returning to their native town in the Syrian desert. The elder seeks official advancement, the younger, the Sheikh Shems-ud-din, accompanies him in search of of peace. When the main story begins, years later, the elder brother has gone back to Constantinople, where he is rising to power amid subterfuges and intrigues, and where the son of

Shems-ud-din has joined him. But Shems-ud-din himself remains in the desert town, diminishing bloodshed and adding a minaret to the mosque. A daughter is all that is left to his old age. He loves her, and when she falls sick he is troubled more than is fitting with hopes of a cure. Although he will not allow her garment to be hung on the Magic Tree, he accepts an aid which is in essence as idolatrous: he journeys up to El Cuds, the city of the Prophet Jesus, in order to consult one of the infidel physicians who live there. A great company journeys with him, including the betrothed of his daughter and a friendly but lawless gang of Circassians. When he learns that his son chances to be a high official at El Cuds the news gladdens him, but the young man meets him furtively at the city gate and explains that open intercourse is undesirable; it would compromise him to be seen with nondescripts from the desert. Shems-ud-din acquiesces without humility and without bitterness; he recognizes his brother's teaching and the spirit of Constantinople. He acquiesces, too, when his daughter's betrothed, who has seen her wasted and ruined face for a moment, falls away, and prefers to enjoy himself among the Circassians. They are natural, these defections, though their result is to leave him alone. With great difficulty does he persuade a Frankish doctor to admit the girl; the hospital is intended for Jews only, and the doctor risks dismissal by his charitable act. The medical verdict is unfavourable; there never has been any hope, but Shems-ud-din cannot face this. Like an idolater who hangs rags on a tree, he clings to gaunt science and wearies God with prayers for his daughter's life, for her mere life irrespective of her happiness or beauty, and at last, in a nightmare, he sees precisely what it is for which he has been praying:

  . . . two wooden boxes united by a thin cord which writhed and twisted between them like a living worm. The tops of the boxes also seemed alive, for they rose and fell regularly, like the breast of a sleeper. He stared terror-stricken . . . realized the stupendous mockery of the hope, inspired by devils, which had led him on through sin after sin – for this.

Then as he glowered upon the fruit of evil the pulse of the barren life grew faint and fainter, the cord more languid in its twistings. . . .

And he awakes to learn with relief that she is dead. Besotted by love, he was asking for a twisting cord, a heaving box, for a hideous stirring of skin and bone. 'Man prays for evil as he prays for good, for man is without understanding.' The infidel science of the West has failed, and he buries his daughter calmly. But in his absence the hospital is attacked; the Circassians believe that the doctor has murdered the girl, and they murder the doorkeeper in revenge. Shems-ud-din is arrested with them and condemned to death. At this point the son intervenes. He can hold back no longer, though it is still shame rather than love that impels him. He telegraphs to his uncle, who is now Grand Vizier at Constantinople, and the miscarriage of justice is averted. But Shems-ud-din is beyond minding. He receives his son's repentance tenderly, because it is part of the Mercy of God, but with indifference, because he can no longer attach himself to any earthly creature. He goes back to his desert town and leads the life of a saint. Thither, after an interval, the son follows him, for his repentance is permanent. Hither, some day, wearied of honours and infamy, will his brother also follow him. They will dwell in the House of Islam instead of in the House of Strife, and they will meditate upon the littleness of man, all whose activities are but as a speck on the ocean of God's mercy, and whose schemes for power and for length of days are equally vain.

This solemn and beautiful book has indeed the effect of a gesture. It is an avowal of faith. 'Life is good,' runs its creed, 'but only good when it imitates the Divine Attributes. Life is not great, God alone is great.' To the West, attracted by the promises of science on the one hand and of Christianity on the other, it seems a meagre creed. We cannot translate Shems-ud-din into an Anglican man who retires to his country parish; the latter, though equally a saint, would develop differently, because to him God would be fundamentally Love. God is not Love in the East. He is Power, although Mercy may temper it. Of this power, in any solemn moment, the Oriental becomes conscious even if he be unorthodox, and it gives him a spiritual hardness that is often intimidating. People love one another as profoundly and as variously as elsewhere – with lust, passion, sentiment, sublimation; with abnegation even; but they do not believe that a Deity approves or transcends their love. To quote from *The Early Hours:*

> The goal of life is surely not communion with a fellow-creature. That search must end in disappointment always. The soul of every living man and woman is solitary from the cradle to the grave unless it finds, by service, that communion with Allah for which, in truth, it was created. When that is found it is at one with all the other servants of Allah, but not before.

An appendage of bodily life, Love could only be an appendage in Paradise.

So if we say of the Oriental, firstly, that personal relationship is most important to him, secondly, that it has no transcendental sanction, we shall come as near to a generalization as is safe, and then it will only be safe in the nearer East. Farther afield, in Persia and India, another idea, that of Union with God, becomes prominent, and the human outlook is altered accordingly. Neither Shems-ud-din nor the Sheikh in *Goha le Simple* sought that union, and the latter '*frissonna de peur quand il se surprit à admirer les mots pour lesquels Halladj fut brûlé vif.*' They do not seek to be God or even to see Him. Their meditation, though it has the intensity and aloofness of mysticism, never leads to abandonment of personality. The Self is precious, because God, who created it, is Himself a personality; the Lord gave and only the Lord can take away. And a jealous guarding of the Self is to be detected beneath all their behaviour even when they are most friendly or seem most humble.

But what is the use of generalizing? Based on a few memories and a few contemporary novels, what can the above remarks be worth? And even if the experience had been wide and the reading deep, what would the remarks have been worth? Syria isn't Egypt nor Turkey Arabia; what is true of the Moslem is only partly true of his Christian compatriot; classes vary, conditions alter; to greet the Orient is an agreeable exercise; but what good does it do, and who cares? Sound objections; yet the effort is desirable, partly because all who love the East ought to testify at the present moment, however great their ignorance, and partly because it recalls, scattered over so many classes and countries, one's Oriental friends.

[1923]

THE MOSQUE

MOST of us see our first mosque at Woking. As the train slackens a small bulbous building appears among the fir trees to the left, and perhaps someone in the railway carriage says, 'That's Oriental'. Our attitude is vague; and years afterwards, despite visits to the East, the vagueness remains. Whereas a Christian church or Greek temple wakens definite sentiments, a mosque seems indeterminate. We can recall its component parts and memorize it architecturally or can make a pretty picture of it against the blue sky, but its central spirit escapes. And before we grapple with such a book as the late Commendatore Rivoira's on Moslem Architecture it may be worth while to do what he would scarcely think of doing: to question our memories, and through them the mosque itself, and to listen to what it has to say.

'I was built,' comes the answer, 'in the first place at Medina where I was a courtyard, and if you would understand me today you must still think of me as a courtyard, decorated by the accidents of history. Attached to the Prophet's house, I was the area to which he proceeded when he would worship God, and where his companions joined him, summoned for this purpose by a cry from the top of my wall. I contained no ornament or shrine, nor was one part of me more holy than another. Near me was a well for ablution; in me was a fallen tree whereon the Prophet stood to preach; and against my north wall lay a stone to indicate the direction of Jerusalem, city of the prophets Abraham and Jesus. My inmates prayed northwards at first, but afterwards turned south, their aspiration being Mecca. Before long I was built at Mecca also, but (strange though this may sound) you should not think of Mecca if you would understand me, because there, contrary to my spirit, I enclosed a sacred object and became a shrine. Dismiss the Caaba with its illusion of a terrestrial goal. Recall the courtyard of Medina, construct upon its wall a tower for the crier, raise a pulpit upon its fallen tree, contrive from its well a lavatory or tank, and encloister the sides of the courtyard, in particular the side that indicates the direction for prayer. Then you will see me as I am today at Cairo, Mosque of Ibn Touloun.'

In the above reply the Mosque sets itself against a profound tendency of human nature – the tendency to think one place holier than another – and this is why it is rather a vague and unsympathetic object to a westerner, and why its own architects have tended to modify its arrangements. It does not fulfil what is to most of us the function of a religious building: the outward expression of an inward ecstasy. It embodies no crisis, leads up through no gradation of nave and choir, and employs no hierarchy of priests. Equality before God – so doubtfully proclaimed by Christianity – lies at the very root of Islam; and the mosque is essentially a courtyard for the Faithful to worship in, either in solitude or under due supervision. In the later centuries, under the influence of idolatrous surroundings, the original scheme was overlaid, and it is instructive to glance at the changes. The mosque that the Emperor Akbar built in 1560 for his new city near Agra is a good example. It has moved very far from the Medina model, and its air is almost that of a temple or church. The prayer niche, usurping the functions of an altar, has become the core of a vast and gorgeous building to which the eye and heart naturally turn, while the uncovered part of the courtyard sinks into the unimportance of a cathedral close and is dotted with tombs. When we leave the courtyard and pass through the 'west door' of the façade and through the smaller and darker apertures in the red sandstone beyond, we seem to near a sanctuary; and when the prayer niche at last appears and our eyes discern the ravishing but delicate colours that adorn its chamber, we have emotions appropriate to Canterbury or Chartres, and should not be surprised if priests arrived from the subordinate chapels on either hand, to mediate between the world and God. The emotion in such a mosque is religious, but scarcely Islamic; we do not experience it in the buildings of earlier date.

Since the edifice under consideration is a courtyard and not a shrine, and since the God whom it indicates was never incarnate and left no cradles, coats, handkerchiefs, or nails on earth to stimulate and complicate devotion, it follows that the sentiments felt for his mosque by a Moslem will differ from those which a Christian feels for his church. The Christian has a vague idea that God is inside the church, presumably near the east end. The Moslem, when his faith is pure, cherishes no such illusion, and, though he behaves in the sacred enclosure as tradition and propriety enjoin, attaches no sanctity to it beyond what is conferred by the presence of the devout. Such mystery as accrues is the work of men. A Tunisian who visited Cairo in the thirteenth century found the famous mosque of Amr there littered with dirt; 'nevertheless,' he adds, 'I experienced in it a soft and soothing influence without there being anything to look upon which was sufficient to account for it. Then I learned that this is a secret influence left there from the fact that the companions of the Prophet (may God accept them!) stood in its court while it was building.' He was conscious of an atmosphere which, though supernatural, was not divine; men had produced it. And whereas men may perfume some mosques, they may defile others; for example, the mosque which Aurangzebe built at Lahore upon the ground of his murdered brother Dara, and which is reckoned unfavourable for prayers. Legends such as these, though they lapse from the spirit of Medina do not oppose it. Islam, like Christianity, is troubled by the illogical and the idolatrous, but it has made a sterner fight against them. The Caaba, the worship of saints, the Mecca-position, do not succeed in obscuring the central truth: that there is no God but God, and that even Mohammed is but the Prophet of God; which truth, despite occasional compromises, is faithfully expressed in Moslem Architecture, and should be remembered by those who would understand it.

[1920]

WILFRID BLUNT

1. *The Earlier Diaries* (1888–1900)

WHICH side are you on, Gog or Magog? O solemn question. Behold the two worthies, each a little moth-eaten but still hale and trailing a venerable beard. Fine work can be done under either banner, but which is it to be? Choose. Gog stands for – well, you can see what he stands for, and Magog stands for opposition to Gog. So choose, and having chosen, stick, for such is the earthly destiny of man.

Hypnotized by the appeal, we choose. Sometimes we choose without thinking, sometimes sort our memories, prejudices, interests, and ideals into two heaps, call one Gog and the other Magog, and plump for the larger. In the first case our choice is known as instinctive, in the second as rational, but in either we are duly enrolled under one of the banners. It is seldom, very seldom, that a dreadful thing happens – an almost unmentionable scandal – and one of us refuses to choose at all, says: 'I don't understand,' or 'Dummies don't interest me,' and strolls away. He might, at all events, have the decency to keep away. But sometimes he will not even do that. He strolls back and begins interfering, just as if he had never forsworn his birthright. He sees what shouldn't be seen and says what shouldn't be said, he taps Magog's head and, lo! it sounds hollow; he slits Gog's breeches and out pours the bran. 'Go away,' everyone shrieks, but he won't go away. There is a flower he wants to pick, and a friend he wants to help irrespective of banners, and menaced by such an intruder Gog and Magog relinquish their hoary feud and make alliance. Here is the real enemy – the man who does not know how to take sides – and they agree that such a man shall never become powerful. He never does – giants can effect thus much. But he may be the salt of his age.

Wilfrid Blunt would never choose. He was drawn towards Liberalism through his hopes for Ireland and Egypt, but he did not really like it, and when it bowed to Jingo in the South African War he threw it over. He was drawn to Islam, and at one time thought of professing it, but his experiences with the Senussi led him to conclude: 'The less religion in the world perhaps, after all, the better.' Shortly after which he was saying prayers to St Winifred. All men exhibit such inconsistencies, but most of them are ashamed, which endears them to us: it was the misfortune of Blunt never to be ashamed. As he felt, so he acted. And incapable of cant himself, he was intolerant of it in others. He could not stand the insincerities that are customary between officials, he refused to make use of the face-saving apparatus that they so liberally provide and employ. This vexed them. Sir William Harcourt – to take an example – once remarked to him that perhaps one oughtn't to interfere with Cromer in Egypt since he 'seems to have his horses well in hand'. Blunt replied: 'I have no doubt he has, and is driving merrily, but even a timid passenger, when he finds the coach is going to Brighton when it ought to be going to York, may be excused for taking the reins. He will drive you merrily to annexation.' Harcourt was indeed that timid passenger, and the Egyptian coach has in our own day arrived at Brighton instead of York, and has even plunged beyond, to the verge of the sea. But it was useless saying so to Sir William. Deep in his heart he knew it, and deeper still he didn't care: he had the cynicism that seems inseparable from high office. Blunt only pricked the stuffing in him, and what was the use? A little bran trickled out, and that was all.

During the years that these diaries cover Blunt was the *enfant terrible* in politics, just as Samuel Butler was in art and literature. *Enfants terribles* of any ability are so rare that those of us who can stand them at all are apt to overrate them, and to assume that to be fresh and mischievous is to be great. Blunt wasn't great. One must make that reservation. He was sensitive, enthusiastic, and sincere, but he had not within him the fiery whirlwind that transcends a man's attitude, and sweeps him, whatever his opinions, into the region where acts and words become eternal. His life, like his poetry, lacked this supreme quality. It was – one speaks of it in the past tense, because he chooses thus to speak of it himself – it was rather the life of an English gentleman of genius, who ignored the conventions of his race and rank, but remained, in the best sense of the word, an amateur – a lover of intellect, generosity, liberty, and tradition, all lovable things, but alas! no more capable of dwelling in unity than are butterflies with fish. Blunt recognized the disunion without bitterness, as a gentleman would. His vision was aesthetic though his career was practical. He cared most about earthly grace, whatever form it took, and conceived even of heaven as a garden:

To be laid out to sleep in a garden, with running water near, and so to sleep for a hundred thousand years, then to be woke by a bird singing, and to call out to the person one loved best, 'Are you there?' and for her to answer, 'Yes, are you?' and so turn round and go to sleep again for another hundred thousand years.

The hope that the Creation may be a garden, wherein the nations and the worlds blossom sweetly each after its kind is the deepest he knows. An exquisite hope; but he who holds it cannot be classed with those who have seen the same Creation's flaming ramparts or have heard its inexpressive nuptial song. So much we must admit, whether our bias be for Blunt or against him.

Never was such a delightful book. One doesn't know where to begin. So much humour – not only the general ragging of Gog and Magog, but a charming good temper that flickers into all corners of life. Such knowledge of men, such opportunities of seeing them, and such power of describing them – Boulanger, Herbert Spencer, Louise Michel, Riaz Pasha, Queen Victoria, Oscar Wilde ('I never walk'), the Grand Mufti, the Comte de Paris, the Poet Laureate, the Sultan of Johore, Lord Cromer, Francis Thompson, Mr Asquith on his wedding day, Miss Margot Tennant on hers, pilgrims and ambassadors, cardinals and fellahin, Poles and Tunisians: all pass before us, and not as oddities but as recognizable human beings who continue to live after they have made the gesture that caught our eye. It is a wonderful gift, this of writing about one's fellow creatures as if they were alive; and so rare. The modern novelist, who while professing to create is generally cataloguing his personal likes and dislikes, may well envy this perennial stream where a comment occasionally splashes in but whose essence is the water of life. To make extracts is difficult. Perhaps the most brilliant sketch is that of the Grand Old Magog himself with the characteristic verdict 'I carried away the mixed impression I have had of him before, one of disappointment at finding less than I should have found to worship.' But it is rather long and not very respectful. Instead, take the following:

Morris is dead. . . . He is the most wonderful man I have ever known, unique in this, that he had no thought for any thing or person, including himself, but only for the work in hand. He was not selfish in the sense of seeking his own advantage or pleasure or comfort, but he was too much absorbed in his own thoughts to be either openly affectionate or actively kind. . . . He liked to talk to me because I knew how to talk to him, and our fence of words furbished his wit, but I doubt whether he would have crossed the street to speak with me. . . . Thus while all the world admired and respected him, I doubt whether he had many friends: they got too little in return to stimulate their affection. I should say half-a-dozen were all the friends he had. I do not count myself among the number, intimate as I was with him, and much as I loved him. It will be a great grief for Jenny, a great break-up for Janey, and a great loss for the world at large, for he really was our greatest man.

These sentences, though more striking might easily be found, illustrate the wealth of Blunt's mind. He had both feeling and detachment, qualities rarely conjoined, and so he could see far into the minds of others, and he had the power of selection, so that he can make us see too. He leaves a portrait gallery, invaluable for students and delightful for all.

To continue the eulogy. How wisely and how poetically he travelled! Sometimes with introductions to the great ones of the earth, sometimes – and then he was happiest – incognito. It was thus that he reached the Oasis of Siwah, and the chapter describing his arrest there by the Senussi is the most thrilling in the book. He broke his health travelling, but home remained, and how sensitive is he to a house, and, of course, to a garden!

My first twenty hours at Shekyh Obeyd were a dream of light-hearted happiness such as I do not remember since a child: It was a physical feeling of perfect pleasure, perfect health, and perfect powers of enjoyment without the least shadow of annoyance. . . . Everything on the way was a pleasure, even the new houses built at Koubbah and our little railway station, lovely and familiar in its palm grove. Inside the garden all was paradise. No misadventure this year of any kind, but a blooming look of extravagant growth, trees, crops, and flowers. The house so shut in with green that we can hardly any longer get a glimpse out into the desert, hardly even from the house top. Cows prosperous, mares in foal, every servant happy. Each year decides me more to spend the remnant of my days in the East, where old age is respected and its repose respectable.

So much for the amateur, the cultivated and travelled Englishman to whom Gog and Magog have no great objection. A word now on the man of affairs.

In this volume his main interest is Egypt. The failure of Arabi and the virtual renunciation of the French had brought England and the Khediviate face to face there – England being represented by Sir Evelyn Baring (Cromer) and the Khediviate by young Abbas II. Was England also to renounce? That was the question at issue. Was she to keep her promises and, having established order, to retire? We all know that she broke her promises and we are now experiencing the result. But in Blunt's day the tragedy was only beginning, and might still be averted. His first impressions of Cromer and of the Khedive were favourable. Later he saw that each in his way was going wrong – Cromer becoming the tool of the Imperialists, the Khedive degenerating into a shifty intriguer. Then came Omdurman, Fashoda, the mutilation of the Mahdi's body, the Boer War, and the final collapse of Gladstonian Liberalism. It is true that Blunt did not 'do' anything for Egypt – he was always, despite his smart connexions, quite without weight – but he tried to 'do', and the record of his effort is here. He also foretold the future – a melancholy accomplishment, and one that seems to be reserved for unimportant men. He knew that we were bound either to lose Egypt or to hold it as in July, 1919, mistrusted and detested by all its inhabitants.

I bid goodbye to the old century, may it rest in peace as it has lived in war. Of the new century I prophesy nothing except that it will see the decline of the British Empire. . . . It all seems a very little matter here in Egypt with the Pyramids watching us as they watched Joseph when, as a young man, four thousand years ago, perhaps in this very garden, he walked and gazed at the sunset behind them, wondering about the future just as I did this evening. And so, poor wicked nineteenth century, farewell!

The twentieth century, which can already teach the nine-teenth century so much, may smile at the concluding sentence. And it may retort that the British Empire has not yet declined. But it seems improbable that a rule which now rests avowedly upon force can endure for eighty-one years more. If its end ever comes and Egypt is granted 'full independence within the Federation of the Seven Seas', or whatever the face-saving phrase of the moment may be, then the protest of Blunt will be remembered and Gog and Magog, wagging their beards, will say: 'Ah, that Blunt was a great statesman. What use we would have made of him if only we had been alive at the time!' and will vote him a statue, Arab dress and all, to be executed by the dullest sculptor that money can command, and will wreathe these diaries with official laurel. He is a failure now: and only those who know actively or imaginatively what failure is will understand his book.

[1919]

2. *The Later Diaries* (1900–1914)

Wilfrid Blunt, among other remarkable qualities, had the power of alluring the East, and one can test his power by mentioning his name today to any educated Indian or Egyptian. It is not that the East always agrees with him: Egyptians often find him too pro-Turkish and Indians too anti-British. But it recognizes in him two qualities which it values – friendliness and kingliness; it discerns behind his desire to be intimate and kind the transfiguring background of the grand manner; and it has given him in return unrestricted enthusiasm and love. He lives in its unwritten chronicles as one of the few really noble Englishmen, as one who not only championed the weak, but championed them in the right way and upheld their dignity without compromising his own, who was religious without fanaticism and cultivated without disillusionment, who had the sense of the appropriate, who was impressed by coincidence and not averse to omens, who appreciated conversation and horses, and who yearly observed, among the amenities of his Sussex home, the anniversary of the bombardment of Alexandria. Traits such as these have endeared him to the Oriental heart, and in the most unexpected places – perhaps on a roof-top among the Patna bazaars – one may suddenly awake a eulogy upon him.

Let us leave the Oriental standpoint for a moment, and turn upon this romantic figure the cold and envious gaze of a fellow citizen. There still remains much to admire – unless, indeed, the gazer be an official, when he will be convulsed with official irritations. Wit, imagination, warmth of heart, courage, generosity, acuteness of judgement – one endorses all these, but on the adverse side must note touches of vanity and dilettantism, touches which an Oriental critic would palliate and probably overlook. The vanity is never obtrusive, yet it weakens the cumulative effect of his work; 'they neglected my advice with the result that . . .' There are too many entries of this type in the 'Diaries', and though it may be well to have directed the policy of Lord Randolph Churchill or anticipated the Monism of Häckel it is not well to be too conscious of such achievements. As for the dilettantism, it appears not so much in the variety of interests as in the quality of the philosophy; Blunt's views on the universe continually melt and waver, but undergo nothing that can be termed development, and though he occasionally draws up an imposing syllabus, it does but express the emotional attitude of the moment. So much by the way, and by way of distinguishing an Occidental admirer from an Oriental. Now one can get back into the cart.

All the characteristics that were so delightful in the first volume of his *Diaries* reappear in the second, though in soberer garb, owing to the advance of old age. The stage is narrower, the opportunities less, but the vivacity and sensitiveness remain, and there is added a tragic unity that was lacking before, for all the entries, so various and so dispersed, gradually flow together like little rills until they form the deathly torrent of the Great War. That war, according to Blunt's interpretation, is essentially Oriental. Germany is indeed the chief villain, but the chief victim is not Belgium but Islam. In the slow, agonizing prelude the Germans and French intrigue in Morocco, Cromer rivets English rule upon Egypt, Italy attacks Tripoli, England and Russia apportion Persia, the Balkan Confederacy nearly captures Constantinople: and Turkey, obliged to choose between two gangs of robbers, chooses the Teutonic. Then is the grim perversion of Calvary accomplished, and the followers of Christ, who have developed economic imperialism and scientific warfare, spoil the followers of Mohammed, who have developed neither and were hoping to

live the lives of their fathers. Blunt would not have dreaded a
purely European conflict, because it would only have shattered
the industrial civilization that he disliked and avoided, and
that, in his opinion, brings no happiness to men. His detachment is amazing. He dreaded a war because it must involve
Asia and Africa, and complete the enslavement of the conservative Oriental nations, whom he loved and who loved
him. It is an interesting conception and one to which his
temperament naturally inclines him. It is the conception not
only of an 'Easterner', but of a poet. Partly by achievement
and wholly by temperament Blunt is a poet, for whom graci-
ousness and beauty are the supreme good, and squalor the
supreme evil, and who yearns, like his dead allies the pre-
Raphaelites, for a world that shall be small and fruitful and
clean. He always tended to conceive of the world as a garden,
and now he sees its lilies and roses defiled beyond redemption,
and he feels that his own efforts have failed. His pessimism
is logical. We can only avoid it by supposing, with Walt
Whitman, that the world is not a garden, but an athlete who
learns while he suffers, and who will some day understand his
own passions and cleanse his limbs. That day is far off. But if
it ever dawns it will lighten not only the graceful nations of
the East, but the dull plebian places of Europe – factories,
mines, commercial offices, suburban drawing-rooms – and its
radiance will be stronger than a king's because the whole of
humanity will contribute to it.

Such is the main theme of the diaries: the approach of a
great war, recorded by a man who combines the acuteness of
a political observer with the vision of a poet. And the war itself
is seen as the last of a series of onslaughts that the West has
made upon the East, and as a squabble between two gangs of
robbers over their plunder. These points established, let us
proceed to the pleasures of quotation.

The volume is less brilliant in detail than its predecessor, for reasons already indicated: there is nothing, for instance, so mischievous and so complete as the account of Mr Gladstone. But there is mischief enough, and perhaps rather too much for the taste of certain celebrities. Mr Shaw gets as good as ever he gave, Mr Belloc may learn that he lives for immediate applause, one Cambridge professor that he is prim in his manner, another professor that his house is in poor taste, and the wife of a prominent statesman may read the following specimen of her epistolary style: 'I personally think the women criminal as they threaten people's lives and incite the rotters in the street to storm anything and anybody'; it is true that she penned the sentence under deep emotion, induced by the suffragettes. These are but scraps; for completer summaries let us turn to the longer entries. Both shall be about monarchs. The first deals with Isabel II of Spain, and is a good example of the pictorial power which would have made Blunt's fortune as a novelist:

It is just forty years since I first saw her at Madrid, but the recollection of her and her court remains a vivid picture in my mind, while so much else is forgotten. It gives me the image of a great, fat, colourless woman, with arms like rounds of raw beef. Beside her, her husband, Don Francisco de Assiz, a little stiff man in a much embroidered coat, and the two royal children, the Ynfanta, a thin anaemic girl of thirteen, and her brother, the little Prince of Asturias, a child of six (he afterwards became king), all four personages sitting on great gilt chairs in a row, having their hands kissed by a long procession of Spanish Grandees and Officers, the child fast asleep. We of the Diplomatic Corps had to stand just opposite the throne and watch the *besa-manos* for an hour or more together, thus it is all photographed upon my memory.

And here, in another strain, is a finely balanced judgement on the character of Edward VII:

His reign began with a fair promise for the world, or at least for the British Empire, of peace; and there was good reason to hope that a more reasonable foreign policy would be pursued than that which had so violently disturbed the last years of Queen Victoria's reign. . . . It was disagreeable to him that persons of his Court with whom he came in contact and in whom he felt an interest, should be on ill terms with each other, and he had long felt a pride in bringing them together. His own life had not been altogether free from domestic storms, but these had not been due to faults of temper on his part, rather of conduct, for he was a lover of pleasure and allowed himself wide latitude in its indulgence. This had involved him in more than one scandal out of which he had always managed to emerge without serious injury to his reputation. These irregularities had indeed rather added to his popularity, for they showed him to have a kindly heart, and he had always proved faithful to his friends. His experience, too, had made him a good judge of character, both with men and women, and gave him a certain facility in his intercourse with both which was not without its diplomatic uses.

There is great good sense in this picture; it is as firm as an eighteenth-century 'character'. And the breath of life is added to it by an imaginative touch, such as only a poet can give: after the king's death Blunt sees a great fallen beech-tree on the way to the station, 'a symbol of the dead King, quite rotten at the root, but one half of it clothed with its spring green.'

But one must return to the East and quote from the most entertaining entry in the book. Blunt had a great Egyptian friend who was Grand Mufti at Cairo; the greatest friend he ever had perhaps, so strong was their mutual love and respect. He also knew the Mufti's brother, a Mohammedan gentleman of the old-fashioned type, who had gone in an evil moment to a ball given by the Khedive. What the Mufti's brother expected to find in the ballroom is not recorded. What he did find he described to the Englishman as follows:

I went with two friends, men like myself in the legal profession, and we arrived among the first, none of us ever having been at such an entertainment before. As we were depositing our coats and umbrellas, for it had rained, in the vestiary, suddenly I saw in a mirror a sight reflected such as I had never in my life beheld, two women were standing behind me, naked nearly to the waist. I thought it must have been some illusion connected with my illness, and I was very much frightened. Their faces and arms and everything were displayed without any covering, and I thought I should have fallen to the ground. I asked what it meant and whether perhaps we had not come to the right house, and they told me 'these are the wives of some of our English officials.' – 'And their husbands,' I asked, 'do they permit them to go out at night, like this?' – 'Their husbands,' they answered, 'are here,' and they pointed out to me Mr Royle, the Judge of Appeal, before whom I had often pleaded, a serious man and very stern, as the husband of one of them. This judge I saw dancing with one of these naked ladies, gay and smiling and shameless, like a young man. 'And he is here,' I said, 'to see his wife thus unclothed? and he dances with her publicly?' – 'That,' they answered, 'is not his wife, it is the wife of another.'

Horror is piled upon horror, until the Mufti's brother flees; he can, he says, understand everything except that the husbands did not send their wives home. This last remark is illuminating. The West has again failed to lure the East, and the nature of its failure is here accurately defined. *Le livre de Goha le Simple* is actually written by Orientals, and its valuable pages express shades of harem-mentality that can scarcely be recorded by an outsider. But Blunt, with his flair for the essential, comes very near, and his pages do throw light on that difficult but important subject – the social emotions of the Mohammedans.

The time to sum up his career has not yet come, and he tells us that no more material upon it will be published in his lifetime. It is the career of one whose birth and education destined him to be a high official, but who spent all his life tilting against officialdom. Socially, he belonged to the governing aristocracy, and he never forwent the advantage that this accident gave him. In England it gave him the *entrée* to any society he chose to frequent; in the East, conjoined with his personal charm and warmth, it ensured him still more profitable experiences. Perhaps only for an Englishman, and only in the nineteenth century, was such a career possible. The chivalrous free-lance, who loves justice and beauty, and is drawn to a distant quest, will doubtless be born in the future, but he will not have enough money to effectuate himself. The age of independent travel, though no one realizes it yet, is drawing to an end, and Blunt is essentially the child of that age. In the future, few of us will be able to afford a visit to the East, except in some 'capacity', and as soon as one is enclosed in a capacity one's last chance of being attractive to the Oriental disappears.

[1920]

FOR THE MUSEUM'S SAKE

THE objects lay quiet for thousands of years, many of them in tombs where love or superstition had placed them. When they were golden they sometimes tempted thieves; brick, stone, marble – when they were of these materials they built houses; when they contained animal matter or lime they were broken up to fertilize the fields; now and then they served as amulets. But they did not work on the general imagination of the living, or disturb sober governments, until the fifteenth century after Christ. It was then that Italy began to take an interest in 'the antique'. 'I go to awake the dead,' cried Cyriac of Ancona; and an evocation began which seemed tremendous to contemporaries. The objects – mainly statues – were routed out of the earth, treated with acids and equipped with fig-leaves and tin petticoats; they were trundled about to meet one another, until they formed collections, which collections were presently dispersed through death or defeat, and the trundling recommenced. In the eighteenth century Egyptian objects also weighed in – not heavily at first, but Napoleon's expedition drew attention to them; and then the pace quickened. In the nineteenth century the soil was scratched all over the globe, rivers were dammed, rocks chipped, natives tortured, hooks were let down into the sea. What had happened? Partly an increase in science and taste, but also the arrival of a purchaser, wealthier than cardinals and quite as unscrupulous – the modern European nation. After the Treaty of Vienna every progressive government felt it a duty to amass old objects, and to exhibit a fraction of them in a building called a Museum, which was occasionally open free. 'National possessions' they were now called, and it was important that they should outnumber the objects possessed by other nations, and should be genuine old objects, and not imitations, which looked the same, but were said to be discreditable. Some of the governments – for example, the French and the Italian – were happily placed, for they inherited objects from the connoisseurship of the past; others, like the German and our own, had less; while poor Uncle Sam started by having none, and Turkey relegated all to the will of Allah. The various governments passed laws restricting exportation, and instructed their custom officials accordingly; and they also hired experts to buy for them and to intrigue against other experts. But an example will make the situation clearer. Let us follow the fortunes of B.M. 10470, or the 'Papyrus of Ani'.

Ani lived at Thebes about one thousand and five hundred years before the birth of Christ. He was chancellor to Pharaoh and overseer of the royal granaries at Abydos, and, like all ancient Egyptians, he was troubled by the certainties of death. There was nothing vague in that river beneath the Nile, over whose twelve reaches Ani would have to make the voyage to the palace of Osiris. Its course was only too clear: there were

myriads of details in it, and woe upon him if he forgot one!
for he would be expelled from the god's boat and be damned.
Everything spoke in that world of the under-waters. Even the
lintel of the palace of Osiris said, 'Who am I' and the bolts,
'Who are we?' The four Apes at the prows of the boat were
vocal, and it was necessary to address them in precisely the
following words: '. . . Let me pass through the secret doors of
the Other World. Let cakes and ale be given to me as to the
Spirits, and let me go in and come out from Rastan,' so that
they might reply: 'Come, for we have done away thy wicked-
ness and put away thy sin, and we have destroyed all the evil
which appertained to thee on earth. Thou shalt enter Rastan
and pass through the secret doors of the Other World. Cakes
and ale shall be given unto thee. . . .' Ani could not hope to
address the apes with accuracy. His memory was but human;
so, buying a strip of papyrus eighty feet long, he had it inscribed
with all he would have to say, and it was placed in a square
niche in the north wall of his tomb, and was tied with a cord
of papyrus and fastened by a clay seal. No apes and lintels
would trouble him now, for his 'Book of the Dead' would
undertake every dialogue, and having reached the palace he
would himself become Osiris, Osiris-Ani, an immortal.

The papyrus lay in its niche during the flash of time that we
call history, not seeing the sunlight until A.D. 1886. It was then
discovered by some natives. Egypt was still a nation, and had
so far advanced as to have a Museum at Cairo and a Director,
M. Grébaud. Britain had become a nation with a Museum in
Bloomsbury, and had sent her Mr (now her Sir Wallis) Budge
to take what he could from Egypt. It was to Sir Wallis that
the natives turned, because he paid more than M. Grébaud,
although they risked imprisonment and torture. Going by
night with them to the tomb, he broke the clay seal, and was
'amazed at the beauty and freshness of the colours of the
human figures and animals, which, in the dim light of the

candles and the heated air of the tomb, seemed to be alive.'
From that moment Ani was dumb. His voice, his 'Book of the
Dead', was taken, and he can no longer reply to questions in
the Under World. Sir Wallis put his find into a tin box, and
hid it in a house whose walls abutted on the garden of a hotel
at Luxor. M. Grébaud sailed in pursuit, but his boat stuck.
However, he sent on a messenger, who told Sir Wallis that he
was arrested on the charge of illegally acquiring antiquities,
and then asked for bakhshish. 'We gave him good bakhshish,
and then began to question him.' As a result, the native dealers
gave a feast to all the policemen and soldiers in Luxor, and an
atmosphere of good-fellowship was created. The house containing the Papyrus of Ani and other stolen objects had been
sealed by the police, pending M. Grébaud's arrival; guards
were posted on its roof, and sentries at its door. The dealers
invited the sentries to drink cognac or to take a stroll, but they
refused. However, the manager of the Hotel was more sympathetic, and his gardeners dug by night through the abutting
wall into the house, so that Sir Wallis could remove all the
antiquities – though he left a coffin which belonged to the
British military authorities, in the hope that it would make
bad blood between them and M. Grébaud. Next day the
Papyrus reached Cairo, and was smuggled across the Kasr el
Nil bridge as the personal luggage of two British officers, to
whom Sir Wallis related his trouble. The officers loved doing
the Egyptian Government. Even more helpful was Major
Hepper, R.E., met in the Mess. Major Hepper thus expressed
himself: 'I think I can help you, and I will. As you have
bought these things, which you say are so valuable, for the
British Museum, and they are to be paid for with public
money, they are clearly the property of the British Government.' He then placed the Papyrus of Ani in a case which was
labelled in sequence with some government property, and
took it, in his military capacity, to England, where he gave it

to the British Museum. It may not be on exhibit, but we have it, which is what matters. It would be humiliating to think it was on exhibit at Cairo.

The above yarn, and many another, are told by Sir Wallis in the jolliest way in his reminiscence *By Nile and Tigris*. He has something of the Renaissance desperado about him, and one can well imagine him 'collecting' for Sismondo Malatesta or Isabella d'Este with the assistance of a poignard. He enjoys being cruel to M. Grébaud, whose honesty and simplicity he despises; he enjoys pushing a young Turkish official into the waters of the Tigris. He has written a most delightful book, and yet he leaves an impression of vulgarity at the close. The vulgarity is not personal. It emanates from the system that he so ably serves. The dreariness and snobbery of the Museum business come out strongly beneath this tale of derring-do. Our 'national possessions' are not accessible, nor do we insist that they should be; for our pride in them is merely competitive. Nor do such fractions as are accessible stimulate our sense of beauty or of religion: as far as Museums breed anything it is a glib familiarity with labels. Yet to stock their locked cellars these expeditions and intrigues go on, and elderly gentlemen are set to pick one another's pockets beneath tropic skies. It is fine if you think the modern nation is, without qualification, fine; but if you have the least doubts of your colossus, a disgust will creep over you and you will wish that the elderly gentlemen were employed more honestly. After all, what is the use of old objects? They breathe their dead words into too dead an ear. It was different in the Renaissance, which did get some stimulus. It was important that the Laocoon should be found. But the discovery of the Hermes of Praxiteles and the loss of the sculptures of Sargon II are equally meaningless to the modern world. Our age is industrial, and it is also musical and one or two nice things; but its interest in the past is mainly faked.

Sir Wallis's own interest is no doubt genuine; he is certainly interested in his fellow-men and there are moments when one feels him the ideal Oriental traveller. He is accommodating over bakhshish: 'I found that in Baghdad a "little gift in the bosom made blind the eyes"'; and yet he can treat the Oriental respectfully. On one occasion he was entertained by some thieves:

My difficulty of the previous day repeated itself, and not a man, old or young, would accept a gift from me: when I pressed them each said it would be a 'shame'; and the shêkh refused even tobacco. Just as we were going to mount the shêkh come up to me and said, 'Knowest thou how to write?' I said, 'Yes.' – 'Then,' said he, 'take thy pen and write in thy book this: "I and my camels nighted in the house of Sulâmân ibn Khidr, shêkh of the thieves, and when I rose and left him at daybreak, of all my possessions I had lost nothing except the service of Sulâmân ibn Khidr."' When I had rendered his words to the best of my ability I took out my knife and began to cut the leaf out of the book, stupidly thinking that he wanted to have the paper as a witness of his honesty towards his guests. But he stopped me saying, 'Cut not, cut not; keep the writing and thou shalt remember Sulâmân.' Then I realized that all he wanted was that I should not forget the most opportune service which he had rendered me, and that he had treated me as a friend and wished to be remembered as a friend.

Indeed, Sir Wallis makes friends all over the East, who appear when most he needs them, and turn his career into an unending triumph. In practice it was probably a tousled compromise, like most careers, but he does not tell us so; and when he does come a crash (as in the Rassam libel case) he carries it off with a swagger. Of his adventures on rafts and in caves; of the old man who said Hû until he dislocated the traffic of Mosul; of the lady in the same city whose garment was unwound by a dog; of the stewponds of Abraham and Potiphar's wife; of the Nile boatmen who grounded, and cultivated melons upon the mud until the river rose again; of the parrot that cried,

'Damn the minor Prophets!' – of these and of other treasures the book is an inexhaustible mine; while the archaeologist will find in it a convenient résumé of the excavations in Mesopotamia, together with much other information. Despite its formlessness, it is the most fascinating travel-book that has appeared for years, for Sir Wallis has not only learning and vitality, but the sense of fun and the sense of beauty.

The afternoon was bright, and the view one of the finest I have ever seen. The buildings of the city stood out clear with their domes and minarets, and the setting sun painted the stonework a blood-red hue. . . . The city was surrounded with living green, and lay like a great green fan on the living desert which hemmed it in. The sight of it thus made it easy to understand why Arab writers and poets have raved about Damascus and called it the 'garden of the East,' the 'spot where beauty passeth the night and taketh its rest,' 'the region the stones of which are pearls, the earth ambergris, and the air like new wine,' 'the beauty spot on the cheek of the world, an eternal paradise with a Jahannum of anemones that burn not,' 'the city which is so truly a paradise that the traveller in it forgetteth his native land,' etc. To the sun-scorched and desert-weary Arab, Damascus, with its waters and its green fields and gardens and its fruits and flowering trees, was the Earthly Paradise. And Muhammed the Prophet, who stood on Mount Kasyun one evening and gazed over the city for a long time, decided not to go down the mountain and rest there lest its delights should spoil his enjoyment of the Paradise of God in Heaven.

Of the Missions recounted, by far the most thrilling is the third (1888–9), in which Sir Wallis, accompanied by a Mr N. White, sails from Constantinople to Alexandretta and thence goes overland to Mosul. The position of the British Museum was different in Mesopotamia from what it was in Egypt: the injured rather than the injurious party, it was trying to stop the leakage of objects from sites that the Turkish Government had given it to excavate. Sir Wallis's adventures were tremendous, and his description of the caravan which slowly accreted round himself and Mr N. White, and was finally robbed by the murderous Shammar, is a masterpiece of cumulative effect. Mr N. White is also a masterpiece. Though nothing definite is told us about that young gentleman, one knows him through and through. He was the son of our ambassador at Constantinople, who obliged Sir Wallis to take him as the price of his diplomatic assistance. Handsome, clever and generous, but utterly selfish, he came as near as a human agent may to thwarting the British Museum. Sometimes he hurt his knee, sometimes he strayed with Turkish officers, sometimes he arrived with masses of petitions and petitioners from the neighbouring villages and wished Sir Wallis to take them to Europe. He tried to break loose in India, but was brought as far as Egypt, where his father's agent met him and put him on a boat which sailed, not to Constantinople, as he expected, but to Manitoba! Mr N. White must have been a great drag on Sir Wallis, and perhaps for that reason our hearts go out to him. For, delightful as these volumes are, they lack one quality: they fail to enlist our sympathies with the author – the touch of the filibuster in him prevents it. It is fun when he pushes the Turk into the Tigris, but it would have been funnier had he fallen in himself. We part from him with admiration, but without tenderness, and with an increased determination to rob the British Museum. 'The Keeper of the Egyptian Antiquities is understood to be entirely prostrated as a consequence of the daring theft of the celebrated Papyrus of Ani.' Would that one was in a position to write such a sentence and to post it to M. Grébaud for his use in the Under World!

[1920]

315

MARCO POLO

WHILST Dante wrote his *Vita Nuova* at Florence, and transformed his love for Beatrice into the love that moves the stars, a book of a very different character was being compiled in the neighbouring city of Genoa. Two men, collaborators, were at work there upon a mass of notes and memoranda – notes scribbled upon every kind of material and dealing with every variety of subject, from the pearl fisheries of Southern India to the banquets in Russia and from the Ark on Mount Ararat to the arrangements for infant welfare in China. 'Orientalia', we should now call them. The owner of the Orientalia – a queer-looking middle-aged man – would read them out and expand them and reminisce, speaking in the Venetian dialect, but speaking with an outlandish accent which made him rather hard to follow. His companion – who spoke Tuscan and was of a literary turn – wrote down from his dictation, asked questions, made corrections, inserted explanatory passages, and pulled things into shape. Both the men were prisoners of the Genoese state, but conditions were comfortable, and when a man of action and a man of letters are immured together for several years with facilities for writing it is probable that a book will result. It resulted in this case, and in consequence of their imprisonment we have got the book we call *Marco Polo*.

Have we got it in its original form? Certainly not. We are not even sure in what language the original was written. The literary man – Rustichello or Rusticiano of Pisa – was an Italian, yet it seems probable that he wrote out his fair copy in French. His manuscript has been lost, but various versions of it were made, in French, Italian, and Latin, and a vast critical literature has grown up round these versions, through which, very dimly, we see the two collaborators at their work – far more dimly than we see their contemporary Dante. For we have Dante's actual words. We know what he thought of people and things, and we can build up his character. But we are vague as to the character of Marco Polo. And the limitations in his book – for it has limitations, and it has been foolishly overpraised – may be due to the vicissitudes of transmission. Had we the original manuscript, we might get more vivid impressions of him. This original may yet be discovered; Professor Benedetto is searching all over Europe, and has actually unearthed a new Latin version at Milan, which contains some additional matter.

Marco Polo belonged to a Venetian family of merchants and diplomats. At the time of his birth, his father and uncle were away in the Far East, at the court of Kublai Khan, the Mongol emperor, who ruled over Mongolia, China, Burma, and Thibet, and they ˙ l not return until Marco was nearly sixteen. They then set out on their second expedition, in which he joined, and which he has recorded. They travelled overland to Kublai Khan to give him some holy oil which had been sent by the Pope, they spent seventeen years in his service, and were employed by him on missions to various parts of China and India and finally they took charge of a princess who was betrothed to a ruler in Persia. Beginning their homeward journey, they travelled by sea, voyaged round the south of Asia *via* Sumatra and Ceylon, deposited the princess, and reached Venice after an absence of twenty-five years. A war between Venice and Genoa then broke out, and Marco was captured, but the Genoese allowed him to send for his memoranda and notes and released him in 1298. His story made a great impression, for it woke Europe up to the existence of the farther East. People realized for the first time that, beyond the barrier of Islam there existed another power, neither Moslem nor Christian, and highly civilized. They read with excitement of enormous walled cities, of roads planted with trees, of bank-notes, pleasure-lakes, hot baths, and the book, though so different from Dante's, also ushers in a New Life.

Yet it is not a first-rate book, for the reason that its author is interested in novelties, to the exclusion of human beings. Herodotus was interested in both, and he is a great traveller in consequence. Marco Polo is only a little traveller. He could bring back thrilling statistics, he could also discourse quaintly about oddities, such as the one-eyed cobbler who moved a mountain near Mosul, or the exportation of dried pygmies from India, but he could not differentiate between men and make them come alive, and the East that he evoked is only a land of strange customs. He could manage men and conciliate them and outwit them, but they never fascinated him; he remained the merchant-diplomat, and it is significant that even his interest in 'novelties' seems to have been due to a whim of Kublai Khan's; the Emperor had complained that his envoys usually did their work and nothing else; he would have liked, he said, out-of-the-way information about the countries they visited, and Marco determined to win his favour here. We get, indeed, the impression of a somewhat unpleasant character, shrewd, complacent, and mean. He despises idolatry, but is glad to benefit by it; when the witches recover some lost property for him, he experiences pleasure but declines to pay the usual fee. The East will not reveal itself wholly through a mind of this type, and we have to wait two hundred years more before we can see it in its full splendour, in the autobiography of the Emperor Babur. A land of riches and curios is all that Marco Polo unveils, and it is appropriate that his book should have been nicknamed by its enthusiastic contemporaries 'il Milione', or the Millionaire.

[1931]

THE EMPEROR BABUR

AT the time that Machiavelli was collecting materials for *The Prince*, a robber boy, sorely in need of advice, was scuttling over the highlands of Central Asia. His problem had already engaged the attention and sympathy of the Florentine; there were too many kings about, and not enough kingdoms. Tamurlane and Gengis Khan (the boy was descended from both) had produced between them so numerous a progeny that a frightful congestion of royalties had resulted along the upper waters of the Jaxartes and the Oxus, and in Afghanistan. One could scarcely travel two miles without being held up by an Emperor. The boy had inherited Ferghana, a scrubby domain at the extreme north of the fashionable world; thinking Samarkand a suitable addition, he conquered it from an uncle when he was thirteen. Then Ferghana revolted, and while trying to subdue it he lost Samarkand, too, and was left with nothing at all. His affairs grew worse; steal as he might, others stole quicker, and at eighteen his mother made him marry – a tedious episode. He thought of escaping to China, so hopeless was the block of uncles, and cousins, and aunts; poisoned coffee and the fire-pencil thinned them out, but only for a moment; up they sprang; again he conquered, lost, conquered, and lost for ever Ferghana and Samarkand. Not until he was twenty-one, and had taken to drink, did the true direction of his destiny appear; moving southward, he annexed Kabul. Here the horizon expanded: the waters flow southward again from Kabul, out of the Asian continent into the Indian; he followed them, he took Delhi, he founded the Moghul Empire, and then, not to spoil the perfect outline of his life, he died. Had Machiavelli ever heard of Babur? Probably not. But if the news had come through, how he would have delighted in a career that was not only successful, but artistic! And if Babur had ever heard of Machiavelli, how gladly he would have summoned him and shown him a thing or two! Yes – a thing or two not dreamt of in that philosophy, things of the earth mostly, but Machiavelli didn't know about them, all the same.

These sanguine and successful conquerors generally have defects that would make them intolerable as companions. They are unobservant of all that does not assist them towards glory, and, consequently, vague and pompous about their past; they are so busy; when they have any charm, it is that of our Henry V – the schoolboy unpacking a hamper that doesn't belong to him. But what a happiness to have known Babur! He had all that one seeks in a friend. His energy and ambition were touched with sensitiveness; he could act, feel, observe, and remember; though not critical of his senses, he was aware of their workings, thus fulfilling the whole nature of man. His admirers – and he has many – have called him naïf, because they think it somewhat silly of an emperor to love poetry and swimming for their own sake, and to record many years afterwards that the first time a raft struck, a china cup, a spoon, and a cymbal fell into the water, whereas the second time the raft struck, a nobleman fell in, just as he was cutting up a melon. Charming and quaint (they say), but no more: not realizing that Babur knew what he was about, and that his vitality was so great that all he had experienced rang and glowed, irrespective of its value to historians. It is the temptation of a cultivated man to arrange his experiences, so that they lose their outlines: he, skilled in two languages and all the arts of his day, shunned that false logic, and the sentences in his Memoirs jostle against one another like live people in a crowd:

Zulnun Arghun distinguished himself among all the other young warriors in the presence of Sultan Abusaid Mirza by the use of the scimitar, and afterwards, on every occasion on which he went into action, he acquitted himself with distinction. His courage is unimpeached, but certainly he was rather deficient in understanding. . . . He was a pious and orthodox believer, never neglected saying the appointed prayers, and frequently repeated the supererogatory ones. He was madly fond of chess; if a person played at it with one hand he played at it with his two hands. He played without art, just as his fancy suggested. He was the slave of avarice and meanness.

No one of the above sentences accommodates its neighbour. The paragraph is a series of shocks, and this is characteristic of Babur's method, and due to the honesty of his mind. But it is not a naïf paragraph. He desires to describe Zulnun Arghun, and does so with all possible clearness. Similarly, when he is autobiographical. No softening:

When, from the force of youthful imagination and constitutional impulse, I got a desire for wine, I had nobody about my person to invite me to gratify my wishes; nay, there was not one who suspected my secret longing for it. Though I had the appetite, therefore, it was difficult for me, unsolicited as I was, to indulge such unlawful desires. It now came into my head that as they urged me so much, and as, besides, I had come into a refined city like Heri, in which every means of heightening pleasure and gaiety was possessed in perfection, in which all the incentives and apparatus of enjoyment were combined with an invitation to indulgence, if I did not seize the present moment I never could expect such another, I therefore resolved to drink wine.

Here is neither bragging nor remorse; just the recording of conflicting emotions and of the action that finally resulted. On a subsequent page he does feel remorse. On still a subsequent he drinks himself senseless. Fresh, yet mature, the *Memoirs* leave an ambiguous and exquisite impression behind. We are admitted into the writer's inmost confidence, yet that confidence is not, as in most cases, an enervating chamber; it is a mountain stream, arched by the skies of early manhood. And since to his honesty, and energy, and sensitiveness, Babur added a warm heart, since he desired empire chiefly that he might advance his friends, the reader may discover a companion uncommon among the dead and amongst kings. Alexander the Great resembles him a little, but Alexander is mystic and grandiose, whereas there are neither chasms nor fences in Babur, nothing that need hinder the modern man if he cares to come.

Nevertheless . . . old books are troublesome to read, and it is right to indicate the difficulty of this one.

Those awful Oriental names! They welter from start to finish. Sometimes twenty new ones occur on a page and never recur. Among humans there are not only the Turki descendants of Tamurlane and the Moghul descendants of Gengis Khan, all royal, and mostly in motion; long lists of their nobles are given also. Geography is equally trying; as Babur scuttles over the earth a mist of streams, and villages, and mountains arises, from the Jaxartes, in the centre of Asia, to the Nerbudda, in the centre of India. Was this where the man with the melon fell overboard? Or is it the raft where half of us took spirits and the rest *bhang*, and quarrelled in consequence? We can't be sure. Is that an elephant? If so, we must have left Afghanistan. No: we must be in Ferghana again; it's a yak. We never know where we were last, though Agra stands out as the curtain falls, and behind it, as a tomb against the skyline, Kabul. Lists of flowers, fruits, handwritings, head-dresses. . . . We who are not scholars may grow tired.

The original manuscript of the *Memoirs* was in Turki, and this brings us to our concluding point, that Babur belongs to the middle of Asia, and does not interpret the mind of India, though he founded a great dynasty there. His description of Hindustan is unfavourable, and has often been quoted with gusto by Anglo-Indians. 'The people,' he complains, 'are not handsome, have no idea of the charms of friendly society, of frankly mixing together, or of familiar intercourse . . . no good fruits, no ice or cold water, no good food or bread in their bazaars, no baths or colleges, no candles, no torches, not a candlestick.' Witty and unphilosophic, definite and luxuriant as a Persian miniature, he had small patience with a race which has never found either moral or aesthetic excellence by focusing upon details. He had loved details all his life. Consequently, his great new empire, with its various species of parrots, concerning which he failed to get reliable information, and its myriads of merging gods, was sometimes a nightmare, and he left orders that he was to be buried at Kabul. Nothing in his life was Indian, except, possibly, the leaving of it. Then, indeed, at the supreme moment, a strange ghost visits him, a highly unexpected symptom occurs – renunciation. Humayun, his son, lay sick at Agra, and was not expected to recover. Babur, apprised that some sacrifice was necessary, decided (who told him?) that it must be self-sacrifice. He walked ceremonially three times round the bed, then cried, 'I have borne it away.' From that moment strength ebbed from him into his son, a mystic transfusion of the life-force was accomplished, and the five senses that had felt and discriminated so much blended together, diminished, ceased to exist, like the smoke from the burning ghats that disappears into the sky. Not thus had he faced death in the past. Read what he felt when he was nineteen, and his enemies closed round the upland garden in Ferghana. Then he was rebellious and afraid. But at fifty, by the banks of the sacred Jumna, he no longer desired to continue, discovering, perhaps, that the so-called Supreme Moment is, after all, not supreme, but an additional detail, like a cup that falls into the water, or a game of chess played with both hands, or the plumage of a bird, or the face of a friend.

[1921]

ADRIFT IN INDIA

1. *The Nine Gems of Ujjain*

'THERE is the old building,' said he, and pointed to a new building.

'But I want the ruins of which the stationmaster spoke; the palace that King Vikramaditya built, and adorned with Kalidas, and the other eight. Where is it? Where are they?'

'Old building,' he repeated more doubtfully, and checked the horse. Far out to the left, behind a grove of trees, a white and fantastic mass cut into the dusty horizon. Otherwise India prevailed. Presently I said, 'I think you are driving me wrong,' and, since now nothing happened at all, added, 'Very well, drive me in that direction.' The horse then left the road and proceeded with a hesitating step across the fields.

Ujjain is famous in legend and fact, and as sacred as Benares, and surely there should have been steps, and temples, and the holy river Sipra. Where were they? Since leaving the station we had seen nothing but crops and people, and birds, and horses as feeble as our own. The track we were following wavered and blurred, and offered alternatives; it had no earnestness of purpose like the tracks of England. And the crops were haphazard too – flung this way and that on the enormous earth, with patches of brown between them. There was no place for anything, and nothing was in its place. There was no time either. All the small change of the north rang false, and nothing remained certain but the dome of the sky and the disk of the sun.

Where the track frayed out into chaos the horse stopped, but the driver repeated 'Old, very old,' and pointed to the new building. We left the horse to dream. I ordered him to rejoin it. He said that he would, but looking back I found that he, too, was dreaming, sitting upon his heels, in the shadow of the castor-oil plants. I ordered him again, and this time he moved, but not in the direction of the horse. 'Take care; we shall all lose one another,' I shouted. But disintegration had begun, and my expedition was fraying out, like the track, like the fields.

Unencharioted, unattended, I reached the trees, and found under them, as everywhere, a few men. The plain lacks the romance of solitude. Desolate at the first glance, it conceals numberless groups of a few men. The grasses and the high crops sway, the distant path undulates, and is barred with brown bodies or heightened with saffron and crimson. In the evening the villages stand out and call to one another across emptiness with drums and fires. This clump of trees was apparently a village, for near the few men was a sort of enclosure surrounding a kind of street, and gods multiplied. The ground was littered with huts and rubbish for a few yards, and then the plain resumed; to continue in its gentle confusion as far as the eye could see.

But all unobserved, the plain was producing a hill, from the summit of which were visible ruins – the ruins. The scene amazed. They lay on the other side of a swift river which had cut a deep channel in the soil, and flowed with a violence incredible in that drowsy land. There were waterfalls, chattering shallows, pools, and to the right a deep crack, where the whole stream gathered together and forced itself between jaws of stone. The river gave nothing to the land; no meadows or water weeds edged it. It flowed, like the Ganges of legend, precipitate out of heaven across earth on its way to plunge under the sea and purify hell.

On the opposite bank rose the big modern building, which now quaintly resembled some castle on the Loire. The ruins lay close to the stream – a keep of grey stone with a water-gate and steps. Some of the stones had fallen, some were carved, and crossing the shallows, I climbed them. Beyond them appeared more ruins and another river.

This second river had been civilized. It came from the first and returned to it through murmurous curtains and weirs, and in its brief course had been built a water palace. It flowed through tanks of carved stone, and mirrored pavilions and broken causeways, whence a few men were bathing, and lovingly caressed their bodies and whispered that holiness may be gracious and life not all an illusion, and no plain interminable. It sang of certainties nearer than the sky, and having sung was reabsorbed into the first. As I gazed at it I realized that it was no river, but part of the ruined palace, and that men had carved it, as they had carved the stones.

Going back, I missed the shallows and had to wade. The pools, too shallow for alligators, suggested leeches, but all was well, and in the plain beyond a tonga wandered aimlessly. It was mine, and my driver was not surprised that we had all met again. Safe on the high road, I realized that I had not given one thought to the past. Was that really Vikramaditya's palace? Had Kalidas and the other eight ever prayed in those radiant waters? Kalidas describes Ujjain. In his poem of *The Cloud Messenger* – a poem as ill-planned and charming as my own expedition – he praises the beloved city. He feigns that a demi-god, exiled from his lady, employs a cloud to take her a message from him. An English cloud would go, but this is Hindu. The poem is occupied by an account of the places it might pass if it went far enough out of its course, and of those places the most out-of-the-way is Ujjain. Were the cloud to stray thither, it would enter the city with Sipra, the sacred stream, and would hear the old country people singing songs of mirth in the streets. While maidens clapped their hands and peacocks their wings, it might enter perfumed balconies as a shower, or as a sunset radiance might cling round the arm of Shiva. In the evening, when women steal to their lovers 'through darkness that a needle might divide,' the cloud might show them the way by noiseless lightning-flash, and weary of their happiness and its own might repose itself among sleeping doves till dawn. Such was Kalidas' account of his home, and the other eight – was not one of them a lexicographer? – may have sported there with him. The groves near must have suggested to him the magic grove in *Sakuntala*, where the wood nymphs pushed wedding garments through the leaves. 'Whence came these ornaments?' one of the characters inquires, 'Has the holy hermit created them by an effort of his mind?' The conclusion, though natural, is wrong. 'Not quite,' answers another. 'The sweet trees bore them unaided. While we gathered blossoms, fairy hands were stretched out.' Cries a third, 'We are only poor girls. How shall we know how such ornaments are put on? Still, we have seen pictures. We can imitate them.' They adorn the bride . . .

But it is only in books that the past can glow, and Kalidas faded as soon as I felt the waters of the Sipra round my ankle. I thought not of Sakuntala's ornaments, but of my own, now spread on the splashboard, and I wondered whether they would dry before we reached the railway station. One confusion enveloped Ujjain and all things. Why differentiate? I asked the driver what kind of trees those were, and he answered 'Trees'; what was the name of that bird, and he said 'Bird'; and the plain, interminable, murmured, 'Old buildings are buildings, ruins are ruins.'

[1914]

2. *Advance, India!*

The house of the rationalistic family (Mohammedans) lay close below that of my friends (English). We could see its red walls and corrugated iron roof through the deodars, and its mass cut into the middle distances though without disturbing the line of the snows. It was a large house, but they were not, I believe, prominent in their community, and only flashed into notoriety on the occasion of this marriage, which was the first of its kind that the province had seen. We did not know them, but had received an invitation, together with the rest of the station, and as the sun was declining we clambered down and joined the crowd in their garden.

A public wedding! It would actually take place here. In the centre of the lawn was a dais on which stood a sofa, an armchair, and a table, edged with torn fringe, and round this dais a couple of hundred guests were grouped. The richer sat on chairs, the poorer on a long carpet against the wall. They were of various religions and races – Mohammedans, Hindus, Sikhs, Eurasians, English – and of various social standings, though mainly subordinate Government clerks; and they had come from various motives, friendship, curiosity, hostility – the ceremony nearly ended in a tumult, but we did not know this until the next day. The snows were seventy miles off in front, the house behind; the less rationalistic part of the family remained in purdah there and watched the marriage through the blinds. Such was the setting.

After long delay the personages mounted. The Moulvi took the armchair – a handsome, elderly man robed in black velvet and gold. He was joined by the bridegroom, who looked self-possessed, and by the unveiled bride. They sat side by side on the sofa, while guests murmured: 'This is totally contrary to the Islamic law,' and a child placed vasefuls of congested flowers. Then the bridegroom's brother arrived, and had a long conversation with the Moulvi. They grew more and more excited – gesticulated, struck their breasts, whispered and sighed at one another vehemently. There was some difficulty, but what it was no one could say. At last an agreement was reached, for the brother turned to the audience and announced in English that the marriage ceremony would begin with verses from the Koran. These were read, and 'the next item,' said the brother, 'is a poem upon Conscience. An eminent poet will recite on Conscience in Urdu, but his words will be translated.' The poet and his interpreter then joined the group on the dais, and spoke alternately, but not very clearly, for the poet himself knew English, and would correct the interpreter, and snatch at the manuscript. Arid verities rose into the evening air, the more depressing for the rags of Orientalism that clothed them. Conscience was this and that, and whatsoever the simile, there was no escaping her. 'The sun illumines the world with light. Blessed be the sun and moon and stars, without which our eyes, that seem like stars, could not see. But there is another light, that of conscience—' and then conscience became a garden where the bulbul of eloquence ever sang and the dews of oratory dropped, and those who ignored her would 'roll among thorns'. When she had had her fling the pair were made man and wife. Guests murmured 'Moulvi is omitting such-and-such an exhortation: most improper.' Turning to the company, and more particularly to those upon the carpet, he said that it was not important how one was married, but how one behaved after marriage. This was his main point, and while he was making it we were handed refreshments, and the ceremony was more or less over.

It was depressing, almost heartrending, and opened the problem of India's future. How could this jumble end? Before the Moulvi finished a gramophone began, and before that was silent a memorable act took place. The sun was setting, and the orthodox withdrew from us to perform their evening prayer. They gathered on the terrace behind, to the number of twenty, and prostrated themselves towards Mecca. Here was dignity and unity; here was a great tradition untainted by private judgement; they had not retained so much and rejected so much; they had accepted Islam unquestioningly, and the reward of such an acceptance is beauty. There was once a wedding in England where a talented lady, advanced, but not too advanced, rewrote her daughter's marriage service. Bad there, the effect was worse in India, where the opportunities for disaster are larger. Crash into the devotions of the ortho-dox birred the gramophone—

> I'd sooner be busy with my little Lizzie,

and by a diabolic chance reached the end of its song as they ended the prayer. They rejoined us without self-consciousness, but the sun and the snows were theirs, not ours; they had obeyed; we had entered the unlovely chaos that lies between obedience and freedom – and that seems, alas! the immediate future of India. Guests discussed in nagging tones whether the rationalistic family had gone too far or might not have gone further. The bride might, at all events, have been veiled; she might, at all events, have worn English clothes. Eurasian chil-dren flew twittering through the twilight like bats, cups clinked, the gramophone was restarted, this time with an Indian record, and during the opening notes of a nautch we fled.

Next morning a friend (Sikh) came to breakfast, and told us that some of the guests had meant to protest against the innovations, and that the Moulvi had insisted in justifying himself to them; that was why he had argued on the dais and spoken afterwards. There was now great trouble among the Mohammedans in the station, and many said there had been no marriage at all. Our friend was followed by the bride-groom's brother, who thanked us for coming, said there had been no trouble in the community, and showed us the mar-riage lines. He said – 'Some old-fashioned gentlemen did not understand at first – the idea was new. Then we explained, and they understood at once. The lady is advanced, very ad-vanced. . . .' It appeared that she had advanced further than her husband, and the brother seemed thankful all was over without a scandal. 'It was difficult,' he cried. 'We Moslems are not as advanced as the Hindus, and up here it is not like Bombay side, where such marriages are commoner. But we have done what we ought, and are consequently content.' High sentiments fell from his lips, conscience shone and flowered and sang and banged, yet somehow he became a more dignified person. It hadn't at all events been an easy thing for two bourgeois families to jerk out of their rut, and it is actions like theirs, rather than the thoughts of a philosopher or the examples of kings, that advance a society. India had started – one had that feeling while this rather servile little clerk was speaking. For good or evil she had left the changeless snows and was descending into a valley whose farther side is still invisible.

'Please write about this' were his parting words. 'Please publish some account of it in English newspaper. It is a great step forward against superstition, and we want all to know.'

[1914]

3. Jodhpur

There must be some mistake! It was surely impossible that a dragon, flapping a tail of stone, should crouch in the middle of houses; that, having reached an incredible height, his flanks should turn to masonry; that he should be ridged with a parapet and bristle with guns; and that upward again a palace should rise, crowning the dragon, and, like him, coloured pearl. This was in the dawn, when a belt of mist cut off the mountain from the lower earth. Later in the day there were contrasts between sun and shade. After the sun set the vision was one colour again – olive-black, merging into night – and the dragon's crown rested among stars.

It was a vision of which the English community, stationed three miles off on the plain, had never lost sight. They had none of the indifference to their surroundings that is considered good form elsewhere. They loved the city and the people living in it, and an outsider's enthusiasm instead of boring them, appeared to give pleasure. Men and women, they shared the same club as the Indians, and under its gracious roof the 'racial question' had been solved – not by reformers, who only accent the evils they define, but by the genius of the city, which gave everyone something to work for and think about. I had heard of this loyalty at the other end of the peninsula – it was avowedly rare. But no one had described the majesty that inspired it – the air blowing in from the desert, the sand and the purple stones, the hills with quarries and tanks beneath, and the palace-fortress on the highest hill, an amazement for ever, a dragon's crown. 'I love these Rajpoots,' an English official cried. 'They have their faults, and one takes steps accordingly, but I love and respect them, and always shall.' It was as if each race had made concessions. Ours seemed more sensitive than usual, the Indian more solid. A common ground for friendship had been contrived, 'but if we were all somewhere else,' he said, 'I don't expect it would be the same.'

Next morning I went to the fort. My companion was a landscape gardener from Bombay, who had been commissioned by the Ruler to contrive a park out of some of the low ground. He shook his head, and remarked, 'A place like this doesn't want a park.' We had to make a wide circuit, since only a path approached the mountain on the city side. The citadel joined on to a wild country, covered for miles with walls that followed the tops of the hills. Below it were many smaller forts, one wider than the pedestal that bore it, and half-way up lay a green tarn and the marble tomb of a prince. The fortress seemed part of the mountain – the distinction between Nature and Art, never strong in India, had here become negligible. The first gateway – there were five or six lines of defence – lay between cliffs of masonry, in whose sides had been hollowed caves for the guard. Each turn of the ascent was commanded by a window, and there were ambushes innumerable. At Daulatabad, in the Deccan, the defences must have been even stronger, for there the enemy had to climb a tunnel cut in the living rock and closed at the upper end by a bonfire. But Daulatabad is not crowned by romance, like this city. Presently the quality of the stone grew finer, and we walked beneath precipices whose upper ranges had been carved. 'We must be getting up in between the palace somehow,' said my companion. 'I've been all these years, and didn't know there was such a place in India, or indeed in the world. What next?' Transepts like honeycomb answered him, and, cramped but splendid, the courtyard of the palace came into view.

We were met by the Keeper of the State Jewels, which were, as so often, stupid and ugly. No lady wears her predecessor's ornaments, and the gems had been recut and reset according to Regent Street. One necklace of emeralds – loot from the Mohammedans – had escaped emasculation. After the Treasury, we saw some other rooms, and admired the painted ceiling of the Durbar hall and its mirrored sides. But the best was to come.

The passage continued by walls of increased elaboration – they concealed the zenana, and how they smelt! – and emerged on to a platform of several acres, wind-swept and baked by the sun. The sense of space returned. On one side, far below, were vultures, on the other, still farther, lay the world of men. We could peer into their secrets with princely arrogance – a wedding procession, a family asleep, policemen drilling in a closed churchyard, camels, two women quarrelling on a housetop. The plans of the temples became clear: we could see their size and symmetry and their relation to the tanks. Then, tired of detail, we could glance at the grey-green bush, or overleaping civilization, rest on the encircling desert, and the ruins of forts ours had destroyed. A Rajpoot army idled on the platform. It was young and insolent, and played among the guns. These were of great age, some Dutch, others Indian, and cast in the shapes of fish, alligators, and dragons. The more reliable were fired in official salutes, and bursting occasionally would throw back the soldiers dead into the fort. Plenty were left, both of guns and Rajpoots, so no change was contemplated, though some day reform may come along with an electric button and a Babu. Beyond the soldiers, on the downward slope, stood a shrine to a goddess. She had some usual name – Chamundi – but she lives here and not elsewhere, and is the daughter of the rock, if not the rock. Beyond Chamundi's appeared the Western city, with the dragon's tail flapping across it, and dividing it into wards, and hidden in the creases of the tail were deep pools of water, where Brahmans scattered flowers or fed the fish.

This is the land of heroism, where deeds which would have been brutal elsewhere have been touched with glory. In Europe heroism has become joyless or slunk to museums: it exists as a living spell here. The civilization of Jodhpur, though limited, has never ceased to grow. It has not spread far or excelled in the arts, but it is as surely alive as the civilization of Agra is dead. Not as a poignant memory does it touch the heart of the son or the stranger. And when it does die, may it find a death complete and unbroken; may it never survive archaeologically, or hear, like Delhi, the trumpets of an official resurrection. One would wish for the sand to close in on the city, and the purple stones to show more frequently than they do through the soil; for the desert to resume the life it gave, and unobserved by men take back the dragon's crown. The wish may be granted. The kindred State of Jaisalmer struggles up to its throat against such a death, and 'will only be saved by a railway'. Railways can create. They cannot save, and for my own part I would leave heroes to heroic graves, and

334

concentrate the blessings of progress upon the new Canal Colonies in the Punjab.

Midday. A loud and unscientific explosion. Everyone remains alive. The soldiers run laughing into the cool of the passage, and fall asleep there.

[1914]

4. *The Suppliant*

Our friend – I will call him Obaidulla and give the account, which, greatly agitated, he poured forth to us on the roof of his house – our friend and his brother had been sitting in the verandah unpacking some books, when an old man approached. His appearance was ruffianly. 'Good evening, gentlemen,' he said. 'Will you please subscribe to my son's railway journey, in order that he may reach Calcutta?' and he produced a forged subscription list. But he was a suppliant, a Moslem, and old. 'I am a poor man myself,' said our friend. 'However, if your son will accept two rupees' – and he gave them.

'I think you have come here to practise as a barrister,' remarked the old man, as he sat down.

Obaidulla replied that he was correct; he had but recently arrived from England.

'I think you need a clerk.'

'No, I do not need a clerk. I have as yet no connexion in the city, and can do such work as I get unaided. We live very simply, as you see.'

'You need a clerk. I will be your clerk.'

'You are most kind, but at present I do not need a clerk.'

'When's dinner?'

The theory that a suppliant leaves after a meal proved correct, and the brothers spent the evening arranging books with the help of their hall-porter, a dictatorial child of ten. They had acted courteously and felt happy. But towards midnight a ghari rolled up piled with luggage. A dirty white turban stuck out of its window. 'I am your clerk,' said the old man. 'Where is my room?' and he left them to pay the driver.

'But what could I do?' Obaidulla protested in answer to our cries. 'What else could I do? One cannot be inhospitable, and he is old. He kept my servants up all night cleaning his hookah, and today he complains of them.' He sighed, then said, laughing, 'Alas! poor India! What next?'

We walked up and down, now scolding him, now joining in the lament. The roof seemed an exquisite place. It rose above the dust of the city into a world of green. The mangoes and toddy-palms and bel-trees pushed out of a hundred little gardens and courtyards, and expanded at our level into a city for the birds. The sun had set, an amazing purple bloomed in the orange of the western sky. Yet not even on the roof were we free. If we walked on its left side, we overlooked our next-door neighbour, a fat Hindu tradesman, and he would call up in English, 'Gentlemen! Gentlemen! Go further away, please! These are lady-women quarters.' And if we walked on the right we came in sight of other lady-women, less supervised or supervisible, who ran about on the top of their roof and waved long scarves. 'A two-storey house is dangerous for a beginner,' said Obaidulla elliptically, so we walked midway, while out of his own courtyard rose the growls of the suppliant – he corpulent mercifully and the staircase narrow.

We left depressed – partly because our friend did not urge us to stop to tea. Tea there was always delicious – peas done in butter were served with it, as were tangerines, as were guavas, sliced and peppered, and sometimes his married friends had sent sweets. But he could not well press us – the suppliant's table manners were too awful – nor could he come to tea with us, not liking to leave his brother alone, nor could they both come, fearing to leave the house. Our depression increased when we caught sight of the old man himself. A thousand insults (I was told) were implied in his salaam. And from inquiries in the bazaar we had news that he really was a bad lot. Nothing could be done, for Obaidulla, though humorous and gentle, allowed no interference with his hospitality. We could only wonder for how long he would sacrifice his friends, his liberty, and his career, and reflect on the disadvantages of keeping house in the medieval style.

Next morning the suppliant called on us. We repelled him before he could speak, and soon afterwards Obaidulla tumbled up on his bicycle, radiant with joy. 'A most fortunate thing has happened,' he cried. 'He has stolen one rupee four annas six pies from my servant's clothes and gone.'

We congratulated him, and asked for details.

'Ah! ah! at last we are happy again. Now I can tell you. When the little boy caught him I did not know what to do. One cannot be impolite. I said: "There seems to have been some misunderstanding," and I waited. Very luckily he grew warm. He said: "I never stop in a house where I am not trusted." I answered: "I am sorry to hear you say such a thing, and I have never said I do not trust you." – "No, but your servants. Enough! Enough! I am your clerk no longer. I go." I told him I was sorry to hear his decision, but perhaps he was wise. So he came straight round to you, having got all he could out of us! Oh, the old villain! The monster! It is a disgrace to India that such men exist! However, it cannot be helped, I suppose.'

'And the money?'

'Oh, he took it, of course; of course. But I might have had to replace as much as fifty rupees. Well, that is all over, and today will you both come to tea?'

He was really too silly, and we gave him a good British talking. He listened in silence, his eyes on the ground. When we had finished he raised them to mine and said:

'It is natural you should laugh at me. You are English, and

have other customs. I should not have behaved like this in England myself. No doubt it all seems jolly funny.' Then turning to his other critic, who was Indian, he added in sterner tones: 'But you – I am ashamed of you. You ought to have understood. As long as we have money and food and houses we must share them, when asked, with the poor and the old. Shocking! Your heart has cooled. You have forgotten our traditions of hospitality. You have forgotten the East. I am very much ashamed of you indeed.'

[1914]

5. Pan

In the silence of the noontide heat, I came, as so often, to a secluded glade among low, scrub-covered hills. The hills were not unfamiliar, and the glade had received its due minimum and meed of cultivation, in the absence of which all manifestations of the cosmic remain imperceptible. The universe cannot roll its eye without a socket. Outraged nature must have something to kick against. And these hurdles would do well enough, woven out of wattles perhaps, and certainly ominous, and that village quivering by the horizon was the asylum to which shepherds and visitors might terrified repair. The hurdles were seven feet high. They were corded together and covered with mats, and they formed an impenetrable palisade, which enclosed an area of one or two acres in extent. From the higher ground I could see over their top, on to a confused web of string and lightly strewn awnings, which were supported on poles. A vulgar observer might have thought he was in Kent. We know better. Something far more mysterious than that was brewing in the enclosure. Hops need a certain amount of protection from the wind, but none from the sun, nor do they retreat to a glade among scrub-covered hills, and further defend themselves by an elaborate system of straw-

padded entrances heavy and hinged, which bang behind the
visitor like the doors of a continental cathedral.

I have entered. Ah! A universe of warmth and manure, a
stuffy but infinite tent whose pillars and symmetric cordage
are flecked with gold and green. Vistas that blend into an
exhalation. Round each pillar a convolvulus twines, aromatic
and lush, with heart-shaped leaves that yearn towards the sun,
and thrive in the twilight of their aspirations, trained across
lateral strings into a subtle and complicated symphony. Oh,
and are those men? Naked and manure-coloured, can they be
men? They slide between the convolvuli without breaking
one delicate tendril, they squat upon the soil, and water flows
out of it mildly and soaks the roots. What acolytes, serving
what nameless deity? I wonder. And a passage from Dr John
Fryer (1650–1733) comes into my mind:

> These Plants set in a Row, make a Grove that might delude the
> Fanatick Multitude into an Opinion of their being sacred; and were
> not the Mouth of that Grand Imposter Hermetically sealed up, where
> Christianity is spread, these would still continue, as it is my Fancy they
> were of old, and may still be the Laboratories of his Fallacious Oracles;
> For they masquing the face of Day, beget a solemn reverence, and
> melancholy habit in them that resort to them; by representing the
> more enticing Place of Zeal, a Cathedral, with all its Pillars and
> Pillasters, Walks and Choirs; and so contrived, that whatever way
> you turn, you have an even prospect.

Exactly; I think I know now; but to make sure, I stretch out
my hand, I pluck a leaf and eat. My tongue is stabbed by a
hot and angry orange in alliance with pepper. Exactly; I am
in the presence of Pan.

Pan; pan-supari; beetle, bittle, bettle, betl, betel: what an
impression it made upon the early visitors to the East, and
how carefully they described it to their friends at home! Dr
Fryer took the most trouble, for he had read Sir Thomas
Browne before sailing, so much so that it is uncertain to what

plants the above passage really refers – he may have been endeavouring to adumbrate palm trees. Marco Polo had my convolvulus in view. Less of a stylist, he says straight out that Pan is 'salutary', and may have recommended it to Dante on his return. Pan soothed the belly and brain of Duarte Barbosa, and he was a contemporary of Luther's. Jan Huygen van Linschoten took it also. Growing as it did in an admired soil, in 'the most famigerous region of the world, the ample and large India', entwined as it was among the customs of an ancient people – Brachmans, Parsies, Moormen, Gentues, Banianes, Xeques – it appeared to our forerunners as a subject for inquiry and indeed for sympathy. We take a purer view. Anglo-India will have no truck with Pan, and roundly condemns the 'natives filthy chewing betel nut', although the natives would rather not be called natives, and what they chew is not the betel or filthy or even a nut. A few of our officials master the technique for ceremonial purposes – they droop stubby fingers over a tray on which little green packets are piled – but actually to consume the mixture would be un-British. What a pity! For it is a good mixture, and in its slight and harmless way it is a sacrament. The early visitors realized this too: 'It is the only Indian entertainment, commonly called Pawn.' In a land so tormented over its feeding arrangements, anything that can be swallowed without being food draws men into communion. Strictly speaking, Pan is a pill, which the host administers to the guest at the conclusion of the interview; it is an internal sweetener, and thus often offered with the external attar of roses. Actually, it is a nucleus for hospitality, and much furtive intercourse takes place under its little shield. One can 'go to a Pan', 'give a Pan', and so on: less compromising than giving a party, and on to the Pan tea, coffee, ices, sandwiches, sweets, and whisky-sodas can be tacked, and be accidentally consumed by anyone who happens to notice them. I have been to a Pan, which, as far as I was concerned, was an enormous meal. But it was not food technically. And there are other conveniences. An 'allowance for Pan' is a delicate excuse for benevolence: 'He gives her rupees five for Pan' – for pin-money, as we might say – cracking another witty jest, this time on the similarity between the words 'pan' and 'pin', a pun which causes laughter when carefully explained.

But that green leaf, the betel-leaf as it is best called. It loses its violence after it has been gathered, and in a short time it is merely fragrant, pleasant, and cooling. Ready for use, it is smeared with lime. Perhaps the lime was originally a preservative and has gradually established itself as a delicacy – there would be a parallel to this in the turpentine which now plays so overwhelming a part in the native wines of Greece. Authorities differ over the lime; doctors think it may cause cancer, and deprecate it, and there is a general inclination to regard it as the least honourable of the ingredients, although it is useful in sticking the others together. Pan's original home was Southern India, as the etymology shows, and the first lime was procured from the oyster shells of the pearl fisheries. On to the lime is sprinkled a most important item – the shredded seed of the areca palm, popularly called a nut, though it has no shell. An areca seed is about as large as a breakfast egg, but otherwise recalls the iron pyrites one used to pick up on beaches at school; it is fabulously hard, darkling without, and radiates spokes within. To have even a fragment of areca in the mouth is alarming; afterwards one gets used to it, and can chew it neat. These three – betel, lime, areca – make up Pan's trinity; but more ingredients can be added, for example cardomum seeds. When all is ready, the pliant leaf is folded upon itself, until it looks like a green jam-puff or the cell of a leaf-cutter bee. There are many ways of folding the leaves; some are tucked in, *billet-doux* fashion; others are fastened at the angle by a clove. There are so many ways of doing everything, all over India, that descriptions quickly shade into falsehood. My own betel grew at Garhi, Bundelkhand, but it may be cultivated differently round the corner.

Now for the operation. To unfold a Pan or to bite it off its end would be improper. It must go entire into the mouth, and consequences be awaited there. The leaf is mild enough, the crisis coming when its fibres tear and the iron pyrites fall about and get under the tongue. Now the novice rises in disorder, rushes in panic to the courtyard, and spatters shrapnel over the bystanders; it is as if the whole mineral kingdom has invaded him under a vegetable veil, for simultaneously the lime starts stinging. If he can sit still through this a heavenly peace ensues; the ingredients salute each other, a single sensation is established, and Pan, without ceasing to be a problem, becomes a pleasure. The cardomums crack, the formidable areca yields, splinters, vainly takes refuge in the interstices of the gums, and is gone. Warm and cleanly, one's mouth beats in tune with the infinite, while the harmony, moving within, slowly establishes its reign in the regions Barbosa indicated. Nothing intoxicating has been swallowed; the kindly angels of Eupepsia are at work, spreading their benison on all that has gone before them. It is incredible that Anglo-India should condemn the innocent practice – incredible until one looks into a looking-glass. Another shock has to be borne then: golly, I am bright red! Why this happens, when the betel was green, the areca brown, and the lime white, I do not know; the writers say that a 'bloody saliva is promoted,' but why should nothing else promote it? It is easily rinsed away, but there is always a danger that one may forget, go to play bridge at the Club with vermilion jaws, and be ruined for ever. Indians who take Pan night and day for years, and never clean afterwards, do indeed get red permanently, and their teeth blacken. They are hideous until one gets used to them, which no doubt one oughtn't to do. Their looks are against them, but their breath is sweet. They are the exact antithesis of Italians, and crowd for crowd I would rather be among them.

The serving of Pan is in itself a little art – and the arts of littleness are tragically lacking in India; there is scarcely anything in that tormented land which fills up the gulf between the illimitable and the inane, and society suffers in consequence. What isn't piety is apt to be indecency, what isn't metaphysics is intrigue. A ritual which avoids all, which coquets with religion yet never lifts her glum veil, which eludes the meshes of taboo without falling into the pit of grossness, has one valuable work, and the sight of the pretty little apparatus arriving makes the heart hop up – that hop that is more human than a leap, because it welcomes a joy of the earth. Generally the Pan comes ready-made upon a covered tray, the invisible hostess emits it, and if the occasion is ceremonial, scent, thick and brown, is offered first, and smeared on the handkerchief or the hand. At informal communions the actual box containing the ingredients may appear, a box on the lines of the spice-boxes one sees in a western kitchen – or possibly the spice-boxes are on the lines of it. It is divided into compartments where the ingredients are stored. Sometimes it is circular – the compartments radiating, and the lid domical; sometimes rectangular; sometimes in two storeys, the upper storey lifting out like the dress-tray of a lady's trunk, and the lower, which has no divisions, containing the areca in large lumps, for chewing. Modern boxes are usually weakly ornate. The older work is often beautiful. Bidar, a forgotten city in the Deccan, has produced beautiful pan-boxes of a lead alloy inlaid with silver. I went there, hoping to see one being made, but the industry had been 'revived', and all hands were consequently at work upon a metal portrait of the Prince of Wales.

The Indian hostess, though almost invisible, is not entirely so, and no one who has once seen her preparing a Pan will speak of 'chewing filthy betel nut' again. It is a gracious and exquisite performance – not even the much advertised tea-making of the Far East can be daintier. Her first labour is to find a perfect leaf. One after another she rejects, fantastically disdainful, and seeking that which grew not upon any earthly stem. Pursing up her lips, she takes the best available, trims it with a pair of scissors, lays it upon the palm of her hand, which it more than covers, and seems to think, 'This is a disgraceful leaf, a humiliating leaf; can I possibly proceed?' Pulling herself together, she seizes a little quill or spoon, and plunges it into the compartment of the pan-box that contains the liquid lime. The areca – which she has already shredded with jewelled clippers – comes next, then the cardomum seeds, and what else she thinks seemly. As she proceeds, her movements grow quicker and her spirits improve, she forgets her disappointment and becomes all anticipation, she is every inch a hostess, and doing up the difficult fastening like lightning, she bends forward and presents the gift. Little gestures, and a little gift. To think of the Mystery of the East in connexion with Pan is to falsify the whole proceeding. The East is mysterious enough, mysterious to boring point. But now and then a tiny fact detaches itself from the Everlasting All, and our common humanity is remembered.

Such is the main outline of a neglected subject. Other aspects exist. There is Comic Pan, which contains salt. It is given to buffoons. Oh, how they splutter, sometimes being positively sick! Not even a pun is such fun. And, to end all, there is Tragic Pan, which contains ground glass, and is given to enemies.

[1922]

HICKEY'S LAST PARTY

WHEN Mrs Smith, fresh from England, entered Mr Hickey's dining-room at Calcutta, she 'gave a violent start and drew back'. The company were apprehensive she was indisposed, but as soon as she got to know them better she explained: 'Such a large party of gentlemen assembled, such a crowd of attendants, a table splendidly covered, and such an extraordinary blaze of light, coming, too, as she did, from utter darkness, she was wholly overcome, feeling as if she could faint.' Well might she start, and even we, who should be accustomed by now to Hickey's lavishness, can scarce restrain a nervous reaction. It is volume four of the Memoirs – the fourth and last – yet still the spell works. Never mind if the table is vulgar and the lights garish, and the gentlemen second-rate. Never mind the fevers and duels that carry them off, never mind if their mistresses and illegitimate children expire in agonies. Suffering from the toothache, Mr MacNaughten seizes a carving knife and hacks at his gums. Septic poisoning results, but never mind. Colonel Auchmuty shouts up the stairs to his wife, 'Shela, my jewel, why Shela, I say, take care, I say, of the spoons and silver forks, count them up carefully, my honey, for by the Holy Jesus we have got some tight boys here today!' The servants steal as well as the tight boys; the trusted Chaund imports prostitutes and all get dead drunk upon the master's claret and sprawl over his furniture. And young Mr Blunt – being a clergyman, will he not exercise a moderating influence? No. Mr Blunt is even more remarkable than his lay colleagues. Appointed to a chaplaincy, he rushes stark naked from his cabin after he has been two days at sea and dances before 'both soldiers and sailors, singing scraps of the most blackguard songs.' When he comes to himself, his concern is extreme; not even Colonel Wellesley, the Commanding Officer of the regiment, can comfort him. Colonel Wellesley puts off expressly from another boat to say, 'that what had passed was not of the least consequence, as no one would think the worse of him, and no blame ought to attach to a cursory debauch.' But Mr Blunt will not take this sensible view, the shadows of the nineteenth century fall on him; he frets, and ten days later is a corpse – but never mind! Mrs Smith, fresh from her northern twilight, may start, but we should be inured by this time to the jollity and vulgarity and death.

Did Hickey himself ever mind anything, as he sat at Beaconsfield invalided 'home', and writing up his extraordinary journal? There had been two great emotions in his life, Charlotte Barry and Bob Pott, but Charlotte is dead and Bob dies unchronicled. Jemdaree has died, too, and so have the friends who called her 'the gentle and kind Fatty'. As the old boy looked back at his jumble of a career and particularly at the Indian fragments of it, what significance could it have to him? Why, none at all, no significance at all, he is not that type of observer. He is not philosophic or profound. He just writes ahead, remembering vividly when necessary, but never concerned to discover a meaning, or to draw lessons from his failure or success. He had been, on the whole, a Calcutta attorney, and had ended as Under-Sheriff and Keeper of the Jail. Some men have achieved less; others more. He puts it all down, unmoved in spite of his liveliness. No yearnings disturb him. He is so second-rate that he does not realize the difference between seconds and firsts, and this makes him happy, restful, dignified. Turn off the raptures of heaven and hell. Leave, as sole illumination for its universe, the 'extraordinary blaze of light' that falls upon a bachelor dinner-table. Hickey looks very well now. He does not want to be anywhere else or among better people, and when Miss Seymour cries, 'Mr Hickey, you are an old man now. I need not lock my bedroom door,' he cannot understand why Sir Henry Russell should look shocked.

Well, this is the last party he will ever give. Back he goes to his Maker, in the middle of compiling a list of passengers who have been drowned at sea. Where he himself died, and what he looked like, we do not know. Off he goes without offering any opportunity for reflection, which is one of the reasons why we like him so much. He had never been pretentious or insincere; he has never regretted or repented or said 'I have lived' or 'I have served England in my little way', or 'I, too, have felt the lure of the East'. How pleasant it would have been to have met him, and how strange it is to realize that one has often met him and fled from him. For he must be reincarnate today in many a smoking-room, many an overseas dining club or tenth-rate military mess. Though somewhat overlaid with newspapers and a bit bothered by the necessity of being all white, he is with us still. Is he still writing everything down? Ah, that we cannot know, nor did his contemporaries know it. As a rule, Hickey does not care to keep a journal, or, if he does keep one, it is unreadable. Only now and then does he develop that strange excrescence, the power to write. The same in other ways, as soon as he takes up his pen, he enters the temple of the Muses and addresses posterity.

[1925]

TWO BOOKS BY TAGORE

1. *Chitra*

To hearken is better than the fat of rams, but seldom as popular. It requires a silent atmosphere, and, when the voice is Apollo's, an ear attentive to beauty. Rare in all places, it is almost unknown in cultured London, where there is noise without and deafness within. The Londoner, and still more the Londoness, prefers adoration to attention. It proves less fatiguing in the long run, and induces a more pleasing glow. It implies enthusiasm, and enthusiasm is surely what we all need. It implies elevation and breadth. Consequently London is the City of booms, of transient fanaticisms that raise the spirit to fever heat and pass leaving it a little weaker. There is no connexion between one boom and the next. The rams are driven hurriedly from altar to altar, and their blood has scarcely cooled to Emil Reich before it is poured in unexampled profusion to Mr Tagore.

The reviewer, while affecting to be above such hysteria, is really involved in it, and it is difficult to listen through the noise and the nonsense of the last two years and catch the authentic voice of Tagore beyond. He is a good writer. All must assent to this minimum. But how good? To that there can be no answer until the adoration and the reaction all adoration entails have passed away, until the mess of the sacrifices has been cleared up, and Beauty can pronounce across the subsiding dust.

Meanwhile, here is *Chitra*, a fairy play in nine scenes. Does it contain any hints for a verdict? It was written long before the boom, to be acted by villagers in India.

This is the story. Princess Chitra, of manlike appearance and garb, loves the ascetic Arjuna, and to win him prays the gods for female grace. It is granted to her for one year. At the close she tells him that the form he has loved is illusion, and that she is only Chitra, ugly, the daughter of a king. Arjuna replies, 'Beloved, my life is full,' and turns from illusion to reality. The story is told with faultless delicacy and grace. Its action is no stronger than a flower, and the fragrance of blossom clings round every phrase. But, of course, there is 'something behind', that something for which the worshipper pants. Allegories stalk in the background, not always upon all fours. The contrast between the material and the immaterial, the contrast between pleasure and action, the nature of wedded joy, which, though only to be gained through youth and beauty, knows how to survive their departure – *Chitra* symbolizes all three ideas in turn. It is true that the play is not the least spoilt by the symbolism. An allegory may be as lame as it likes if it walks quietly, and Tagore's always do that. Indeed, one's enjoyment is increased by the sense of half-audible stirrings in the midst of the jasmine bowers. But to drag the allegory from its retirement, and proclaim it has importance in itself is to brutalize the atmosphere and pay no real honour to the author. Tagore is a poet who, like any other, must contrive some sub-structure on which to exhibit beauty, and, being an Indian poet, he has turned to general ideas more readily than does his English brother. That is all. He is not a seer or a thinker. He is not to be classed with Nietzsche or Whitman, or others of whom he occasionally reminds us. Such, at all events, is the verdict suggested by *Chitra*.

Nor is the poetry strong stuff. Despite allusions to immensities, our flight through the air is quiet, and we alight in some gracious grove. Here all is consideration and charm and tenderness, and though sincerity blows, it is as a breeze wherein champak odours linger. In this grove we see men as flowers walking. Their speech is gentle.

I felt like a flower, which has but a few fleeting hours to listen to all the humming flatteries of the woodlands, and then must lower its eyes from the sky, bend its head, and at a breath give itself up to the dust without a cry, thus ending the short story of a perfect moment that has neither past nor future.

The inmates of the grove are modest and reasonable. They make no high claims for themselves, no criticisms of men who may walk as trees and mountains and everlasting suns.

Take to your home what is abiding and strong. Leave the little wild flower where it was born; leave it beautifully to die at the day's end among all fading blossoms and decaying leaves. Do not take it to your palace hall to fling it on the stony floor which knows no pity for things that fade and are forgotten.

This exquisite plea might be Tagore's own. Whatever his claim to divinity, he has, at all events, nothing in common with his worshippers. He has known how to hearken, and to what, and the noise of London may have vexed, but cannot mislead him.

[1914]

2. *The Home and the World*

When a writer of Tagore's genius produces such a sentence as 'Passion is beautiful and pure – pure as the lily that comes out of the slimy soil; it rises superior to its defilement and needs no Pears' soap to wash it clean' – he raises some interesting questions. The sentence is not attractive – in fact, it is a Babu sentence – and what does Tagore, generally so attractive, intend by it? Is he being dramatic, and providing a Babu of his creation with appropriate English, or is he being satirical, or was there some rococo charm that has vanished in the translation, or is it an experiment that has not quite come off?

Probably an experiment, for throughout the book one is puzzled by bad tastes that verge upon bad taste. The theme is so beautiful; here it is, beautifully stated:

While the day is bright and the world in the pursuit of its numberless tasks crowds around, then it seems as if my life wants nothing else. But when the colours of the sky fade away and the blinds are drawn down over the windows of heaven, then my heart tells me that evening falls just for the purpose of shutting out the world, to mark the time when the darkness must be filled with the One . . . that work alone cannot be the truth of life, that work is not the be-all and the end-all of man, for man is not simply a serf—even though the serfdom be of the True and the Good.

But when the theme is developed, one receives inappropriate emotions, and feels that the contrast is not so much between the Home and the World as between the well-bred and the ill-bred. The Home is not really a home, but a retreat for seemly meditation upon infinity. And the World – it proves to be a sphere not for 'numberless tasks', but for a boarding-house flirtation that masks itself in mystic or patriotic talk. The action is laid in Bengal, during the Swadeshi movement, and it leads up to the theft of Rs. 6,000. How, why, and by whom were the Rs. 6,000 stolen from the safe? Tagore is scarcely at his soundest when speculating on such problems. Not here, O Nirvana, are haunts meet for thee, and we learn without emotion that they were stolen by a wife from her husband for the Cause, that they were misappropriated by an amorous and amoral Babu, and that they led to the death of another Babu, who was chivalrous and young. The tragedy is skilfully told, but it all seems to be about nothing, and this is because the contrast does not work out as the writer intends. He meant the wife to be seduced by the World, which is, with all its sins, a tremendous lover; she is actually seduced by a West Kensingtonian Babu, who addresses her as 'Queen Bee', and in warmer moments as 'Bee'. In spite of the beautiful writing and the subtle metaphor and the noble outlook that are inseparable from Tagore's work, this strain of vulgarity persists. It is external, not essential, but it is there; the writer has been experimenting with matter whose properties he does not quite understand.

Why should he care to experiment? Here is a more profitable but more difficult question. Having triumphed in *Chitra* or *Gitanjali*, why should he indite a '*roman à trois*' with all the hackneyed situations from which novelists are trying to emancipate themselves in the West? These Bengalis – they are an extraordinary people. Probably this is the answer. They are more modern and mentally more adventurous than any of the other races in the Indian peninsula. They like trying, and failures do not discompose them, because they have interest in the constitution of the world. They have in a single generation produced Tagore and Bose, innovators both, and the people that has done that will not rest content. In literature, as in science, they must work over the results of the West on the chance of their proving of use, and one expects that the younger writers will reject the experiment of *The Home and the World*, and will adopt some freer form.

[1919]

THE MIND OF THE INDIAN NATIVE STATE

I

WHETHER the Princes of India are safer now than they were ten years ago* is questionable, but they are certainly having a pleasanter time. Both socially and politically they receive from the British authorities increased civility. The Political

* I have been twice to India: this article was written in 1922 after my second visit.

Agent, the British official with whom smaller rulers most frequently collide, was formerly an imposing figure. News of his coming stirred the State to its depths. He represented the Agent to the Governor-General who represents the Viceroy who represents the Emperor. Girt with vicarious authority, he laid down the law on every conceivable subject, including deportment, and freely criticized everything and everyone who did not minister to his comfort. Meanwhile his servants blackmailed the court officials. But the Political Agent of to-day is a wilted and almost pathetic figure. He retains his title of Colonel and his tendency to bluster, but at the slightest resistance he collapses, becomes abjectly polite, and attempts to see the point of an Oriental joke even when it is directed against himself. He is housed with decreasing splendour, and the Government of India has instructed him to instruct his chuprassies not to rob his hosts. And as with him, so with the upper grades of his hierarchy. They have orders to treat the Princes of India as if they were princes and not naughty boys. Nor is the change in policy merely sentimental. When there is a dispute between a ruler and his feudatories, it is usually decided in the former's favour; there is even a tendency to restore to Native States territory that they have lost; there is even a notion of re-creating Native States, like Satara, that have disappeared. Both by words and deeds the Government of India has reversed the policy which was in favour a decade ago, and which a hundred years ago produced British India.

There are two reasons for the change. The Native Princes have shared in the increased consideration accorded to Indians generally, and they are also encouraged because of their usefulness as counter-weights against the new Nationalism. It is neither in their tradition nor to their interests that India should become a nation; even if they survived, they would lose their importance and local variety. It is only the modern democratic Indian who boasts of being an Indian; the majority still say 'I am Afghan, or Persian, or Rajput; my ancestors entered the country under so-and-so'; and the Princes, whose mentality is anything but modern, and whose views of the present are always coloured by visions of the past, go further than most in their separatism, and like to suppose themselves invaders, holding their lands by the sword, even when they relegate the invasion to the Golden Age. The Government of India, while not sharing such a view of history, has naturally profited by it, and as its own troubles grow and a Gandhi succeeds to a Tilak, it becomes more polite than ever to men who have no sympathy with Nationalist aspirations, whether legitimate or anarchical, and who applaud any attempts to suppress them. Curious alliances result. Certain Anglo-Indians now speak of the Native States as certain Englishmen spoke of Germany during the war, with a morbid envy: 'They stand no nonsense over there,' is their attitude, 'they clap agitators all right into prison without a trial, and if your servant's impudent you can strafe him without getting hauled into the Courts.' And Sir Frederick Lugard, in the ripeness of his Imperial wisdom, has lately suggested that we should apportion British India among the loyaller rulers, and control the whole peninsula through them. Before we do this there are one or two points to consider.

The Princes have studied our wonderful British Constitution at the Chiefs' Colleges, and some of them have visited England and seen the Houses of Parliament. But they are personal rulers themselves, often possessing powers of life and death, and they find it difficult to realize that the King-Emperor, their overlord, is not equally powerful. If they can exalt and depress their own subjects at will, regard the State revenue as their private property, promulgate a constitution one day and ignore it the next, surely the monarch of Westminster can do as much or more. This belief colours all their intercourse with the Government of India. They want to get through or behind it to King George and lay their troubles at his feet, because he is a king and a mighty one, and will understand. In the past some of them nourished private schemes, but today their loyalty to the Crown is sincere and passionate, and they welcomed the Prince of Wales, although his measured constitutionalisms puzzled and chilled them. Why did he not take his liegemen aside and ask, in his father's name, for the head of Gandhi upon a charger? It could have been managed so easily. The intelligent Princes would not argue thus, but all would have the feeling, and so would the reader if he derived extensive powers under a feudal system and then discovered that it was not working properly in its upper reaches. 'His Majesty the King–Emperor has great difficulties in these days': so much they grasp, but they regard the difficulties as abnormal and expect that a turn of the wheel will shake them off. However cleverly they may discuss democratic Europe or revolutionary Russia with a visitor, they do not in their heart of hearts regard anything but Royalty as permanent, or the movements against it as more than domestic mutinies. They cannot understand, because they cannot experience, the modern world.

One of the annual festivals, the Dessera, may help to explain their psychology. The Dessera falls in October, at the end of the rains, and was in its origin a preparation for war against an enemy state. There is no enemy now, nor always an army, but the Dessera is still celebrated by many a Hindu ruler with archaic pomp. During the day various warlike implements are worshipped, and in the evening a military expedition sets out, partly in landaus, to the boundaries of the city. Here a halt is called round a Tree of Victory, planted for the occasion, and a document is read out which enumerates the territories, feudatories, revenue, and expenditure of the State. This document is of a satisfactory nature, because it bears no relation to facts. It is a faery budget, such as might occur in the parliaments of Gilbert and Sullivan. The actual budget may display an income of ten lakhs and secretly anticipate an expenditure of eleven; the Dessera budget announces an income of thirty lakhs and an expenditure of twenty, mainly upon arrows and elephants. The State may actually cover only a few hundred square miles; in the Dessera it swells to a mighty Empire, so that the various Maratha States each possess the whole of the country that was at any time occupied by Maratha bands, and the Rajput Maharana of Udaipur owns all India from top to toe. The document is then signed by the Finance Minister, and the military expedition moves back to its base. The participators smile at the absurdities, yet probably take the Dessera more seriously than a Westerner realizes. To the ruler and his family it is an assertion of the eternity of their State. It belongs to that broad border region between reality and dreams where so much of the spiritual life of the Indian proceeds, be he conservative or extremist; occurring year after year, it subtly reinforces a habit of mind.

The taste for unrealities (as we call them) also appears in the grotesque pride which imprisons some of the shyer rulers in their own jungles lest they be snubbed, and which led the Maharajah of Alwar, I am told, to promenade the deck of a P. & O. with a crown upon his head, under the belief that it was expected from him. The pride is not always personal. Though modest himself, a ruler may feel that he represents his State and family, and must uphold their honour – e.g., must insist on being received half-way down a strip of carpet instead of at the top for their sake. If he forgets, and advances too many steps, the story of his failure will be whispered in a dozen palaces and be magnified by his enemies. On the other hand, if he can trick his host into advancing too far to meet him, he has scored a triumph which may be used as a precedent in the future, and enable his heir to be received at the bottoms of carpets instead of half-way down them, after he himself is dead. His argument is: 'No doubt I seem trivial, but the eyes of my brother rulers are upon me, and I must behave in a way that they will understand,' and, since the brother rulers feel the same, it is not surprising that they meet each other with caution, and part with relief.

One or two of them, e.g., the Gaekwar of Baroda, exact and accord the minimum of ceremonial, but the rest try to get it both ways, in spite of the practical disadvantages. There is a story about Holkar (not the present ruler of Indore, but a predecessor) who wished to visit Hyderabad, but could not go because the ceremonial which the then Nizam accorded him was insufficient. He therefore planned an oriental joke. He went to Hyderabad secretly, and drove in a shabby carriage along the route that the Nizam was accustomed to frequent. When the Nizam's carriage approached, he managed to graze against its wheels and fling himself out, as if dislodged by the concussion. The late Nizam had a compassionate nature, and, seeing a stout old gentleman rolling in the dust, jumped out to assist him. Holkar immediately arose. 'At last,' he said, 'the Nizam of Hyderabad has descended from his carriage to greet the Maharajah of Indore.' Fortunately the host thought the joke equally delightful. Roaring with laughter, he seated his mischievous guest beside him, and they drove on to the palace together. The story may be untrue, like other Holkar stories, but it illustrates the difficulties with which Princes have to contend. Although their interests are identical and threatened by the same tide of Nationalism, they find it hard to combine or even to meet one another, lest they compromise their prestige.

The Chamber of Princes, one of the many stillborn children of Lord Chelmsford, attempted to give them a meeting-place where they could discuss matters affecting their class. The smaller rulers, who had nothing to lose, repaired to it in shoals. Not so the larger fish. The Nizam, for intance, with dominions as large as France and as populous as Egypt, does not want to hobnob with chieftains who may be far less powerful than his own vassals. The little Rajput chiefs alone are so numerous that they can outvote any combination that can be brought against them, and do outvote, since they are organized under an able leader, the Maharajah of Bikanir. Until the Rajput block is broken by some device – e.g., by the introduction of a system of group-votes – the leading Mohammedans and Marathas do not care to attend. Thus history and mythology intervene at every turn. The hand of the past divides the rulers whenever they attempt to discuss the present. They forget the common enemy as soon as they see one another, and waste their time in discussing the form of their organization, in exchanging insincere courtesies, in cracking jokes of a symbolic nature, and in being photographed either officially or semi-officially or informally. The Maharajah of K—, for instance, always likes to stand in the back row of a photograph, but modesty is not suspected as the cause, his Highness being of a bulky build, and dominating from his high position such Princes as are perched on chairs. The Nawab of L— pushes for the front; serve him right when the humorous Maharajah of M— obscures him, quite by accident, during the exposure of the plate. The Rajah of N— takes a side seat himself, but brings in his children at the last moment and spreads them along the carpet, so that they lean against their Highnesses' legs, and appear to be heirs of the whole continent of India. Fortunately the Viceroys say: 'Who are these children?' And so on and so forth . . . while the New Spirit knocks with increasing irritability upon the door. The Chamber of Princes, and all that it connotes, seems absurd not only to the politically minded Indian, but to him who pursues the more elusive goals of science and art. 'For what reason are such people important?' asks the Bengali painter or the Punjabi poet. 'What are they doing, what have they ever done, that is either beautiful or interesting?'

2

The rulers are kept in touch with criticism by their agents, but the measures they take against it are mainly negative. They particularly dislike being criticized by British India newspapers, and have begged the Government of India to strengthen the Press Act in their favour. They desire to be immune to the extent that the King–Emperor is immune, although they have no status in British India, and consequently no claim to special protection. With more right, if no more wisdom, they sometimes take matters into their own hands, and forbid peccant newpapers to be read in their dominions. Such a censorship is too complicated to be worked. One State may prohibit the *Bombay Chronicle*, while its neighbour is indifferent, and the territories of the two States may be peppered in and out of one another so that the road passes to and fro back again every few miles, and there may be a railway station, close to them both and situated in British India, where the *Chronicle* can be bought freely. Hitherto the extremists have attempted no serious propaganda in the Native States, but if an attack comes, the rulers will be in the same difficulty as they are over the newspapers.

There is, of course, another line of defence, and the more intelligent adopt it: to fortify themselves by internal reforms, by spreading education, and by granting constitutions. But let no one suppose that they adopt it with enthusiasm, or will carry out more changes than are imperative. If the menace from British India subsides, they will return to their old ways. Some of them may like to have an efficient system of administration, or to be surrounded by cultivated men, but these no more than the others wish power to pass out of their own hands. Mysore and Baroda are the two most 'progressive' States, but the constitution in the former and education in the latter are both said to be of the nature of decorations – showy exhibits that flower in the capital, but have no roots in the country districts. An education that frees the mind, a constitution that gives effect to such freedom, can never be tolerated by a man who believes in autocracy and possibly thinks it divine.

During the recent visit of the Prince of Wales, several constitutions burst into sudden bloom. The Maharajah of Gwalior – a clever investor and hard worker, and from that point of view the most modern of the Princes – produced a specimen, and his neighbour, the aged Begum of Bhopal, held out another. It may be of interest briefly to examine one such constitution as a sample of the crop. We may learn a little more from it about the external problems that occupy the Princes, and a little about their internal difficulties also. Trained in Western history, we tend to assume that a Prince is a lonely despot whose word is law, and our knowledge of the particular acts of Princes seems to confirm this: they can make or break an individual subject. But they cannot make or break a class. Aged, and often sacred, traditions prevent them, and something more tangible than traditions – the land. Land binds all the members of the State together, from the labourer to the ruler. Every class has its share in it, and one class – the hereditary nobles – will be even more averse than the ruler to reform, and he will have to consider their feelings even when he does not wish to, because he can no more get rid of them and replace them by more enlightened men than he could turn the hills they own into valleys. He must live with them, for better or worse.

The Constitution that we will examine was promulgated last January. The State in question* is quite small (income about seven lakhs, area about 450 square miles), but notable owing to the high character and ability of its ruler. The preamble to the constitution implies that there is no demand for reforms, indeed the contrary, but the ruler thinks fit to

* Dewas Senior, near Indore.

anticipate the wishes of his subjects in the matter, since a demand is bound to come. He recognizes six main factors in his State: the two most important are himself and his relatives (the Ruling House); then come the nobles, the officials, the townsmen, the villagers. These six factors are provided for in a tripartite constitution consisting of the Ruler, a State Council of six, and a Representative Assembly of about sixty.

The composition of the Representative Assembly is more remarkable than its powers. It includes one official to represent the Ruler, one member of the Ruling House, 20 nobles of various grades (total number of nobles in the State being about 80), 21 officials, 8 members elected by the towns (each representing 2,000 electors), and 15 village members (each representing 4,000 electors). It has no executive or legislative power, and though it may send up suggestions to the State Council, that body is not obliged to discuss them. It may ask the Council questions, provided that the question does not criticize the Ruler or any member of the Ruling House; such a question can only be asked when the Assembly is unanimous on the point, and if we glance back at its composition we see that unanimity is unlikely to occur. It may act as a referee when there is a dispute between the Ruler and the Council, but, as we shall see, such a dispute is unlikely to occur. The town and the village members in it each co-opt one of their group to be a member of the Council.

The Council consists of one member nominated by the Ruler, one member of the Ruling House, one noble, one nominated official, and the two town and village members co-opted from the Assembly. The council is a legislative body, all real legislation requiring the assent of the Ruler. It also has executive powers, the Ruler distributing the portfolios among its six members.

The Ruler is 'the fountain of all the power in the State', and he retains all powers that he does not expressly delegate. The annual grant for his household expenditure is fixed, but he can get an extraordinary grant for any special occasion, provided that two thirds of the Council agree.

Such are the chief provisions of our sample Constitution. We may sum them up by saying that the Assembly is negligible, and that two thirds of the members of the Council are dependent on the Ruler's favour, and so unlikely to withstand him on any vital point. We may even say as much about those modest heralds of democracy the town and village members. They are after all not to be elected! A final clause enacts that for the first five years all the members both of the Assembly and the Council shall be nominated, not elected, since the population is not yet sufficiently educated to work the constitution! We are not told what steps will be taken to educate it. The whole document is from the Western and the British Indian point of view as unreal as a Dessera Budget, but this does not mean that it is unstatesmanlike. On the contrary, it is a clever move. When the extremist campaign begins, those rulers who can point to a constitution will be in a stronger position than those who can't. They will have a framework into which they can introduce realities without compromising their dignity. And any change, however trifling, is to be welcomed which lessens the gulf between the States and the rest of India – a gulf which sometimes seems even more menacing than that which divides Indians from Europeans.

History is full of ironies, and it is strange to reflect that those parts of India which the British deprived of independence are now the most independent. Not only is the individual safer and freer in them, but he has, if he chooses to take it, a greater share of political power. He may hate the British and have good reason for doing so, but he would not exchange their yoke for an Indian Prince's; so that the Native States can only be enlarged or re-created if the principle of self-determination is ignored. A few years ago there was question of restoring to Indore a small district populated by Bhils. Someone thought of asking the Bhils what they would like, and they implored to be left as they were. Satara and Berar would answer likewise. An alliance between the British and the Princes against the rest of India could only lead to universal disaster, yet there are people on both sides who are foolish enough to want it.

So long as his subjects are uneducated peasants, a Prince is in a strong position from every point of view. They revere him with the old Indian loyalty, and a glimpse of his half-divine figure brings poetry into their lives. And he understands them even when he is indifferent or unjust, because like them he is rooted in the soil. He has an instinctive knowledge which no amount of training or study can give. If he takes too much of their money or imprisons their bodies without a trial, they are pained but not outraged; he is no more incomprehensible to them than a hostile sky. But his instinctive knowledge only works so long as their obedience is also instinctive. As soon as they feel the impulse of the outside world which believes in, or at all events talks about, principles and duties and rights, the spell breaks and they begin to question. The troubles which overtook the Nawab of Tonk and the Maharana of Udaipur last year, and which threaten other rulers, need not be ascribed to Non-cooperative agitators. Non-Cooperation is only one aspect of a wider tendency that envelops not India in particular but all the globe – the tendency to question and to protest. The Maharana of Udaipur is the premier prince of Rajputana and a semi-sacred figure, yet an armed mob of his subjects besieged him because the extortions of his officials wearied them. It was nothing to them that during the Dessera he owned the whole of India. He fled to one of his island-palaces in disarray, and was obliged to delegate his powers to his son. The matter was tidied up, and Udaipur was duly visited by the Prince of Wales. But the immemorial majesty of its dynasty has been outraged, more fatally than when it withdrew from Chitor before the advancing Moghul armies. A new spirit has entered India. Would that I could conclude with a eulogy of it! But that must be left to writers who can see into the future and who know in what human happiness consists.

[1922]

HYMN BEFORE ACTION

ARJUNA stayed his chariot between the two armies. He saw in either relatives, benefactors, and friends. He saw kindred civilizations opposed, and destruction certain for one of them, and perhaps for both. His limbs trembled, his purpose weakened and instead of proclaiming battle, he spoke thus to the god Krishna, who was his charioteer:

I desire not victory nor kingdom nor pleasures; what is kingdom to us, O Krishna, What is enjoyment, or even life? Those for whose sake we desire such things – they stand opposite to us in the battle now. I desire not to kill them even if the kingship of the three worlds were my reward; how then for earth? Slaying these poor sinners, we shall fall ourselves into sin. They, blinded by greed, see no guilt in the destruction of kindred, no crime in hostility to friends, but we, we who have seen, why should we not refrain? When kindred are destroyed, the immemorial traditions perish; when traditions perish, anarchy falls on us all. Were it not better for me to go unarmed, unresisting, into the battle and be slain by them instead.

Krishna's reply to this question of Arjuna's at the opening of the Bhagavad-Gita – a question that has never been answered decisively by Christianity – is to be found in the subsequent cantos of the poem. Arjuna must fight; for three reasons.

The first reason can never appeal to the Westerner. It assumes death is negligible – not even a gate leading to a new universe, but merely a passage leading back through birth to this. Why hesitate to traverse such a passage? Why hesitate to send others down it, since they must soon return? The body kills or dies; the 'dweller in the body' does neither, being immortal, and to regret or to retard its occasional disappearances would be childish. 'The dweller in the body slayeth not, nor is it slain when the body is slaughtered. Weapons cleave it not, nor fire burneth it, nor waters wet, nor wind drieth; it is perpetual, all pervasive, immutable, and knowing it to be such, thou shouldst not grieve. And even when thinking of its constant entrances and constant exits – even then, O Arjuna, thou shouldst not grieve, for certain is death for the born, and certain is birth for the dead.'

Now the Westerner will argue that though such a doctrine may inspire heroes, it is equally an excuse for cowards. All incentives to action, all rules for conduct, are made void by it. If nothing that is done in the body matters, then why need we do anything? If to slay and to be slain are the same, then to be fled from and to flee are also the same, and dishonour is as negligible as death. But, as if expecting this criticism, the divine charioteer proceeds at once to his second reason for bloodshed: – Duty. Whatever Arjuna has been or may be, in this present life he is a soldier, and as such it is his duty to fight. This duty has not been assigned to him by chance, though in his ignorance he may suppose so. It has been conditioned by his performances in past lives, just as its performance will condition his duty in lives to come. Action is indeed unimportant. But the impulses that produce action and could not exist apart from it – they are important, and their consequences eternal. The soldier must follow his soldierly impulses, and the Brahman his priestly, neither envying the other's task. 'Better one's own duty though destitute of merit than the duty of another, however well discharged; better death in the discharge of one's own duty than the perilous success that comes from discharging another's.' It is Arjuna's duty not to save life but to destroy it; were he trivially to show mercy now, he might check the flow of his development and debar himself from showing perfect mercy in some existence to come.

Yet how shall the hero escape the inevitable stains of war – the insolence of victory, the venom of defeat? He remains unconvinced. The remainder of the poem is concerned with Krishna's third reason, which deals with the problem of renunciation, and attempts to harmonize the needs of this life with eternal truth. The saint may renounce action, but the soldier, the citizen, the practical man generally – they should renounce, not action, but its fruits. It is wrong for them to be idle; it is equally wrong to desire a reward for industry. It is wrong to shirk destroying civilization and one's kindred and friends, and equally wrong to hope for dominion afterwards. When all such hopes and desires are dead fear dies also, and freed from all attachments the 'dweller in the body' will remain calm while the body performs its daily duty, and will be unstained by sin, as is the lotus leaf by the water of the tank. It will attain to the eternal peace that is offered to the practical man as well as to the devotee. It will have abjured the wages of action, which are spiritual death, and gained in their place a vision of the Divine. Towards the close of the poem Krishna reveals himself in full glory. 'Destroyed is my delusion,' Arjuna cries, 'I have gained knowledge (literally, 'memory') through thy grace, O immutable One. I am firm, my doubts have fled away. I will do according to thy word.' He drives into the battle rejoicing, and wins a great victory. But it is necessarily and rightly followed by disillusionment and remorse. The fall of his enemies leads to his own, for the fortunes of men are all bound up together, and it is impossible to inflict damage without receiving it.

[1912]

PART V

THE ABINGER PAGEANT

THE ABINGER PAGEANT*

Foreword to Visitors

ABINGER is a country parish, still largely covered with woodland. It is over ten miles long – one of the longest parishes in England – but very narrow, and it stretches like a thin green ribbon from the ridge of the North Downs right away to the Sussex border in the South. The Old Rectory Garden, where our pageant is held, lies so to speak about a third of the way down this ribbon. To your left, as you are sitting, the parish land falls away from you towards the valley of the Tillingbourne, then it rises on to the Downs. The larger and the wilder part of the parish is on your right; here the strip of land rises over Leith Hill and Abinger Commons, then it falls steeply into the Weald.

The church, on whose behalf the pageant is held, stands a quarter of a mile beyond you, at the Hatch or entrance to the Common. It was built in the reign of William the Conqueror (about 1080) and added to in the days of Archbishop Stephen Langton (1220), and again in the nineteenth century. It is dedicated to St James, the saint of pilgrims. Close to it are the Village Stocks and the old Hatch Inn. On the farther side of it stands the former Manor House of Abinger.

You see a large house on your right. This is the Old Rectory, parts of which go back to the fifteenth century. The great

* This is the programme of a pageant which was performed on July 14 and July 18, 1934, in aid of the Abinger Church Preservation Fund. The people concerned in it were nearly all connected with the parish. Mr Tom Harrison was the producer; the general conception is entirely due to him. Dr Vaughan Williams wrote the music. Mr Wilfred Grantham was the narrator.

tree showing behind it is a tulip tree, which according to tradition was planted there three hundred years ago by the diarist, John Evelyn.

Straight ahead of you lie the lands of Wotton parish, the Evelyns' home.

Our Pageant is not planned quite on ordinary pageant lines. It is rural rather than historical and tries to show the continuity of country life. It consists of a short Prologue and six Episodes, linked together by a Narrator. There is also, in this programme, a short explanatory note before each episode, dealing with points of local interest.

THE PAGEANT

Prologue

As the audience gather, the arena is occupied by a flock of sheep. Presently they are driven away, and a Woodman appears. This Woodman is the Narrator, and he will speak between each episode, sometimes visible, sometimes behind the scenes, to link up the action. Now he speaks the Prologue:

Welcome to our village and our woods. I welcome you first to our woods, because they are oldest. Before there were men in Abinger, there were trees. Thousands of years before the Britons came, the ash grew at High Ashes and the holly at Holmwood and the oak at Blindoak Gate; there were yew and juniper and box on the downs before ever the Pilgrims came along the Pilgrims' Way. They greet you, and our village greets you.

What shall we show you? History? Yes, but the history of a village lost in the woods. Do not expect great deeds and grand people here. Lords and ladies, warriors and priests will pass, but this is not their home, they will pass like the leaves in autumn but the trees remain.

The trees built our first houses and our first church, they roof our church today, they are with us from the cradle to the grave.

And that is why I speak to you this afternoon, I the Woodman. The sound of my axe is the beginning of history at Abinger. Before I came and cleared the fields he (*pointing after the shepherd*) could not pasture his sheep. And now the Britons are coming down the paths I have cut, then you shall see the Romans come, then the bugle will sound and, like the falling leaves, the Romans will go back to Rome. Then the Saxons will come, and after them monks and the Coming of Christ. We will show you a great battle next – and then the Normans will come, and at the end of that trouble there will be peace for a little – Domesday and its Book, and the settling of the land.

EPISODE I

From Briton to Norman

(NOTE.—There are several relics of this early period in the district. The most impressive is the huge neolithic camp on Holmbury Hill, date unknown. A small Roman villa stood near the present Abinger Hall. The Roman 'Stane Street' or Stone Street passes by the parish. The Saxons in 851 won a great victory over the Danes at Aclea, which may well be 'Ockley', just over the boundary. The nave of the church dates from Norman times, and the church itself is mentioned in Domesday.

The opening episode does not deal directly with any of these scattered facts, but you might bear them in mind – more particularly the great fact of the camp on Holmbury Hill.)

Scene: The Woodland. *Time:* From the beginning of history to the Norman Conquest. A rapid imaginative survey, passing by with music. When the Woodman has finished his Prologue, Ancient Britons appear, collecting fire-wood, hunting. 'The Romans, the Romans,' they cry, and the Roman legions enter, take possession, and make themselves at home. Soldiers, formed into a line, symbolize the straight Roman Road. Then the bugle sounds retreat, and the Romans retire to Rome.

The Saxon invasion follows. The Saxons and Romanized Britons are hostile to each other at first, then fraternize. A priest arrives, Christianity is established. The Saxon leader moves with his men into battle, while the women await the event. He is brought back dead. The priest comforts the mourners.

Finally the Normans enter with triumphant music. Grouping themselves round a Saxon scribe, they make the Domesday Survey and the episode closes.

After a short pause the Woodman re-enters to introduce the second episode which consists of two scenes from the Middle Ages:

The trees are growing, the trees are cut down, but there is one great tree that shall not be cut down. It is the Kingdom of England. We will show you a king – King John. He will break into our peace to do evil, you will see him down there (*pointing north*) at our Manor House of Paddington, and the Lord of the Manor will escape him, but the Lady and her son he will put to death. King John is evil; he will fall like a rotten branch, but the tree of the Kingdom of England remains.

And when John has passed and his crimes with him, you shall see another great tree, the tree of the Church. Stephen Langton, Archbishop of Canterbury, comes. Peter des Roches, Bishop of Winchester, comes. Pilgrims come from Canterbury along the Pilgrims' Way. Our own church of St James, the patron of pilgrims, receives them. Here again there is strife and ill-will and the wind stirs the branches. But the tree of the Church stands firm.

The Kingdom and the Church are high matters, and Abinger only a village. Listen for a moment to some of our local names, the names of our fields and woods and roads. They came to us, these names, through centuries of Surrey speech, they are dear to us, they are with us still.

(Raises his hand; a voice recites as if calling a Roll):

The nine acres, the ten acres, the thirteen acres, the old twenty acres, Shoulder of Mutton Field, Hogs Ham, Hellicon Ham, Roundabouts and Upper Chalks, Frogberry Lane, Stane Street and Friday Street, Hackhurst, The Shiffolds, The Dial, The Tolt, Canterbury Field, Great Spleck, Fillebar, Middle Maggots, the Dolly and Shaw in Dolly, Rainbow Field, Crooked Shy Field, Samsatchull, Trumpets, Great Slaughter Field, Angry Field, Ellix and Volvens.

(Woodman continuing): The seven acres, the eleven acres, the thirty acres; and Paddington down by the Tillingbourne, where we wait for King John.

EPISODE II

The Middle Ages

SCENE I

King John at Paddington

(NOTE—Paddington Farm lies down the slope on your left near a big mill pond on the Tillingbourne. There was a Manor House here in the Middle Ages, and in 1188 – that is to say, about thirty years before the incident to be played – the then Lord of the Manor had forfeited his lands for sheltering an outlaw, Avice Wykelin. John, King of England, is also hostile to the actual Lord, William de Braose, and has determined to destroy him.)

Scene: Before the Manor House of Paddington in the year 1210. Lady de Braose urges her husband to depart before the King's vengeance falls. His horse is ready saddled. He refuses to leave. Then, from the trees, comes Avice Wykelin the outlaw, dressed in green. Out of gratitude to the house which has sheltered him he brings warnings that the King himself is approaching.

De Braose now takes leave of his wife and two sons, and rides away. The villagers beg her to hide. She refuses, and she and her elder son remain to confront the King, but the younger son, Giles, is taken away into safety.

Enter the King and his train. Enraged at the escape of de Braose, he seizes Lady de Braose and her son, and carries them away to their death. Giles, the younger son, will appear in the next scene as a novice, and in after years he will become Bishop of Hereford and be installed as Lord of the Manor of Paddington in his father's place.

SCENE II

Stephen Langton at Abinger Church

(NOTE—The previous scene followed history, but this scene is an imaginative reconstruction. An old tradition connects the great Cardinal-Archbishop of Canterbury, Stephen Langton, with the district, and he is here shown returning to the scenes of his youth, to dedicate the new chancel of our church. Ten years have passed since the tragedy at Paddington. King John is dead, and Langton, a patriotic Englishman, represents a newer, better order. Yet still there is conflict. Abinger is in the diocese of Winchester, whose Bishop, Peter des Roches, a Frenchman, belongs to the opposite faction. In the minds of the villagers, des Roches represents the vanished tyranny of John, and this explains the sullenness with which they greet him, and the coldness of the meeting between the two prelates.)

Scene: In the courtyard of the Manor of Abinger, close to the church, in the year 1220. The villagers wait for their beloved Archbishop.

Pilgrims from Canterbury approach, having deviated from the Pilgrims' Way, which runs across the north of the parish. They are the types shown by Chaucer in his Canterbury Tales, and include the Knight, Squire, Yeoman, Prioress, Man of Law, Franklin or Freeholder, Webbe or Weaver, Cook,

Shipman, Wife of Bath, Parson and Pardoner. They sing the Latin Hymn to the Virgin Mary, which Chaucer himself assigns to them. The first verse speaks of the Annunciation, the second implores the Virgin to intercede with Christ so that our sins may be forgiven us and we may enjoy eternal life, after the exile of this world:

Angelus ad Virginem
Sub intrans in conclave
Virginis formidinem
Demulcens inquitare,
Ave regina virginum,
Coeli terraeque Dominum
Concipies et paries intacta,
Salutem hominum
Tu porta coeli facta,
Medela criminum.

Eia Mater Domini
Quae pacem reddidisti
Angelis et homini
Cum Christum genuisti,
Tuum exora Filium
Ut se nobis propitium
Exhibeat et deleat peccata
Praestans auxilium
Vita fini beata,
Post hoc exilium.

These pilgrims bring news of the Archbishop's approach. Children play in the courtyard of the Manor, there is a mock tournament on hobby-horses, and a miracle play on a cart. The Archbishop is seen in the distance, accompanied by a single novice, who is Giles de Braose of Paddington; but before they arrive the unpopular Bishop of Winchester appears with his monks; he converses with a crusader, since he will himself soon be going on a crusade.

Finally the Archbishop comes and is received with joy. He and the Bishop greet one another distantly. A procession is formed and all start for the church, led by the monks, who sing a Latin Chant in Plainsong, appropriate to the dedication of a building. The first verse celebrates the Heavenly Jerusalem, the celestial model of all earthly churches, the second gives glory to the Father, the Son, and the Holy Ghost.

Coelestis Urbs Hierusálem,
Beata pacis visio

Decus parenti debitum
Sit usque quaqu' altissimo

Quae celsa de viventibus
Saxis ad astra tolleris
Sponsae quae ritu cingeris
Mille angelorum millibus.

Natoque patri unito
Et inclyto paraclyto
Cui laus, potestas, gloria
Aeterna sit per saecula.

The entire company enter the church and the episode closes.

As the bustling third episode starts, the voice of the Woodman is heard 'off' to an accompaniment of anvils; he introduces the Elizabethan age.

The trees are growing, the trees are cut down. They are cut down now for charcoal, for the iron works, for the forge. Listen to the hammers at Abinger – Abinger Hammer. England awakes, Elizabeth is Queen, the Armada is coming, and we are part of England. Listen to the anvils, working for peace and war. We are part of the world. And when the Armada is past our trees are cut down again to build a bonfire of joy and thanksgiving.

Listen to the hammers at Abinger, Abinger Hammer!

EPISODE III

The Hammer Forge

(NOTE—Abinger Hammer is a couple of miles to your left, near Paddington but farther down the stream. There used to be a forge here connected with the iron works of the district.

The year selected is that of the Spanish Armada when George Nevill, Earl of Abergavenny, was Lord of the Manor of Paddington. It is worth noting that by this time our Parish Register has started, and that the first marriage recorded in it is that of Richard Edshue (Edser) on October 20, 1559—a name still well known in the neighbourhood.)

Scene: The Hammer Green in the year 1588, with forge and whipping-post. After the Narrator stops, the anvils continue, and the Surrey-Sussex Smiths' folk-song, 'Twankydillo', is sung 'off':

Here's a health to the jolly blacksmith, the best of all the fellows,
Who works at his anvil while the boy blows the bellows;
Which makes my bright hammer to rise and to fall,
Here's to old Cole and to young Cole and to old Cole of all,
    Twankydillo, twankydillo,
    A roaring pair of bagpipes and of the green willow.

If a gentleman calls his horse for to shoe
He makes no denial of one pot or two,
Which makes my bright hammer to rise and to fall,
Here's to old Cole and to young Cole, and to old Cole of all.
Here's a health to good Bess, our glorious Queen
And to all her loyal subjects where'er they are seen,
Which makes my bright hammer to rise and to fall,
Here's to old Cole and to young Cole and to old Cole of all.

Charcoal-burners, apprentices, etc., enter, small boys play, a lady of position walks about.

Enter Lord Abergavenny's steward with a man who is dragged to the whipping-post in spite of the protests of the villagers and the intercession of the Rev. Richard Dean, the Rector. But a hunting-horn is heard, and Abergavenny himself arrives and has the man released. Quickly on this comes the news of the defeat of the Armada, and general rejoicing. There is a country dance, 'Gathering Peascods', and the scene closes to the strains of 'Twankydillo', and to the building of a bonfire.

Before the next episode, the Woodman again speaks 'off', to introduce the troubled times of the seventeenth century.

The trees are growing, the trees are cut down, their branches entangle, and this time we show you in passing the tangle of the Civil Wars, and how Puritans and Cavaliers intertwine in our village life.

Arguments and brawls, strokes and counterstrokes, plots and counter-plots – but the trees are growing all the time, and we shall end with the planting of a tree. But before we begin, remember once more we are only a village, and listen once more to some local names: to the names of some of our people. They come down to us through the centuries, not as old as the woods and fields, but very old, and many of them are with us this afternoon and playing to you in our pageant. Listen to a few of our Abinger names.

(*A voice recites*): Edser, Smallpiece, Longhurst, Overington, Etherington, Jelly, Tickner, Harrison, Cumper, Hoad, Lane, Cole, Wood, Carpenter, Stone, Evershed, Dewdney, Tidy, Worsfold, Snatchfold; and the great name Evelyn from Wotton.

(*Woodman, continuing*): And it is an Evelyn from Wotton who will plant that tree – that great tree above the house, the finest tulip tree in South England.

EPISODE IV

The Days of John Evelyn

(NOTE—By this time the manors of Abinger and of Paddington have both passed into the hands of the Evelyns of Wotton, who still hold them. Towards the close of the episode the most famous of the Evelyn family will appear—John Evelyn, the diarist, author of *Sylva*, a book about trees. The woods had been destroyed owing to the iron works, and he induced people to replant.

There is a fine farmhouse of this period in the parish, Crossways Farm, on the Dorking–Guildford road. George Meredith introduces it into his novel, *Diana of the Crossways*.)

Scene: Outside Abinger Church. *Time:* From 1643 to 1660. Another rapid survey. As it opens, two villagers are about to be married by the rector, the Rev. Anthony Smith, but the Puritans prevent them from entering the church, and marry them at a table instead, much to their bewilderment. The Rector is deprived of his living, and the Puritans and the villagers, now in black, sing the old metrical version of the 68th Psalm:

Let God arise and then his foes will turn themselves to flight:
His en'mies then will run abroad and scatter out of sight.
And as the fire doth melt the wax and wind blow smoke away
So in the presence of the Lord the wicked shall decay.
But let the righteous be glad, let them before God's sight
Be very joyful; yea, let them rejoice with all their might.
To God sing, to His name sing praise. Extol Him with your voice.
That rides on Heav'n by his name JAH before His face rejoice.

While they are singing, a solitary horseman – John Evelyn – rides slowly across the stage. When the Psalm is over, there is a sudden change in the music, to symbolize the Restoration of Charles II, and the villagers, glad enough of the change, throw off their black cloaks and reappear in colours. They sing a song of the period:

Here's a health unto His Majesty;
Conversion to his enemies.
And he that will not pledge his health,
I wish him neither wit nor wealth,
Nor yet a rope to hang himself,
With a fa, la, la.

and follow it by a Country Dance, 'The Triumph', during which the genuine Puritans retire. At the end of the dance they form an aisle up to the church. It is a second wedding. The Rev. Stephen Geree is now Rector of Abinger, and his daughter Elizabeth is marrying Mr Francis Hammond from London. The procession comes down the aisle, followed by guests, among whom are George Evelyn of Wotton and his second wife, Lady Cotton, also John Evelyn and his wife. There is another Country Dance, 'Haste to the Wedding'. When it is over, a gardener hands John Evelyn a small tree.

He goes out to plant it in commemoration of the glad event, and you may, if you will, suppose it to be the tulip tree which stands by the Old Rectory today.

The Woodman, still speaking 'off', now introduces us to some rustic scenes of the eighteenth century and to some changes in the woodland.

A hundred years pass, and a newcomer welcomes you – a new tree comes to our woods: the Larch. While you look at the people whom we are next going to show you, at the smugglers, at the local gentry and their visitors, at lords and philosophers, farmers and footmen, while you watch the dancing and listen to the music – remember that people are not everything at Abinger and never will be, and that just at this moment a new tree, the Larch, has been planted a mile away. The first Larch tree to be planted in South England was at Parkhurst in this parish, and it still stands. The Silver Fir comes too, the wild commons are planted with Scots Pine, and thus the Surrey woods take the forms and the fragrance that we know.

Which is the better – that ancient royal wood of Saxon and Norman, where the oak and the ash were king? Or this later wood of ours republican, where many trees mingle? I cannot tell you. I am only the Woodman, but I know that though the trees alter the wood remains.

EPISODE V

Smugglers and Other Gentry

(NOTE—At Abinger, as elsewhere in Surrey, a number of hollow lanes have worn down deep into the greensand. These were found useful by the smugglers, since they could move their stuff about with little chance of being seen. The smugglers were in league with the villagers, one of whom, John Lane, is going to get caught in the earlier part of this episode.

In the latter part the landed gentry will appear before you, headed by the Dowager Countess of Donegal. She has bought Paddington House, down in the valley, close to the site of the present Abinger Hall. Please also meet Mr Theodore Jacobstein, a retired Dutch merchant, and Mr John Spence, formerly a dyer at Wandsworth. Mr Jacobstein has built the artificial waterfall at Tillingbourne. Mr Spence has bought Parkhurst, where the larch trees will be planted before long; he is at present occupied in entertaining two very queer fish – the French philosopher, Jean-Jacques Rousseau, who is in exile for his opinions, and in a highly nervous state, and Rousseau's mistress, Thérèse Levasseur.)

Scene: Outside the Inn at Abinger Hatch on a summer's day about the year 1760. Scenes of village life. A young woman (Mrs John Lane) moves over the bridge and watches. Then the Smugglers gallop on, and unload their casks. Excise men appear, the casks are hidden by various devices, but when all seems safe the excise men reappear, and John Lane is arrested, and taken off, to be deported.

The casks are now opened, the neighbourhood of the Hatch Inn becomes gay and 'I'm Seventeen come Sunday' is sung.

> As I walked out one May morning,
> One May morning so early,
> I overtook a fair pretty maid
> Just as the sun was rising.
>> With my rum dum day,
>>> Fol de liddle day,
>>> Right fol lol de liddle lido.
>
> Her shoes were black, her stockings white,
> Her buckles shone like silver;
> She had a dark and rolling eye,
> And her hair hung down her shoulder. With, etc.
>
> How old are you, my fair pretty maid?
> How old are you, my honey?
> She answered me right cheerfully,
> I'm seventeen come Sunday. With, etc.

The quality now begin to arrive. Rousseau and his lady are actually stopping with Mr Malthus at Westcott, but Mr Spence is responsible for them in Abinger. The Countess of Donegal drives on last. There is an entertainment of Morris Dances and of other Country Dances. Meanwhile the Curate of Abinger, who has a taste for philosophy, tries to have a little interesting talk with Rousseau. This ends badly, for Rousseau mistakes the Curate for a French spy, and finally dashes off in terror, to the concern of Mr Spence. The gentry leave, and the villagers have another drink, and strike up the Surrey Folk Song, 'The Sweet Nightingale', which has been sung in these parts for generations:

> One morning in May by chance I did rove,
> I sat myself down by the side of a grove;
> And then did I hear the sweet nightingale sing,
> I never heard so sweet as the birds in the spring.
>
> All on the grass I sat myself down
> Where the voice of the nightingale echoed around;
> Don't you hear how she quivers the notes, I declare
> No music, no songster with her can compare.
>
> Come, all you young men, I'll have you draw near,
> I pray you now heed me these words for to hear,
> That when you're grown old you may have it to sing,
> That you never heard so sweet as the birds in the spring.

The singing dies away; the stage is left empty.

When all is silent the Woodman once more speaks 'off' to introduce the last episode:

Again a hundred years have passed, Victoria is Queen, and our Pageant is ending. Two scenes remain before you bid farewell to our woods, and they to you. The first scene is trivial and gay; an excellent Italian gentleman . . . but you shall see the excellent Italian gentleman. And when that little comedy is played you shall see the second scene, which concerns our church and its needs, and hear a psalm of dedication sung, as in the days of Stephen Langton, and then (as happens in a dream) all the characters will re-enter, re-enter and vanish and leave you alone among woods and fields.

EPISODE VI

Towards Our Own Times

(NOTE—It is said that the stocks up by the church have never been used for their proper purpose, so here is an imaginary Italian refugee, Dr Riccabocca, locking himself up in them by accident. Dr Riccabocca has never existed historically. He is a fictitious character, from the pages of Bulwer Lytton's book, *My Novel*, and so are the rector, the squire and the steward. After his mishap, the mood of the episode alters and passes into music. Three restorations of the church took place at this time and are here summarized and symbolized.)

Scene: Outside Abinger church, during the ninteeenth century. The stocks are being repaired, an Eton boy and a village boy squabble, the steward puts the village boy into the stocks. Dr Riccabocca releases him, and experiments with stocks himself until he can't get out. Steward comes out of church with squire, and is much surprised.

Meanwhile the rector arrives, with the farmers who are presenting a new porch to the church. They look at plans, and sing some verses of the 84th Psalm:

'How amiable are Thy dwellings, thou Lord of Hosts! My soul hath a desire and longing to enter into the courts of the Lord. My heart and my flesh rejoice in the living God.'

'Yea, the sparrow hath found her an house and the swallow a nest where she may lay her young, even Thy altars, O Lord of Hosts, my King and my God.'

'Blessed are they that dwell in Thy house, they will be always praising Thee.'

'The glorious majesty of the Lord our God be upon us. Prosper Thou the work of our hands upon us; O prosper Thou our handy work.'

While the Psalm is being sung all the performers of previous scenes assemble on the hill behind, and the hymn 'O God our help in ages past' concludes the active part of the Pageant. The Woodman then comes forward to speak the Epilogue, and the sheep begin to return to the arena.

The Epilogue

Houses, houses, houses! You came from them and you must go back to them. Houses and bungalows, hotels, restaurants and flats, arterial roads, by-passes, petrol pumps, and pylons – are these going to be England? Are these man's final triumph? Or is there another England, green and eternal, which will outlast them? I cannot tell you, I am only the Woodman, but this land is yours, and you can make it what you will. If you want to ruin our Surrey fields and woodlands it is easy to do, very easy, and if you want to save them they can be saved. Look into your hearts and look into the past, and remember that all this beauty is a gift which you can never replace, which no money can buy, which no cleverness can refashion. You can make a town, you can make a desert, you can even make a garden; but you can never, never make the country, because it was made by Time.

Centuries of life amongst obscure trees and unnoticed fields! That is all our Pageant has tried to show you, and it will end as it began among country sights and sounds. Farewell! and take back its lesson with you to your houses, for it has a lesson. Our village and our woods bid you farewell.

At the conclusion of the Epilogue the arena is again occupied by the flock of sheep.

[1934]